Working in a world of hurt

MANCHESTER
1824

Manchester University Press

Cultural History of Modern War

Series editors

Ana Carden-Coyne, Peter Gatrell, Max Jones, Penny Summerfield and
Bertrand Taithe

Already published

Series logo Centre for the Cultural History of War

http://www.arts.manchester.ac.uk/subjectareas/history/research/cchw/

Centre for the
Cultural History
of War

Working in a world of hurt

Trauma and resilience in the narratives of medical personnel in warzones

~

CAROL ACTON AND JANE POTTER

Manchester University Press

Published by Manchester University Press
Altrincham Street, Manchester M1 7JA
www.manchesteruniversitypress.co.uk

British Library Cataloguing-in-Publication Data
A catalogue record for this book is available from the British Library

Library of Congress Cataloging-in-Publication Data applied for

ISBN   978 0 7190 9036 3 hardback

First published 2015

The publisher has no responsibility for the persistence or accuracy of URLs for any external or third-party internet websites referred to in this book, and does not guarantee that any content on such websites is, or will remain, accurate or appropriate.

Typeset
by Out of House Publishing
Printed in Great Britain
by TJ International Ltd, Padstow

Contents

Figures

Acknowledgements

Our shared interests in First World War nursing brought us together as friends and then as co-authors, who have somehow managed to remain friends despite the trials and tribulations of research, writing and numerous trips across the Atlantic. We have benefited greatly from the support of many institutions and individuals over the past five years.

The librarians and archivists at the following collections have been unfailingly helpful and courteous. Without these collections and the institutions that support them this work could not be undertaken: the Department of Documents, the Imperial War Museum, London; the Liddle Collection, Brotherton Library, University of Leeds; the Wellcome Trust Library and Archives, London; the Army Medical Services Museum Archives, Keogh Barracks, Surrey; Library and Archives Canada and the George Metcalf Archival Collection in the Military History Research Centre at the Canadian War Museum, Ottawa; American Folklife Center Archives, Library of Congress, Washington, DC; Archives of the US Army Medical Museum, Fort Sam Houston, Texas; the Huntington Library, San Marino, California. Carol would like to thank St Jerome's University and the University of Waterloo for funding and research leave that made the necessary archival work possible; she also thanks the wonderful librarian at St Jerome's University, Lorna Rourke, for her help in sourcing and buying books and aiding in database searches. We thank our university colleagues who have engaged in discussion on this topic and our students who have shared their enthusiasm for this material, in particular postgraduates in English 780 Winter 2012 at the University of Waterloo and MA and BA Publishing students at Oxford Brookes University.

We would like to thank the following copyright holders for permission to reprint material in the following pages:

Acknowledgements

The Trustees of the Army Medical Services Museum (for the papers of J. B. Reid, Allan Hanson, W. Watson, R. B. C. Welsh, David Westlake and Trevor Gibbens); Ann Kimzey and the Grover Carter Family (for the papers of Grover Carter); the Liddle Collection, Brotherton Library, University of Leeds (for the archives of Katherine Ferguson, Nurse Hitchens and C. McKerrow); Kathy Lowe/the Mary Morris Trust (for the diary of Mary Morris); Peter Randolph (for *An Unexpected Odyssey* by Edgar Randolph); Michael Tattersall (for the papers of Norman Tattersall); the Imperial War Museum (for the oral interview/sound recording of Eileen Joan Nicolson); and the Wellcome Library (for the memoir of Mary Knocker). Permission to quote from Ken Adams, *Healing in Hell: The Memoirs of a Far Eastern POW Medic*, is granted by Pen and Sword Books. Excerpts from Ronald J. Glasser, *365 Days* (Copyright © 1971, 1980 by Ronald J. Glasser), are reprinted with the permission of The Permissions Company, Inc., on behalf of George Braziller Inc., www.georgebraziller.com. Excerpts from *Ruff's War: A Navy Nurse on the Frontline in Iraq* (Annapolis, Md.: Naval Institute Press, © 2005) are reprinted, by permission, from K. Sue Roper and Cheryl Lynn Ruff. Lines from Brian Turner, 'AB Negative' from his collection *Here, Bullet* (Copyright © 2005 by Brian Turner), are reprinted with the permission of The Permissions Company, Inc., on behalf of Alice James Books, www.alicejamesbooks.org. Quotations from the late Lynda VanDevanter's *Home before Morning*, are reprinted with the kind permission of Tom Buckley. Quotations from the late Aidan MacCarthy's *A Doctor's War* are reprinted with kind permission of Nicola and Adrienne MacCarthy. We have made every effort to trace the copyright holders of other sources quoted in the following pages and should be glad to receive details from those to whom we have not made proper acknowledgement.

For many years our families have listened to our endless talk about war and trauma. Last but not least, we thank *them*.

List of abbreviations

AEF	American Expeditionary Force
AFS	American Field Service
ANC	Army Nurse Corps
ARC	American Red Cross
BEF	British Expeditionary Force
BGH	British General Hospital
CBC	Canadian Broadcasting Company
CIA	Central Intelligence Agency
CPT	Captain
DMZ	demilitarized zone
DSM	*Diagnostic and Statistical Manual of Mental Disorders*
ESWS	Ex-Services' Welfare Society
GI	US private soldier
IED	improvised explosive device
LMF	lack of moral fibre
MASCAL	mass casualty
MEDCAP	Medical Civil Action Program
MO	medical officer
POW	prisoner of war
PTSD	post-traumatic stress disorder
QAIMNS	members of Queen Alexandra's Imperial Military Nursing Service
RAF	Royal Air Force
RAMC	Royal Army Medical Corps
RMO	regimental medical officer
SJAB	St John's Ambulance Brigade
USAID	US government aid agency

List of abbreviations

USMC	US Marine Corps
VA	Veterans Association
VAD	Voluntary Aid Detachment
VVA	Vietnam Veterans Association

Introduction

> ... Thalia Fields is gone, long gone,
> about as far from Mississippi
> as she can get, ten thousand feet above Iraq
> with a blanket draped over her body
> and an exhausted surgeon in tears,
> his bloodied hands on her chest, his head
> sunk down, the nurse guiding him
> to a nearby seat and holding him as he cries,
> though no one hears it[1]

Iraq War veteran poet Brian Turner's poem 'AB Negative (The Surgeon's Poem)' is unusual in combatant poetry in bringing us imaginatively into the surgeon's intimate physical and emotional relationship with war injury and death.[2] The poem privileges the surgeon's emotions, making them central to the moment of combatant death. Turner demands that we hear what is unheard, see what is unseen, as he translates not only the surgeon's very physical confrontation with death, but also the grief and loss that arise out of his failure to prevent it, into an arresting visual image. He draws our attention to the silence that exists not because no one speaks, but because the event itself is out of reach, the medevac plane at once a real place and a metaphor for the psychic space – the world of hurt – inhabited only by the surgeon, nurse and dying combatant. Turner's image is not only unusual in war poetry; in the history of war, and especially in discussions of the psychological trauma that can result from constant exposure to war-induced injury and death, the experience of medical personnel is strikingly absent. Historically, the focus on combatant trauma has obscured the trauma of those who care for the injured and dying.[3] Considering such trauma in the First World War, Margaret Higonnet suggests it is a 'history' that 'lies concealed' beneath that of 'combatants' psychological injury.'[4] Furthermore, we find in the writings under discussion that this 'concealment' is compounded by the writings of medical personnel themselves who tend to represent their own emotional pain only obliquely, if at all, instead foregrounding the story of the wounded they care for.

Recently, however, discussion of the emotional price paid by medical personnel who practice in warzones, and who treat war injury immediately outside it, has made its way into the media. A 2012 article on BillMoyers.com entitled 'At a Military Hospital, Warriors Are Not the Only Wounded', reported on 'what's called Combat and Occupational Stress Reaction or Secondary Traumatic Stress Disorder … at Landstuhl Regional Medical Center in Germany which has received many of the severely wounded casualties from the wars in Iraq and Afghanistan.'[5] Reporter Michael Winship notes that '[t]hey compare this hospital to the center of an hourglass; it's the midpoint between combat injury and treatment in the field and then subsequent care back in the States or other home country.'[6] In December 2013 an article in the *Guardian*, 'Canadian Armed Forces Hit by Spate of Suicides', drew attention to the stress carried by doctors in frontline hospitals:

> Major Marc Dauphin, a military surgeon, led the multinational hospital at Kandahar airfield in 2009. 'It was 24/7, one of the busiest trauma hospitals in the world', he told the CBC this week.
> He said: 'War weaponry is designed to tear the human body apart – and it works.' Four months after returning to Canada, he started suffering panic attacks and his marriage began falling apart. He said he considered throwing himself into a freezing river. Instead, he decided to get help. Even he didn't realise he was suffering from PTSD.[7]

Military hospitals, aid posts, casualty clearing stations, and medevac flights among others, are all at the 'center of an hourglass' between combat injury and the return home. Medical personnel have occupied this space between front and home in wars throughout the centuries, whether as camp-followers (very often wives of soldiers who acted as nurses as well as cooks and laundresses), military surgeons or regimental mates, and, as Anthony Babington describes in *Shell-Shock: a History of the Changing Attitudes to War Neurosis* (1997), there is evidence that early medical personnel were profoundly affected by what they saw:

> During the Peninsular War (1808–1814) an ancestor of [Dr Patton of the University of South Wales] was assisting some surgeons with the wounded when he suddenly went blind. It was thought that he had poisoned his eyes

by rubbing them with bloody hands. Although his condition was believed to be incurable, he did eventually recover his sight. Dr Patton has suggested that his ancestor's symptom of blindness was probably 'an unconscious attempt to 'shut out' the sights of mutilation' which he had witnessed at the dressing station.[8]

Florence Nightingale was similarly haunted by what she had witnessed nursing at Scutari. Returning to England in 1856 having contracted Crimean fever or brucellosis during her service, she became an invalid, subject to recurring and often excruciating symptoms such as palpitations, tachychardia, sciatica and spondylitis. Other symptoms, more associated now with post-war trauma, included depression, insomnia and nausea, and one could argue that her incessant letter-writing and obsessive commitment to reform of the Army Medical Services were manifestations of her efforts to assuage and even shut out the memory of the dead:

> She was haunted by the thoughts of the 'living skeletons' ... men, ulcerated and covered with vermin, who wrapped their heads in their blankets, and died without uttering a word. Overwhelming herself with work might at least keep those memories at bay. Almost a decade after the war, she was to look back, and shudder at the memory of the 'slaughter houses' of Scutari. It was like 'a horrid spectre' that she was afraid of conjuring up from the dark corners of her mind, where it was ever present, waiting to spring out on her.[9]

But it was over half a century before the idea of psychiatric illness as a result of war service received formal recognition, as the years 1914–18 became almost synonymous with the concept of psychological 'shock'. In 1919 the Ex-Services' Welfare Society (ESWS, today called Combat Stress) was founded in London 'for the purpose of helping men and women of all ranks who had developed psychiatric illness while serving in the Armed Forces or the Merchant Navy'.[10] The presence of women in this clause would suggest that these included nurses. In *Broken Men: Shell Shock, Treatment and Recovery in Britain 1914–30*, Fiona Reid finds that

> no one had paid much attention to the problems of mentally wounded women ... although by October 1923 it had been established that 71 ex-service women nurses were being held in local asylums ... Records do demonstrate that the ESWS supported Nurses Clappen and Lovejoy, women who required long-term mental health treatment as a consequence of their war service.[11]

There is also evidence that funds were raised by Lady Nellie Martin Harvey at the end of the First World War to create a 'rest home for nurses broken by the war'.[12] Although it is impossible to determine exactly what 'broken' meant – Nightingale was broken in body and at times in mind – based on evidence we present in Chapter 1 we can surmise that some of these were psychiatric casualties. On male doctors there is little information apart from anecdotal accounts passed down in family history, such as a Canadian doctor who returned from the war an alcoholic, brief remarks about breakdown in private letters or diaries, or the occasional historical note:

> Captain B. A. West, an RMO [Regimental Medical Officer] in Gallipoli and later attached to a siege battery in France, broke down in October 1916. After a year of treatment and convalescence, he returned to base duties in the UK but found that contact with patients revived his earlier experiences … Only in November 1917 was West able to return to work in a civilian hospital.[13]

The psychiatric and medical history of war has remained remarkably silent on the subject of medical personnel and the possible traumatic consequences of their work.

Like the First World War term 'shell shock', which referred to injury through combat, the Second World War described combatant breakdown as 'battle fatigue', both terms excluding those who were not immediately in combat, and there are very few references to the breakdown of medical personnel in the latter. In a post-war oral recollection, American James Kirtley reports that 'one of my battalion surgeons … [was suffering] from extreme battle neurosis and had to be strapped to a litter so he could be evacuated to the rear'.[14] It was not until after the Vietnam War, when former nurses such as Lynda Van Devanter, whose memoir, *Home before Morning*, will be discussed in Chapter 5, recognised the description of post-war symptoms in what was being diagnosed as post-Vietnam syndrome and then post-traumatic stress syndrome or disorder in combatant veterans, that members of this medical personnel community came to understand that caring for the wounded, and watching them die, and at times being under attack themselves, could result in a traumatic response to their experience, even though they had not been in combat. It is clear, in reading accounts by medical personnel throughout the twentieth century and from the war in Iraq, that they, too, suffer from the emotional consequences of their work. It is also clear that, like combatants and other groups affected by war, they can be resilient and develop coping strategies that allow them to withstand the rigours of their environment.[15]

Charles Figley, one of the most prominent practitioners in the area of war and trauma, identifies the trauma of a Vietnam veteran medic he treated as 'secondary or vicarious trauma' that is defined 'by the pain and suffering he experienced from treating those in harm's way; by the guilt he felt each time one of his patients died; by being obsessed with reacting quickly enough to save lives'.[16] While Figley draws our attention to the specific stressors that not only medics but all medical personnel face in a warzone, recent psychiatric and psychological discussions of physician and medic trauma would exclude the terms 'secondary' and 'vicarious' from the definition, noting that constant witnessing and participating in severe injury and death are directly rather than vicariously traumatic. This is summed up by US Navy psychologist Heidi Kraft, in her memoir of the war in Iraq, where she asserts that in this war, unlike wars in the past, we understand that in addition to combatants, 'war damages doctors'.[17]

While our approach to these accounts of the 'damage' visited upon medical personnel is to read them primarily in relation to psychological and psychiatric positions on trauma and resilience, we also take into account influential perspectives in the later twentieth and twenty-first centuries by theorists such as Caruth on the way trauma, a condition that belongs in the first instance to medicine as the term for physical wounding and later to psychology and psychiatry as a psychic wound, has become part of literary and cultural theory.[18] In this context, we particularly welcome Carpentier's acknowledgement in *Culture, Trauma and Conflict* that his 'focus on ideology and representation [of trauma] has no ambition to ignore the materiality of war', since theoretical perspectives often seem to lose contact with the lived experience. His connection between the materiality of injury and psychological trauma is extremely pertinent to our discussion:

> War impacts on human bodies with an almost unimaginable force. It destroys or mutilates them. It causes pain to them, and traumatises them. The (individual) trauma is not only physical, but also psychological ... Erikson (1976, 153) defines this individual trauma as 'a blow to the psyche that breaks through one's defences so suddenly and with such brutal forces that one cannot react to it efficiently'.[19]

We extend this connection between physical and psychic to include the medical personnel who treat these wounds.

Yet for Carpentier and theorists like Caruth, this 'blow to the psyche' results in the inability to articulate the trauma, so that the theory relies on defining the traumatic event by the inability to remember fully, resulting in an absent narrative which is replaced by post-trauma fragmented and intrusive images. 'The flashback, it seems, provides a form of recall that survives at the cost of willed memory or of the very continuity of conscious thought.'[20] The problem with focusing on this particular aspect of traumatic experience as a gap or space in memory that cannot be articulated, or exists only as a disconnected flashback, is that it does not adequately offer a way of reading the attempts by writers to articulate their range of experiences and reactions, which importantly include resilience. Nor does it account for the persistent post-event or post-war memories that would be characterised as a normal reaction rather than as traumatic flashbacks, but still haunt the sufferer as a legacy of the chronic traumatic environment inhabited by medical personnel that is the object of our study. These writings thus demand, as Robinett argues, a 'more complex evaluation of the relationship between narrative and experience' than that espoused by the postmodernist position wherein 'traumatic experience resists linguistic representation'.[21]

The importance of Robinett's approach is reinforced by Higonnet's analysis of trauma in nurses' wartime accounts where she argues for the need to 'uncover an alternate history of World War I traumas'.[22] One of the few critics to identify the narratives of trauma contained in medical accounts from the First World War, she suggests that the very terminology used in the First World War, 'shell shock' and its associations with combat, 'seems inappropriate for a discussion of the mental trauma experienced by medical staff', noting that '[p]erhaps the terminology itself impeded this insight'.[23] Over the course of the twentieth century war trauma has been synonymous with combat, a problem that the Vietnam nurses had to contend with when they claimed the legitimacy of psychological wounds received outside combat. Only during the recent war in Iraq has this approach broadened to occasionally include medical personnel, though even now most of the discussion of war trauma still focuses on the combatant.

Given the limitations posed by reading traumatic experience through theorists in the humanities that we have noted above, our analysis draws on psychiatric and psychological approaches to trauma since, as Roger Luckhurst acknowledges, 'psychiatric discourse assumes a plurality of possible responses to traumatic impacts. Cultural theory too often demands that the impossible, aporetic or melancholic response is the only appropriate ethical condition for individuals and communities defined by their post-traumatic afterwardsness.'[24] Especially relevant to our reading is acknowledging 'the different trajectory psychiatric practice is taking from the assertions of trauma theory as it appears in the humanities'.[25] In particular this trajectory acknowledges resilience as a reaction to traumatic experience. Specific approaches to this 'different trajectory' on traumatic breakdown are found in work by Paulson and Krippner and Stein *et al.*, for example, who argue for a combined medico-socio-cultural approach that acknowledges the relationship between cultural constructions and definitions of trauma and traumatic breakdown and for broadening the model to incorporate resilience into the narrative of wartime stress and its treatment.[26] Thus Stein *et al.* argue that 'we need ... to emphasise narratives that celebrate resilience and create the expectation that distress and dissipation of distress after trauma are normal'.[27]

Tensions continue both in the humanities and in psychological and psychiatric discussion about how trauma is expressed or silenced and that expression's relation to the pain carried by individuals, as well as the extent to which individuals suffer long-term consequences from the traumatic experience. The articulation of the traumatic experience is seen as politically important by theorists such as Judith Herman, as it can be therapeutic for the individual and can bear witness to traumatic events that need to be made public.[28] For Kali Tal, '[b]earing witness is an aggressive act. It is born out of a refusal to bow to outside pressure to revise or repress experience, a decision to embrace conflict rather than conformity, to endure a lifetime of anger and pain rather than submit to the seductive pull of revision and repression.'[29] But Tal's valorisation of such witness carries problems even as it identifies the need to employ trauma for political purposes. The survivor's burden arises out of a compulsion to keep the war-shattered combatant or civilian body on public view as well as to bear witness to one's own pain and to the pain of medical personnel as a community. Yet taking on this role can become problematic if it stands in the way of resolving the very real lived experience of post-traumatic stress. As Dominick LaCapra posits

> The invest[ment] of trauma with value ... create[s] a more or less unconscious desire to remain within the trauma: Those traumatized by extreme events, as well as empathizing with them, may resist working through because of what might also be termed a fidelity to trauma, a feeling that one must somehow keep faith with it. Part of this feeling may be the melancholic sentiment that, in working through the past in a manner that enables survival or a reengagement in life, one is betraying those who were overwhelmed and consumed by the traumatic past.[30]

The desire to endure a 'lifetime of pain' may therefore mean that the individual remains trapped in the traumatised state, unwilling to try and resolve it because the pain is a kind of expiation for survivor guilt which is sustained through the constant bearing of witness.

While we are hampered by the problem that psychological investigations into war trauma concentrate primarily on the combatant, it is still useful to offer a brief overview of historical approaches to wartime trauma as well as to consider current approaches to defining trauma that have bearing on our discussion.[31] We recognise that while war experience has been traumatic across time, constructions of trauma have not. The concept of trauma is contentious, fraught with argument between scholars and practitioners and, as Tracey Loughran points out, 'contains, and generates, knotty ethical and political problems'.[32] Attempts to apply defined PTSD [post-traumatic stress disorder] symptoms to historical figures and literature as well as contemporary use of such terms as 'shell shock' in everyday parlance to connote a troubled reaction, may gloss over the specificities of kinds of reaction and diagnoses, and especially the cultural context in which concepts of trauma are defined.[33] Since responses to and thus definitions of trauma are culturally based, definitions of trauma in one culture cannot be imposed on another, whether historically across time, or geographically across cultures at the same time. Thus, for example, as Jones and Wessely, and Young, among others, contend, 'shell shock' and PTSD cannot be conflated since they emerge from different cultural and medical contexts.[34] At the same time, the personal accounts we read in this book do show similarities of emotional response and in coping strategies, which underscore the importance of reading a range of experiences side by side.

The term 'trauma' to denote a mental as opposed to a physical wound was first used in the nineteenth century to describe the effects of what was first known as 'railway spine'. Railway accidents would jar the passenger, causing whiplash or other back injuries, which themselves manifested no visible wounds. With this came concerns that such injuries could be faked and the difference between real sufferers and charlatans hard to distinguish. Thus the syndrome was renamed by Hermann Oppenheim in 1889 as 'traumatic neurosis', and is credited with being the first instance where the term trauma was applied in psychiatry, where 'before that it had been the exclusive purview of surgery'.[35] The symptoms of 'traumatic neurosis' were similar to those of hysteria, a highly gendered diagnosis, since it originated in a theory that women's biology predisposed them to neurosis. Although working in different cities, both Janet and Freud identified that the symptoms of hysteria could be relieved by 'the talking cure', by putting the trauma into words. These origins point to the legacy of stigma that still surrounds wartime trauma, where sufferers may be seen as malingerers and/or as showing 'feminine' weakness, and to the idea that recovery was predicated on expression of the experience.

From the American Civil War onwards, forms of breakdown that are manifest in physical and psychological symptoms have been documented as a response to war stressors, and the medical community of the time variously offered hypotheses, both physical and mental, to try and explain causation. 'Soldier's Heart', coined in 1870 by Arthur Meyers, described a disorder with symptoms such as 'extreme fatigue, dyspnea, palpitations, sweating, tremors, and occasionally complete syncope'. Elaborated on by an American Civil War Army surgeon, Jacob Mendez DaCosta, in 1871 as a 'strictly biological response to the stress of battle',[36] 'soldier's heart' was replaced by the terms 'irritable heart' and 'effort syndrome'.

The culture in which a particular war is remembered also, of course, has implications for constructions of trauma. As Ben Shephard outlines in his historical discussion of war and psychiatry:

> [P]ublic opinion was not constant. In the Great War there was considerable public concern about shell-shock, which led, one eminent psychiatrist believed, to a 'wave of sentimentality' that made 'sane treatment of shell-shock' much more difficult. In contrast, in Britain during the Second World War (though not in the United States) civilians had too many problems of their own – bombing, evacuation, rationing – to spare much sympathy for the soldier who had broken down. During and after the Vietnam War, public attitudes changed several times and the stereotype of the Vietnam veteran in the media went from being a psychopathic baby-killer to an innocent victim.[37]

The cultural context surrounding the trauma of the First World War can be defined by conflicting attitudes in Edwardian Britain that were simultaneously imperialist, stressing 'administrative rationality and masculine civic virtue', and 'feminine and inward looking', defined by 'egalitarianism, "progressivism", consumerism, popular democracy [and] feminism'.[38] In the military wartime context this could translate into execution for the man who, suffering from uncontrollable breakdown, was deemed to have deserted in the face of the enemy, or into a return home for psychiatric treatment.

In spite of growing recognition during and after the First World War that wartime stress could lead to breakdown, little had changed in terms of preparation for this at the outbreak of the Second World War. A British doctor who had served in the First World War was angered by the lack of preparation for psychiatric casualties amongst soldiers when he served in Egypt in 1940. The term 'battle fatigue' originated when this doctor and others found that men suffering from milder forms of neurosis often just needed rest.[39] The term, of course, also avoided any diagnosis of a psychiatric condition, implying, as shell shock did, a physical cause. It also allowed men to be sent back to their units rapidly, rather than being invalided out. Other areas of the British service were not so sympathetic. The RAF defined all breakdown as LMF ('lacking moral fibre'), furthering the surrounding stigma and reinforcing the idea that the origins of breakdown were innate.[40] Although the Americans instigated a form of psychiatric testing for its recruits, aimed at weeding out individuals who might not be psychologically fit, in reality this often involved a three-minute questioning by a psychiatrist or physician.[41] After the war there was a recognition on both sides of the Atlantic that soldiers' families needed to support them in reintegrating into civilian life, but psychiatric treatment still carried stigma. Popular representations of returning soldiers, such as in the American film *The Best Years of our Lives* (1946), placed much of the responsibility for the recovery of returning servicemen at the hands of their wives or mothers, giving women, rather than the state, responsibility for the men's well-being.

The understanding post-Second World War that long-term exposure to war stressors made individuals increasingly likely to break down led, during the Vietnam War, to the American decision to limit the tour of duty to one year; yet this tactic carried some unforeseen morale issues, when individuals rotated in and out of the warzone alone, rather than surrounded by the support of a unit who had trained together. As we will see in Chapters 5 and 6 which discuss the Vietnam War, the cultural context in which the war was fought, including a draft system that worked against poor white youth, African Americans and Hispanics, as well as the reaction against the war at home, adversely affected the psychological well-being of those who fought. Lack of support, actual or perceived, on their return home exacerbated the wartime traumatic experience, as well as the sense of having participated in a highly contentious, lost war.

Yet it was post-Vietnam War psychiatry (linked to treatment for survivors of Second World War concentration camps) that tried to uncover the specific causes behind war trauma, defining it as post-traumatic stress syndrome or disorder, with a listing of stressors and subsequent physical and psychological symptoms in the *Diagnostic and Statistical Manual of Mental Disorders* (*DSM*-III) in 1980. More recently, in the Iraq and Afghanistan wars, PTSD has been reconsidered, and other forms of stress response have been made to distinguish between manifestation of stress that occurs immediately after an event, acute stress reaction, and stress that manifests much later (PTSD). In this war, too, some discussion of concussion caused by high explosives has brought us back to the concept of 'shell shock', so that while we would not want to say that we have come full circle, contention over whether the source of injury is physical or psychological, and to what extent these can be separated given our increasing knowledge of the brain, persists.

These ongoing debates move us beyond the medical and psychiatric and into the way trauma has become a socio-cultural issue. As Loughran writes:

> Shell shock is integral to our ideas of the First World War, and because this conflict has been so crucial in forming our understanding of war in general, that means that histories of shell shock have a vital role to play in determining how we, as moderns, orient ourselves toward war, how in turn these orientations shape the stories we tell ourselves about past and future wars, and what war itself means. Its histories are therefore messy.[42]

Given the 'messiness' of those histories, and the problem that the term 'trauma' has become something of an undefined catch-phrase, it is useful to highlight recent discussions in this area. One crucial element in the reading of these texts is being aware of the distinction between PTSD and 'normal' shock response to traumatic events that is part of the current conversation about war and trauma. Scurfield and Platoni assert that

> [t]rauma *always* has a significant impact on all who experience it, although this does not necessarily result in Post-traumatic Stress Disorder (PTSD) or other psychological disorders. In other words, exposure to trauma is so catastrophic that it will evoke symptoms in almost everyone, regardless of one's background or pre-morbid factors. 'It is abnormal *not* to have strong reactions to trauma.'[43]

This recognition will become evident again in DeCoster's comments on traumatic experience in the Iraq War in Chapter 7. Even while 'almost everyone' will respond with some form of shock reaction, it is important for our reading of texts written in the immediate term, such as letters and diaries, that we also keep in mind the process by which traumatic reaction emerges. Scurfield and Platoni note that

[p]eople seldom 'break down' psychologically or become overwhelmed while in the midst of war ... or in the immediate aftermath. Most survivors are able to 'bury' painful feelings and thoughts and learn how to 'detach' from emotions in order to continue functioning and survive. In fact, typically there is a delay in the onset of problematic emotions and thoughts until sometime after the danger has passed – the battlefield is no place to fall apart or spiral down into a state of emotional dyscontrol. This 'sometime after' could be hours, days, weeks or possibly months, years or decades later.[44]

Many of the writings we consider show how individuals are conscious of employing this kind of detachment, or other forms of coping, but only those written from hindsight can convey the distinction between such coping and long-term resilience. Although researchers still 'differ in their conceptions of resilience as a set of characteristics',[45] currently they define 'the presence or absence of resilience [as] inferred post hoc by the absence of psychological disorder when disorder might otherwise be expected (but cannot be predicted with certainty) in individuals who are presumed to be "at risk" for stress-related psychopathology'.[46] Thus, like breakdown, it is, as Luckhurst notes, intimately linked to the traumatic response.[47] In many instances we find that breakdown and resilience coexist in the same narrative. Reading resilience carries its own problems, however. It is difficult to tease out the distinctions between repression, silence and a resilience that is acknowledged by the individual as the means by which he or she avoided breakdown during or after the war. As Scurfield and Platoni contend, it is important not to confuse detachment with coping or resilience in the long term or coping with a form of repression that entirely avoids the experience: '[f]or most survivors who have become experts at detachment or denial, typically at some point this stops working well.'[48]

There is a range of current thinking around repression and long-term coping. Thus, alongside a certain valorising of emotional pain that we see in Tal, or Scurfield and Platoni's contention that repression rarely works well in the long term, Nigel Hunt's recent exploration of wartime trauma and coping finds that at times suppression and repression of experience may, in fact, contribute to coping and thus to longer-term resilience. At the same time, however, when individuals cannot suppress the experience effectively, Hunt asserts the importance of narrative and its role in resilience. Noting that the main coping strategies people use are 'avoidance and processing', he writes

Most people do most of their coping through avoidance; it is often easier not to think about a problem and hope it will go away, and in the real world, it often does. With psychological problems, including PTSD, effective avoidance means that symptoms are rarely or never experienced, but there is the potential for future problems arising as any trauma-related information (e.g. cognitions, emotions) remains in the memory and is not dealt with. Processing – used by most of us for a minority of the time – concerns the active 'working through' of problems, in our case traumatic recollections. Traumatic memories that are worked through are turned into narrative-explicit memories. *Through narrative, the individual deals with cognitions, emotions and behaviours associated with the memory.*[49] [our italics]

More generally, Hunt summarises a range of responses to war trauma that we find in the works we explore throughout this book. In some instances individuals are traumatised, finding 'their memories emotionally unbearable'. Others 'manage to suppress their memories, whether through conscious or unconscious mechanisms'. Still others ' "work through" or cognitively process their responses, ultimately learning from what happens'. He affirms that many individuals have 'no difficult emotional memories or problems'.[50] While this may seem to contradict Scurfield and Platoni's assertion that '[t]rauma *always* has a significant impact on those who experience it', there is a distinction to be made between 'normal' immediate response and long-term 'post-traumatic' difficulties. Hunt also recognises that in understanding war experience we need to take into consideration what psychologists call 'post-traumatic growth', where individuals report positive outcomes of their traumatic war experience, or, as we often see in the narratives discussed in this book, present a paradoxical response which categorises the experience as both the worst and best experience of their lives. What is particularly important in Hunt's discussion is his call for a new way of examining the particular trauma induced by war, which allows for this often paradoxical nature of the experience:

[T]here is a case for arguing that we need to have a diagnostic category of war trauma distinct from PTSD, as PTSD covers only a proportion of the symptoms experienced by people suffering from war trauma. Rather than take that approach, we may help victims of war more effectively using a narrative approach that takes into account the breadth of their experience. … Many people who have experienced war talk about the excitement, the buzz, and about learning about themselves and the development of new skills that are useful in later life, and these experiences are just as valid as the negative symptoms experienced by others.[51]

What both Hunt and Scurfield and Platoni emphasise that is particularly relevant to our discussion, is that constructing a narrative allows the individual to order and control the experience, whether or not it carries long-term psychological effects. In addition, Hunt notably emphasises the importance of understanding war trauma through 'explor[ing] the experiences of individuals', rather than relying on quantitative studies. 'While nomothetic approaches may recognise that a range of variables impact on psychological outcome ... they cannot reconstruct the complexity as experienced by the individual'.[52] What we are concerned with here is showing the complexities that become visible as we read multiple subjective accounts across the wars under discussion, taking into account both the private role of narrative indicated by Hunt and the public role that allows these voices to be heard across time. As Rippl *et al.* note: 'autobiographical lives are always "relational lives" (Eakin, 'Relational Selves'), that is lives that are related to other subjects as well as to real and imagined communities as small as the family or as large as the nation.'[53]

Lynda Van Devanter's exploration of her own post-Vietnam process of recovery brings together the importance of narrative with the need to bear witness, and draws our attention to writing (creating narrative) as an essential part of the process by which the individual imposes meaning on that experience to 'work through' it, a primary concern in this discussion. She opens *Home before Morning* by announcing that

> I began this book as a form of therapy in early 1979. I was hoping somehow to exorcise the Vietnam War from my mind and heart. What I learned in the intervening years of writing and reliving the pain of that war is that my feelings about the war will never go away. I don't want them to. For if I forget entirely, I may be passively willing to see it happen again. I did learn, however, that the war doesn't have to own me; I can own it.[54]

Coming from a very different position, as a doctor who had been a prisoner of war of the Japanese, Aidan MacCarthy tells us in the prologue to *A Doctor's War* that he wrote on the advice of doctors in London who had removed a benign brain tumour, probably a result of head beatings in captivity, and thought 'that it might be therapeutic for me to tell others the dramatic incidents of "my" war. Thus it is after nearly thirty-five years I have written this book and come face to face with experiences that I would rather have left buried forever.'[55] Like Van Devanter and others, for him therapy is both a public bearing witness and a painful private process.

The importance of these narratives, whether they are letters, diaries or memoirs, is that in them we find articulated the subjective experience. Even when they do not directly describe trauma or breakdown, the very act of narrating these interdependent stories of healer and sufferer, be it in hurried diary entries written during the war or in a considered memoir after the war, is the means by which writers order and control the extreme psychological demands of such wartime experience, allowing us into a private space that cannot be entered by more clinical means. In this context Nussbaum's analysis of the importance of diaries to women's negotiation of their identities under stress can usefully be extended here to apply more generally to the writings under discussion: '[The diary] becomes necessary at the point when the subject begins to believe that it cannot be intelligible to itself without written articulation and representation' and thus 'the diary might arise when the experienced inner life holds the greatest threat'.[56] In his introduction to his wartime diary, *Medicine and Duty* (1928), First World War Medical Officer Harold Dearden posits that

> [The diary] came into being, indeed, without any deliberate plan on my part. It was simply that one's mind at the time was receiving a ceaseless flood of new impressions of so vivid and tumultuous a character as imperatively to demand expression, and one wrote to oneself, as it were, for no other purpose than to make that expression possible.[57]

Two other medical personnel whose writing is discussed here offer possible reasons behind their recording, each suggesting that writing arises out of a psychological need to record for the self and, looking towards the future, to bear witness to events so that they will not be forgotten. Brendan Phibbs tells us that he wrote his memoir to leave a legacy for the next generation: 'What we were, and what we did, at our best, and what happened around us, is slipping out of knowledge. That's a pity. Please, young people, listen to us before we leave'.[58] But in the immediate term, writing the diary which formed the basis for the memoir fulfilled a different function. Phibbs, an American battalion surgeon in the Second World War, tells us that 'I wrote in diaries, on the backs of requisitions and report forms, and even, as the best revenge, on the empty side of Nazi propaganda sheets ... writing was an infinitely better use of thought than brooding about future annihilation'.[59] Queen Alexandra's Nursing Sister, Mary Morris, recounting soldiers' stories from the Battle of Arnhem in the Second World War, records that she writes her diary in spite of its being forbidden because she 'resent[s] having her mail censored', suggesting that the diary fulfils an underlying need to write without constraint for oneself, as well as to integrate the voices of others into that story and to record it for the future.

Poirier, in her study of doctors' autobiographical writings, reflects further on the importance of such 'stories [as] self-contained accounts in which an author attempts to explain the meaning of an experience both to him- or herself and to others ... Storytelling is, thus, simultaneously reflective and rhetorical.'[60] Reading these diaries, letters and memoirs from a multidisciplinary perspective that draws on psychological approaches to war experience alongside life-writing theory and a literary-critical close reading of the texts offers a route into the subjective experience which cannot be reached through an objective analysis of medical history. Moreover, it allows us to take into account not only what is being said and how, but how what is said or not said is positioned in the larger cultural context which give these narratives meaning. The use of language (including repetition, imagery, simile and metaphor), the length of entries and frequency of writing in diaries and letters, what is stated or omitted (from the deliberate use of ellipses or dashes whereby the writer indicates what cannot be said to the complete and unexplained silence surrounding the lack of entries in a diary) together communicate to the reader the nuances of the experience unavailable in any other sources.

Given the lived reality in which these accounts were composed, we also need to be alert to the practical as well as emotional reasons behind silences. Not least was the working context: 'I could tell you for hours, stories ... but they'll be lost, because this kind of life allows only work and sleep.'[61] While the demands of articulating this complex experience are challenging even after the fact, to write fluently and coherently under such conditions was enormously difficult, as many diaries and letters show. In her analysis of literary texts Robinett finds that 'some writers have indeed found eloquent linguistic expression for their traumatic experiences,'[62] but the range of life-writings discussed here are not always sophisticated and in many cases the instances of trauma are to be found 'between the lines', in snippets of commentary, brief references and euphemisms for trauma and breakdown. They are, however, equally important in providing us with ways of understanding such experience. *How* the tale is told is as significant as *what* is being narrated. In the preface to her account of nursing on the Western Front during the First World War, Mary Borden articulates the problems inherent to writing and the limitations that accompany the expression of such extreme experience:

> I have blurred the bare horror of facts and softened the reality in spite of myself, not because I wished to do so, but because I was incapable of a

nearer approach to the truth ... I have dared to dedicate these pages to the Poilus who passed through our hands during the war ... They know, not only everything that is contained in it, but all the rest that can never be written.[63]

Our reading thus keeps in mind the problems inherent in the use of language itself. While we have argued earlier that trauma is not necessarily indicated by what cannot be spoken, we also need to be aware that there may be a gap between what is spoken and our apprehension of it. Exploring the nature of language and the articulation of trauma, Kali Tal asserts that it is not the lack of language to describe the experience that is behind the inability to articulate it, but the breakdown in meaning between signifier and what is signified.

> Traumatic experience catalyzes a transformation of meaning in the signs individuals use to represent their experiences. Words such as *blood, terror, agony* and *madness* gain new meaning, within the context of the trauma, and survivors emerge from the traumatic environment with a new set of definitions. On the surface, language appears unchanged – survivors still use the word terror, non-traumatized audiences read and understand the word *terror*, and the dislocation of meaning is invisible.[64]

As well as being conscious of what can and cannot be transmitted through language, we also need to consider the larger context in which these writings are constructed and to acknowledge the differences of purpose between diaries, letters and memoirs. As we have noted, diaries are usually written in private and to meet the writer's own needs, and thus are arguably less mediated than letters and memoirs. Letters are written for and respond to a recipient, necessarily tailoring the account to the needs of the audience. In wartime, they are also subject to official censorship. The consciousness of the censor, an over-the-shoulder reader, may cause individuals to self-censor not only censorable details but also more personal intimacies. On the other hand, the exchange of letters in wartime is crucial to the sustaining of morale, as Roper, Meyer and Hanna among others have shown; they give insight into a self that may not be present in a diary, indeed that might not exist as a narrative without the need to communicate under wartime conditions.[65] Gibelli says of Italian wartime letters, 'the letter presented a form of therapy, it became a means for self-preservation: to write home and receive mail was first of all a means to alleviate the pain of distance and the horror of the present'.[66] At the same time, when reading any genre, we have to be aware of the narratives that individuals choose. To give a specific example, as Shephard notes, introspection is less culturally acceptable in men than women[67] and thus male writers may omit their emotional responses to situations because of unconscious cultural pressures. This applies especially to memoirs since they are constructed with a public audience in mind, written as a public testimony to the experience, as well as a private therapy.

Unlike diaries and letters which tell an immediate story, memoirs are necessarily more reflective, especially as they are often written years after the war, when the experience and the meaning it carries as a whole can be contemplated from a distance. The lapse of time may offer a necessary space between the traumatic events and their recording. Especially, these may show a very conscious awareness of revealing or seeing that had been shut down during the war. Both Vera Brittain and Brenda McBryde speak of protective 'shutters' that sustained much-needed detachment from the surrounding horror during the war. Brittain notes how what she calls a necessary 'psychological shutter' that operated during the war might 'refuse to operate' at a later time so that individuals were forced to contend with a repressed trauma.[68] In a more positive way, Brenda McBryde credits her autobiography of nursing in the Second World War with lifting the 'shutters' she had kept in place since the war.[69] The importance of seeing as witness returns again and again throughout the works under discussion from Julia Stimson's assertion that '[t]hese frightful sights would work havoc with the brain' in the First World War, to Dave Hnida's Iraq War memoir, *Paradise General*, which he says he wrote because he wanted the public to *see* what could not be revealed in news coverage: 'I knew people back home saw and heard about the deaths and the wounds, but on a screen or in writing it was all sanitized and sterile … They didn't see, feel, or smell what a broken body is like up close and personal.'[70] Seeing, here and in many of the works we read throughout the book, becomes an important metaphor for revealing what is hidden, especially what cannot be entirely comprehended or described, and articulating it to the writing self as well as bringing it to the attention of a public audience.

Memoirs written after the war may, like Van Devanter's quoted earlier, be written out of a psychological need for control over an experience that still haunts the writer. Yet at times a single account may not be enough to contain the trauma. In *Autopsy of War* (2012), Vietnam War veteran surgeon John Parrish's second work to examine his own legacy of the war in the larger context of American politics, the author, conscious of the limitations of expression we have noted previously, claims that he must keep 'writing and rewriting [his] war story' in an attempt to 'get it right'.[71] Returning to the experience to articulate it to the writer him- or herself and then to others is the reason the works discussed here exist. It is precisely that need to write that allows us to enter the subjective experiences of the individuals that tell us the stories we engage with in the analysis that follows.

This discussion is necessarily selective. Only certain individuals leave us with their stories, and complete breakdown may be indicated only by silence. We cannot necessarily generalise from these accounts, but we can examine how individuals tell their stories across time and place and what similarities these reveal when they allow us to enter, however inadequately, the 'center of the hourglass' that is the space in which medical personnel in warzones operate. As Hinton affirms in his discussion of Second World War diaries, 'the luminosity of single cases' can provide 'a point of discovery'.[72] When these single cases are brought together then we find a virtual community made up of these voices.

The voices heard here, with the notable exception of a few professional writers, come from individuals who were made writers by the war, whether they were writing diaries and letters with no thought of an audience more public than themselves or family and friends, or returned to their war experience in its aftermath in memoirs. For the most part these were ordinary individuals writing because they found themselves in extraordinary circumstances. At the same time, in articulating their emotions directly or obliquely, they are unusual in revealing the inner self, especially in a demographic who have been trained to be in control and not to show weakness. Historically the majority of medical personnel have remained silent about their experiences, but that silence makes it even more important to pay attention to those who have spoken. Their drive to articulate the experience, for men and women, British, Canadian and American, is the common denominator that unites individuals beyond sex, wartime role or nationality. Thus, although political and cultural climates set the First World War American volunteers apart from their British counterparts, for example, what is more striking are the similarities we find when these medical personnel struggle to articulate the onslaught of death and dying that surrounds them. Likewise, while those who experienced the Vietnam War carried the particular burden of involvement in that war, their immediate everyday experience of caring for the injured and sick, maintaining their psychological equilibrium in the face of casualties and struggling to fight their post-war demons takes place, as they themselves note, in the context of similar experiences from earlier wars. Reading multiple individual narratives across time arguably brings into being a virtual community that reveals important commonalities. The ensuing chapters show how close examination of personal accounts allows us to see points of intersection that transcend the isolation of separate experiences and specific wars and war cultures.

Because we cannot hope to be exhaustive in this discussion, we have chosen to focus on specific theatres of war or on specifics groups at war in the following chapters. In discussing the First World War in Chapters 1 and 2 we begin with a general examination of accounts by nurses and doctors on the Western Front. The second chapter then focuses more specifically on the particular experience of American nurses and ambulance drivers, both before and after 1917 and the United States' official involvement. In Chapters 3 and 4, we turn to the Second World War and again begin with a general examination of accounts by nurses and doctors, focused on the invasion of Europe from 1944 onwards. Chapter 4 specifically focuses on doctors in prisoner of war camps in Europe and the Far East. In discussing the Vietnam War we focus in Chapter 5 on the Vietnam nurse veterans, the first medical personnel to claim publicly their experience as traumatic, and then examine accounts by doctors and medics in Chapter 6. Finally, in part because of the limitations on available material, we draw on memoirs by American medical personnel of their experiences in the Iraq War, to examine how they write their experiences in the very immediate term. Since this is the final chapter, we focus on how medical personnel negotiate and grieve for the deaths of their patients.[73] Our conclusion draws together the commonalities of experience we find throughout these accounts.

Towards the ending of *Home before Morning*, Van Devanter reminds us that the physically and psychologically dangerous reality of war nursing has been a part of the experience in all wars:

> [E]ven to talk about Vietnam is not the whole story. During World War II, hundreds of women were killed. There were more than sixty-five women who were POWs on Corregidor for years. Women were on the beachhead at Anzio, caring for the wounded while bombs exploded around them. In all of our wars, women have been killed, maimed, disabled, and psychologically injured.[74]

If we extend this to include not just nurses but all medical personnel, then we need to pay attention to how these men and women relate their war stories, and especially their psychological response, whether the narrative is one of breakdown or resilience, or more commonly, a struggle that involves both responses.

Our focus is the twentieth century. But the war that ushered in decades of conflict began as the nineteenth century drew to a close. The 'last of the gentlemen's wars' and the first modern war was the South African War in 1899–1902. The memoirs and letters of its medical personnel serve as snapshots of reactions that are replicated and transformed by their descendants in the wars that followed.

The South African War (also known as the Second Anglo-Boer War) began on 10 October 1899 and ended on 31 May 1902. It was fought between the British Empire, the eventual victor, and the Afrikaans-speaking Dutch settlers of the two independent Boer republics, the South African Republic and the Orange Free State, which eventually became incorporated in 1910 as the Union of South Africa, a dominion of the British Empire. Although tensions had been growing for many years, the real issue was over who would control the lucrative Witwatersrand gold mines. The South African War was 'essentially a modern war',[75] combining tactics of the nineteenth century with new technologies such as field telephones, balloons for aerial reconnaissance, high-velocity rifles and heavy artillery. Barbed wire, trenches and guerrilla warfare were also features along with concentration camps. Of the nearly 28,000 Boer civilians who died in the camps of disease due to poor hygiene, poor administration and neglect, approximately 22,000 were children, and more than 14,000 Africans died in their own camps, the conditions of which were far worse than those in white camps.[76] Seven thousand Boers and 22,000 British combatants died in the war, three-quarters of the British number from disease.[77] The media also played a central part, with newspapers and magazines aimed at audiences from adult to adolescent, emphasizing the cult of the New Imperialism. The press and the government had a symbiotic relationship: just as the press helped to 'sell' the war, the war helped to sell papers.[78]

Memoirs published both during and after the war took time to praise and defend the RAMC (Royal Army Medical Corps, which was formed in 1898) and other medical personnel, who were often the subject of criticism in the newspapers for the rising tide of deaths from disease and wounds. Defenders of the work of medical personnel argued that such criticisms were made by those who had no first-hand experience of the devotion to duty as well as the courage that was constantly on display in South Africa. Redvers Buller asserted that

> No men could have behaved more admirably than my Imperial bearer companies, or 'body snatchers' as the men used to call them. The only fault I had to find with my men was that they were too venturesome and would go right into the firing line after wounded men. Whether for their mercy, their

tenderness, or their endurance my bearer companies deserve the highest praise, and my only regret is that, from the very nature of their duties, their work went more unrecognised than I could have wished.[79]

A rather doggerel poem published in the *Morning Post* and quoted in N. J. C. Rutherford's memoir *Soldiering with a Stethoscope* (1937) praised: 'the man of the RAMC':

Buzzing about on the field like a bee,
Tending the wounded where lead's flying hot,
Biting his lip when he gets himself shot;
Brave as the best of us, hurt and not tell,
Doctor he may be – he's soldier as well.[80]

W. S. Inder further stressed that RAMC orderlies

do all in their power, tending the sick and dying with the sympathy and tenderness of women ... every doctor, nurse, and orderly has had to make personal sacrifices in various ways. Every person here engaged in hospital work, I am sure, starts the day determined to do his level best for the sick and suffering.[81]

Thus medical memoirs of the South African War went beyond being the fact-driven catalogues of bullet wounds and the organisation of field hospitals that make up a large part of their content. In a larger sense, these memoirs act as apologias, vindicating for a sceptical public the work of those who treated the wounded and sick. They situate wartime medical staff at the heart of the nation's combat response. And in this way the South African War of 1899–1902 marked a turning point not only for the reputation of soldiers but also for that of their carers. As Kevin Brown argues,

What no one at the time could know was that the new century so soon to dawn was to be a century of total war in which health and medicine were to assume great importance for good and ill, nor that this colonial adventure straddling the 'Century's corpse outleant' was to prefigure the relationship between medicine and warfare in the years to come.[82]

A key part of this relationship is evidenced in the intimate and at times gruesome details of the effects of war on the body that are highlighted in the South African memoirs. For, as Sir Frederick Treves noted in the preface to his *Tale of a Field Hospital* (1912), 'It may be that the story is a little sombre, and possibly on occasions gruesome; but war, as viewed from the standpoint of a field hospital, presents little that is cheery'.[83] Inder, a member of the Kendal Division of the St John's Ambulance Brigade (SJAB), who, after serving two years at the front, died of pneumonia at Bloemfontein in January 1901, describes in his posthumously published letters treating everything from 'ague, abscess groin and a crushed hip and abdomen' to fractures of the arms and legs, gun-shot wounds and rheumatic fever.[84] Nearly half the doctors in his camp are 'volunteer civilians, scarcely to be distinguished from the military when dressed in khaki uniform'. His own 'idea in volunteering' recalls the influence of popular culture's view of warfare: 'a field stretcher bearer and first aid man at the firing line, where the bullets were spitting, and to treat my comrades in arms when they most needed help, that is, when they fell, and here we are at the base of the front.' But he acknowledges how much he is needed in the less-than-dramatic location of the field hospital: 'I can assure you we have our hands full. There are upwards of 500 English St John men doing duty out here.'[85] The recovery of the men is the best reward for their work.

William Watson's send-off as part of the Preston SJAB recalls the popular enthusiasm for imperial war with 'crowds of people' lining the route to the train, which drew out from the station 'amid the sounds of music and the cheering of the crowds'. In London, too, Watson had 'an exciting time while marching to Waterloo station ... crowds followed our procession cheering, ... we had to fight out way through one by one.'[86] Arriving in Cape Town in December 1899, during the 'Black Week' of British disasters at Magersfontein and the Modder River, Watson is attached to the Wynberg staff of No. 2 General Hospital and on his first morning is sent to meet a convoy of wounded from Magersfontein. He encounters 'a terrible load of mutilated human beings ... some without legs, and some without arms, there were scalp wounds and gun shot wounds of every description'. He assists in operations, describing how 'men were mutilated and cut open like sheep, bullets were taken out of almost every part of the body, and limbs'. His first night duty was 'the most heart-rendering [sic] I ever experienced' and he describes a scene that would become almost commonplace in the twentieth-century war hospital and the emotions that would become familiar to his counterparts whether in Flanders, Changi, Saigon or Fallujah:

> As I walked through the lines of marquees, which in all appearances was a place of human torture and torment, I could hear the moaning and groaning of the wounded and dying, some of whom having got beyond the aid of human skill could be heard uttering some blasphemous curse

against the enemy who had inflicted his wound. ... A prayer came to the lips of many a man that night who never knew what it was to pray before, but finding his life ebbing to a close at last appealed to the only supernatural being of Providence to save his soul from destruction. Many a man died praying that he might see his wife and family once more, which, alas, could not be. Such was the state of the Wynberg hospital after the battles of Magersfontein and Modder River. A place of butchery, terrible agony and extreme suffering. Nobody who has not seen a hospital in time of war has any idea what a terrible price has been paid for the so called honour and glory of Old England. Never shall I forget the early days of the campaign at Wynberg Hospital, when men were dying almost every hour, men who had been in the same corp [*sic*] as myself, and been my playmates at school. They suffered for their countrys [*sic*] sake, not for themselves, for they had everything to lose, and nothing to gain; with the result that they now occupy a soldiers [*sic*] grave so far away from their native land, never to be heard again and deprived of the blessing of seeing their home circle once more.[87]

In Watson's eyes, though, these are the fortunate men. The unfortunate are those who 'lose a limb', for when they return home, 'they are thrown on the streets with a remuneration scarcely enough for their existence'. Such would be the common experience of many war veterans in the decades that followed. And the doctor, nurse, stretcher-bearer, ambulance driver and orderly would continue to be their witnesses and bear the burden of that witness.

Notes

1 Brian Turner, 'AB Negative (The Surgeon's Poem)', lines 33–41, from *Here Bullet* (Hexham: Bloodaxe Books, 2005; 2007), p. 25.
2 The official American term for the Iraq War is 'Operation Iraqi Freedom'. The term Iraq War will be used throughout this book to refer to the war that developed from the American invasion of Iraq in 2003.
3 Even after the war in Iraq this is still the case, even though an article written as long ago as 1989 concludes that '[i]t appears obvious to the authors of this article that there are significant risk factors for stress reactions or PTSD for female nursing personnel assigned to combat areas'. Shirley Menard and Lois Johns, 'The Military Nurse Experience in Vietnam: Stress and Impact', *Journal of Clinical Psychology* 45: 5 (1989): 736–44; p. 744.
4 Margaret Higonnet, 'Authenticity and Art in Trauma Narratives of World War One', *Modernism/Modernity* 9: 1 (2002): 91–107; p. 92. Higonnet focuses primarily on First World War nurses in this discussion.

5 Michael Winship, 'At a Military Hospital, Warriors Are Not the Only Wounded' (15 May 2012), p. 2: http://billmoyers.com/2012/05/15/at-a-military-hospital-warriors-are-not-the-only-wounded (accessed 5 October 2014).

6 Winship, 'At a Military Hospital', p. 1.

7 www.theguardian.com/world/2013/dec/06/canadian-armed-forces-hit-spate-suicides (accessed 5 October 2014).

8 Anthony Babington, *Shell-Shock: A History of the Changing Attitudes to War Neurosis* (Barnsley: Leo Cooper, 1997), p. 10.

9 Mark Bostridge, *Florence Nightingale: The Woman and Her Legend* (London: Viking/Penguin, 2008), p. 299.

10 Babington, *Shell-Shock*, p. 123.

11 Fiona Reid, *Broken Men: Shell Shock, Treatment and Recovery in Britain 1914–30* (London and New York: Continuum, 2010), p. 139.

12 The file of Lady Nellie Martin Harvey in the Imperial War Museum (99/76/1) contains information on various fundraising activities including a concert to raise funds for the nurses' rest home and a pamphlet advertising 'Rest Home for Nurses, Connected with the College of Nursing, at Seaside Cottage, Bonchurch, Isle of Wight'. The list of the committee members includes Lady Martin Harvey, Dame Maud McCarthy, GBE, RRC, and Matron: Miss A. Burgess, RRC. It is not clear whether this is the rest home for 'broken' nurses referred to in the concert advertisement.

13 Edgar Jones, 'Doctors and Trauma in the First World War: The Response of British Military Psychiatrists', in Peter Gray and Kendrick Oliver (eds), *The Memory of Catastrophe* (Manchester: Manchester University Press, 2004), p. 94. In spite of this example, the rest of Jones's discussion focuses on psychiatric responses to combatant trauma.

14 James Marion Kirtley, MD, 'Beanie, Ernie and More', in Patricia Sewell (ed.), *Healers in World War II: Oral Histories of Medical Corps Personnel* (Jefferson, NC, and London: McFarland & Company, 2001), p. 32.

15 For an overview of 'psychological trauma syndromes' and their history with particular reference to carers, see Patrick J. Morrissette, *The Pain of Helping: Psychological Injury of Helping Professionals* (New York: Brunner-Routledge, 2004), pp. 2–9.

16 Charles R. Figley, 'From Veterans of War to Veterans of Terrorism: My Maps of Trauma', in Charles R. Figley (ed.), *Mapping Trauma and Its Wake: Autobiographic Essays by Pioneer Trauma Scholars* (New York and London: Routledge, 2006), p. 52.

17 Dr Heidi Squier Kraft, *Rule Number Two: Lessons I Learned in a Combat Hospital* (Boston and London: Little, Brown, 2007), p. 134.

18 Cathy Caruth, *Unclaimed Experience: Trauma, Narrative, and History* (Baltimore and London: Johns Hopkins University Press, 1996).

19 Nico Carpentier, 'Introduction' in Nico Carpentier (ed.), *Culture, Trauma, and Conflict: Cultural Studies Perspectives on War* (Newcastle: Cambridge Scholars Press, 2007), p. 8, citing Kai Erikson, *Everything in Its Path* (New York: Simon and Schuster, 1976).

20 Caruth, *Unclaimed Experience*, p. 152.

21 Jane Robinett, 'The Narrative Shape of Traumatic Experience', *Literature and Medicine* 26: 2 (Fall, 2007): 290–311; pp. 291, 290. A section of this theoretical discussion has appeared in an earlier form in Carol Acton and Jane Potter, ' "These Frightful Sights Would Work Havoc with One's Brain": Subjective Experience, Trauma, and Resilience in First World War Writings by Medical Personnel', *Literature and Medicine* 30: 1 (Spring 2012): 61–85.

22 Higonnet, 'Authenticity and Art', p. 91.

23 Higonnet, 'Authenticity and Art', p. 96.

24 Roger Luckhurst, *The Trauma Question* (London and New York: Routledge, 2008), pp. 211–12. It should be noted that Luckhurst does not necessarily endorse this perspective.

25 Luckhurst, *Trauma Question*, p. 211.

26 Daryl S. Paulson and Stanley Krippner, *Haunted by Combat: Understanding PTSD in War Veterans Including Women, Reservists, and Those Coming Back from Iraq* (Westport, Conn.: Praeger Security International, 2007); Dan J. Stein, Soraya Seedat, Amy Iversen and Simon Wessely, 'Post-traumatic Stress Disorder: Medicine and Politics', *The Lancet* 369: 9556 (13–19 January 2007): 139–44. See also Brian J. Lukey and Victoria Tepe (eds), *Biobehavioural Resilience to Stress* (Boca Raton, Fla., and London: CRC Press/Taylor & Francis, 2008) on stress and resilience in the military context.

27 Stein *et al.*, 'Post-traumatic Stress Disorder', p. 142.

28 See for example, Judith Herman, *Trauma and Recovery* (New York: Basic Books, 1992).

29 Kali Tal, *Worlds of Hurt: Reading the Literatures of Trauma* (Cambridge: Cambridge University Press, 1996), p. 7.

30 Dominick LaCapra, *Writing History, Writing Trauma* (Baltimore, Md. and London: Johns Hopkins University Press, 2001), p. 22–3.

31 So many works have been written about combatant trauma, on war in general and on specific wars, that we do not need to reiterate this discussion here, except to provide a brief overview. However, many of these works are important to our discussion and will be referenced in the ensuing chapters.

32 Tracey Loughran, 'Shell Shock, Trauma, and the First World War: The Making of a Diagnosis and Its Histories', *Journal of the History of Medicine and Allied Sciences* 67: 1 (2010): 94–119; p. 101.

33 See for example Philip A. Mackowiak and Sonja V. Batten, 'Post-Traumatic Stress Reactions before the Advent of Post-Traumatic Stress

Disorder: Potential Effects on the Lives and Legacies of Alexander the Great, Captain James Cook, Emily Dickinson, and Florence Nightingale', *Military Medicine* 173: 12 (2008): 1158–63; Philippe Birmes, Leah Hatton, Alain Brunet and Laurence Schmitt, 'Early Historical Literature for Post-Traumatic Symptomatology', *Stress and Health* 19 (2003): 17–26; Jonathan Shay, *Achilles in Vietnam: Combat Trauma and the Undoing of Character* (New York: Scribner, 1995) and *Odysseus in America: Combat Trauma and the Trials of Homecoming* (New York: Scribner, 2003).

34 Edgar Jones and Simon Wessely 'War Syndromes: The Impact of Culture on Medically Unexplained Symptoms', *Medical History* 49: 1 (January 2005): 55–78. For a historical overview of symptoms and diagnoses, see also their article 'A Paradigm Shift in the Conceptualization of Psychological Trauma in the Twentieth Century', *Journal of Anxiety Disorders* 21 (2007): 164–75; Allan Young, *The Harmony of Illusions: Inventing Post-Traumatic Stress Disorder* (Princeton, NJ: Princeton University Press, 1995).

35 G. C. Lasiuk and K. M. Hegadoren, 'Posttraumatic Stress Disorder Part I: Historical Development of the Concept', *Perspectives in Psychiatric Care* 42: 1 (February 2006): 13–20; p. 15.

36 Lasiuk and Hegadoren, 'Posttraumatic Stress Disorder', p. 17.

37 Ben Shephard, *A War of Nerves: Soldiers and Psychiatrists in the Twentieth Century* (Cambridge, Mass.: Harvard University Press, 2001), p. xix.

38 Shephard, *War of Nerves*, p. 20.

39 Shephard, *War of Nerves*, p. 183. As we will discuss in the chapter on the Iraq War, this treatment, referred to there as 'three hots and a cot' (three hot meals and a night's sleep), still persists as it seems to help avoid more severe breakdown.

40 Shephard, *War of Nerves*, pp. 286–8.

41 Shephard, *War of Nerves*, p. 199.

42 Loughran, Shell Shock, Trauma, p. 101.

43 Raymond Scurfield and Katherine Platoni (eds), *War Trauma and Its Wake: Expanding the Circle of Healing* (New York and Hove: Routledge, 2013), p. 18.

44 Scurfield and Platoni, 'Myths and Realities about War, Its Impact, and Healing' in Scurfield and Platoni, *War Trauma*, p. 22.

45 Lukey and Tepe (eds), *Biobehavioural Resilience to Stress*, p. xiv.

46 Barbara Palmer and Victoria Tepe, 'Introduction' to *Biobehavioural Resilience to Stress*, p. xiv.

47 Luckhurst, *Trauma Question*, pp. 210–11.

48 Scurfield and Platoni, *War Trauma*, p. 23.

49 Nigel Hunt, *Memory, War and Trauma* (Cambridge: Cambridge University Press, 2010), p. 78. For further discussion with a specific focus on American veterans of wars in Iraq and Afghanistan see Terri Tanielian and Lisa H. Jaycox (eds), *Invisible Wounds of War: Psychological and*

Cognitive Injuries, *Their Consequences, and Services to Assist Recovery* (Santa Monica, CA: RAND Corporation, Center for Military Health Policy Research).

50 Hunt, *Memory*, p. 8.
51 Hunt, *Memory*, p. 59.
52 Hunt, *Memory*, p. 93.
53 Gabriel Rippl, Phillip Schwieghauser and Therese Steffen, 'Introduction: Life Writing in an Age of Trauma', in Rippl *et al.* (eds), *Haunted Narratives: Life Writing in an Age of Trauma* (Toronto: University of Toronto Press, 2013), p. 5, citing Paul John Eakin, 'Relational Selves, Relational Lives: The Story of the Story', in G. Thomas Couser and Joseph Fichtelberg (eds) *True Relations: Essays on Autobiography and the Postmodern* (Westport, Conn.: Greenwood Press, 1998).
54 Lynda Van Devanter (with Christopher Morgan), *Home before Morning: The Story of an Army Nurse in Vietnam* (New York: Warner Books, 1983), p. ix.
55 Aidan MacCarthy, *A Doctor's War* (Cork: The Collins Press, 2005, 2008; Robson Books, 1979), p. 8.
56 Felicity Nussbaum, 'Toward Conceptualizing Diary', in James Olney (ed.), *Studies in Autobiography* (Oxford: Oxford University Press, 1988), p. 135.
57 Harold Dearden, *Medicine and Duty: A War Diary* (London: Heinemann, 1928), p. i.
58 Brendan Phibbs, *The Other Side of Time* (Boston: Little, Brown, 1987), p. ix.
59 Phibbs, *Other Side of Time*, p. viii.
60 Suzanne Poirier, *Doctors in the Making: Memoirs and Medical Education* (Iowa City: University of Iowa Press, 2009), p. 5.
61 K. E. Luard, *Unknown Warriors* (London: Chatto and Windus, 1930), p. 159.
62 Robinett, 'Narrative Shape', p. 291.
63 Mary Borden, 'Preface', *The Forbidden Zone* (London: William Heinemann, 1929).
64 Tal, *Worlds of Hurt*, p. 16.
65 Martha Hanna, *Your Death Would be Mine: Paul and Marie Pireaud in the Great War* (Cambridge, Mass.: Harvard University Press, 2006); Jessica Meyer, *Men of War: Masculinity and the First World War in Britain* (Basingstoke: Palgrave Macmillan, 2009); Michael Roper, *The Secret Battle: Emotional Survival in the Great War* (Manchester: Manchester University Press, 2010). For a comprehensive discussion of wartime letters and diaries across time see D. C. Gill, *How We Are Changed by War: A Study of Letters and Diaries from Colonial Conflicts to Operation Iraqi Freedom* (New York and London: Routledge, 2010).

66 Antonio Gibelli quoted in Sonia Cancian, *Families, Lovers and Their Letters: Italian Postwar Migration to Canada* (Manitoba: University of Manitoba Press, 2010), p. 11.

67 Shephard, *War of Nerves*, p. 19.

68 Vera Brittain, *Testament of Youth* (London: Virago, 1982), p. 384.

69 Brenda McBryde, interview in *The Age*, Wednesday 18 March 1981.

70 Dave Hnida, *Paradise General: Riding the Surge at a Combat Hospital in Iraq* (New York: Simon & Schuster, 2010), p. 163.

71 John Parrish, *Autopsy of War: A Personal History* (New York: Thomas Dunne Books/St Martin's Press, 2012), p. xi.

72 James Hinton, *Nine Wartime Lives: Mass-Observation and the Making of the Modern Self* (Oxford: Oxford University Press, 2010), p. 18.

73 Unfortunately we have been unable to find medical memoirs or other accounts by British medical personnel who served in the Iraq War for comparison with the American accounts.

74 Van Devanter, *Home before Morning*, p. 358.

75 Carolyn Burdett, *Olive Schreiner and the Progress of Feminism: Evolution, Gender and Empire* (Basingstoke, Macmillan, 2001), p. 139.

76 Donal Lowry (ed.), *The South African War Reappraised* (Manchester: Manchester University Press, 2000), p. 2. One of the most outspoken critics of the celebration of imperial manhood and public fascination with the exploits of the war was Emily Hobhouse (1860–1926) who was outraged by the concentration camps that Kitchener set up to intern Boer families. *The Brunt of War and Where It Fell* (London: Methuen & Co., 1902) offers 'an outline of the recent war, from the standpoint of the women and children', and describes the destruction of homes, relief work, life and death in the camps, and agitation in England for humane treatment of the 'enemy'. A royal commission charged with investigating how the war was handled catalogued a lack of army intelligence, mismanaged hospitals and sickly working-class volunteers. The Inter-Departmental Committee on Physical Deterioration found that 60 per cent of all recruits were physically unfit to serve in the Army.

77 Lowry, *South African War*, p. 2.

78 Paula M. Krebs, *Gender, Race and the Writing of Empire: Public Discourse and the Boer War* (Cambridge: Cambridge University Press, 1999).

79 Quoted in W. S. Inder, *On Active Service with the SJAB, South African War 1899–1902: A Diary of Life and Events in a War Hospital* (Kendal: Atkinson, 1903), p. 284.

80 Quoted in N. J. C. Rutherford, *Soldiering with a Stethoscope* (London: Stanley Paul & Co., 1937), p. 45.

81 Inder, *On Active Service with the SJAB*, pp. 151–2.

82 Kevin Brown, *Fighting Fit: Health, Medicine and War in the Twentieth Century* (Stroud: History Press, 2008), p. 13.

83 Sir Frederick Treves, *The Tale of a Field Hospital* (London: Cassell and Co., 1912), p. v.

84 Inder, *On Active Service with the SJAB*, p. 159.

85 Inder, *On Active Service with the SJAB*, p. 60.

86 W. Watson, 'An Account of My Work in South Africa, as an Hospital Orderly attached to the Royal Army Medical Corp during the Boer Campaign from December 1899 to December 1900. Including a Version of My Experiences from Preston to Pretoria', Army Medical Services Archive (ACDMS: 2001: 42).

87 Watson, 'An Account of My Work', 42.

1

'These frightful sights would work havoc with one's brain': First World War writings by medical personnel[1]

In 'Mental Cases', war poet Wilfred Owen depicted the 'men whose minds the Dead have ravished', and in 'Strange Meeting' pointed again to the psychological suffering engendered by war: 'Foreheads of men have bled where no wounds were.' The literature of the First World War is arguably the primary means by which it has been absorbed into cultural memory, and the war's psychological impact on the participants has become central to the way it is perceived. While during the Great War, what became popularly referred to as shell shock or neurasthenia was stigmatised – it is argued that Owen returned to the front after his time at Craiglockhart, a hospital for 'shell-shocked' officers, in part to prove his sanity – in the late twentieth and early twenty-first centuries, the shell-shocked soldier who embodies the psychological trauma of that war has been accorded the status of victim-hero.[2] The Shot at Dawn campaign achieved pardons in 2006 for the 306 men executed for desertion mainly on the basis that these men were suffering from shell shock engendered by the extreme conditions of trench warfare.[3] Post-war, both historians and writers have sought to document and understand the psychological trauma wrought on soldiers. Works such as Leese's *Shell Shock: Traumatic Neurosis and the British Soldiers of the First World* War (2002) and Reid's *Broken Men* (2010) examine the personal and political ramifications of 'shell shock' during the First World War, alongside more general analysis, from Anthony Babington's *Shell-Shock: A History of the Changing Attitudes to War Neurosis* (1997) and Ben Shephard's *A War of Nerves* (2001) to Edgar Jones and Simon Wessely's *Shell-Shock to PTSD: Military Psychiatry from 1900 to the Gulf War* (2006) among others. Fiction, too, has valorised the suffering of the shell-shocked soldier, most prominently Pat Barker's *Regeneration* trilogy (1991, 1993, 1995). In contrast, Michael Roper's *The Secret Battle: Emotional Survival in the Great War* (2009), which explores the tactics soldiers employed to avoid breakdown and maintain emotional well-being, offers an important move towards foregrounding resilience and survival as an alternative response to traumatic collapse. Yet these analyses focus on the combatant experience; as we point out in the Introduction, there is a marked lack of discussion of the response to extreme emotional stress borne by those who treat the casualties of war: medical personnel. This is in spite of the assertion in Remarque's *All Quiet on the Western Front* that 'a hospital alone shows what war is'.[4]

To examine healers' responses to their own service that put them in the front lines of caring for wounded and the dying during the First World War, this chapter foregrounds the autobiographical writings of the men and women who worked in those hospitals, as well as casualty clearing stations, ambulance trains, field aid-posts or dressing stations, hospital ships and ambulance units. Our reading of published and unpublished accounts written during and after the war draws on medical history, psychology and life-writing theory, as well as more literary textual analysis, to understand these individuals' often oblique representation of an experience that can be defined as traumatic, and, equally importantly, their construction of narratives of resilience that offer an alternative to breakdown. These accounts, at times fragmented, ambiguous and contradictory, defined as much by what is left unsaid as by what is said, arguably constitute the first body of writing to document and legitimise an experience of war that remains largely unacknowledged: how medical personnel perceived and negotiated the physical and psychological context in which they worked. In doing so they become the starting point that reaches through the wars of the twentieth century and into those of the twenty-first. Unlike later writers they had little or no precedent for articulating their experiences. Even though each war is different and in each instance medical personnel to some extent must reinvent themselves as witnesses and writers, the Great War established medical personnel accounts as an identifiable part of the war-writing genre, both during and after the war. While there are medical accounts from both the Anglo-Boer war (as we have shown) and the American Civil War, they do not constitute such a defined body of material. In many ways, as with combatant accounts, the initiation of these men and women into technological warfare on a vast scale also becomes ours, since we understand it in large part through their accounts and we necessarily read accounts from later wars in the context of the 'First' World War. While their articulation of their experience is grounded in the cultural context in which these medical personnel wrote, their representation of their experience, in the daily entries of a diary for example, is written without recourse to any prior tradition in which to situate themselves, or which could offer them a means of negotiating the emotional and physical impact of their experience.

When we examine how medical personnel articulate the psychological stresses of their novel situation we find a range of responses, from the heightened language of sacrifice and duty and the desire to endure to utter despair at the apparent futility of the war as it is manifest in the thousands of dead and wounded who pass through their aid posts, casualty clearing stations, ambulances and hospitals. Drawing on the subjective experience as it is represented in letters, diaries and memoirs offers a way of understanding the nuances and contradictions involved in a highly complex response to extreme psychological strain as well as highlighting the extent to which medical personnel bear a huge burden of the psychological cost of war. Yet while their experience is undeniably traumatic, their writings do not invite a reading through theories of trauma that see such experience as defined by a breakdown in meaning or lack of a coherent narrative. In spite of silences and fragmentation, the life-writings of these doctors, nurses and ambulance drivers demonstrate a determination to make meaning out of their experiences and, alongside the possibility of breakdown, indicate remarkable resilience and the ability to endure, challenging any attempt to understand this experience in terms of an either/or narrative.

Medical care in warzones positions personnel as both witnesses to and participants in the carnage of war and nowhere, arguably, is the relationship between sufferers and healers more intense. The American doctor Harvey Cushing prefaced his First World War journal with the words of an earlier 'wound dresser', Walt Whitman, to claim the hospital as the place that reveals the essence of war: 'The marrow of the tragedy is concentrated in the hospitals.'[5] Yet while, as Robinett demonstrates, 'writers often turn intuitively to writing as a way of confronting and surviving trauma suffered in their own lives,'[6] historically medical personnel have, perhaps, been unwilling to 'write' their own suffering in a world where that of the combatant is perceived to be so much greater. Being 'particularly prone to survivor guilt, incapable of remembering the people they saved, blaming themselves for the deaths of even hopeless cases,'[7] their narratives focus more on the suffering they see and attempt to mitigate than they do on the psychological burden they themselves carry. In place of the writer's suffering, it is common for First World War medical life-writings, especially those published during the war years, to exalt and thus foreground the courage of Tommy Atkins – the enlisted or conscripted soldier – and officer alike. Their writing presupposes that the wounded combatant is the reason for their existence at the front, and thus it is he who is central to the narrative.[8] Disembedding medical practitioners' wartime representations of trauma from these texts can thus be problematic. When their accounts bear witness to the physical and psychological trauma of those they care for (and tend to be read in this context), they obscure their own psychological wounds. Describing her work on an ambulance train in a series of diary-letter entries published in 1915, Nurse K. Luard, for instance, veers the narrative away from her own emotion to 'the outstanding shining thing [which] was the universal silent pluck of the men'.[9] Such a form of witness seems to want to atone for an inability to save so many of the wounded and sick as well as to pay tribute to then. As Medical Officer Geoffrey Keynes would later admit, ' "doing our best" was often distressingly inadequate'.[10]

In addition to foregrounding the wounded soldier and thus obscuring their own pain, accounts by the men and women who cared for him were subject to gendered constructions of their roles (heightened in wartime) that necessarily have bearing on how they perceived those roles and thus how they write their stories. Male doctors, who might otherwise have been combatants, needed to maintain an appropriately masculine endurance, particularly in the face of the stoicism of the men they tended – 'like the army, the medical profession has its own version of the stiff upper lip'.[11] Where the emotional and psychological experience of male medical personnel is noted in historical discussion, the reference often appears matter-of-fact, as in Ian R. Whitehead's *Doctors in the Great War* (1999): 'The unavoidable risks attached to their work inevitably placed a great strain on RMOs [Regimental Medical Officers], contributing to a high incidence of nervous disorders.'[12] Women, on the other hand, needing to prove themselves in a male-dominated world to which they had been grudgingly admitted, likewise took their cue from the suffering that surrounded them in being unwilling to acknowledge their own psychological pain. Recent books on women's medical experience in the First World War identify psychological stress and even breakdown as inherent to the war nursing experience, but do not offer close analysis of nurses' wartime accounts to examine how this is played out, articulated or represented in their subjective responses. These works tend to focus instead on the nursing process as well as the nurses' role in 'containing' combatant trauma and their own emotional response.[13]

Perhaps not surprisingly, contemporary wartime discussion, such as that carried out in the *British Journal of Nursing*, maintained that, as Yvonne McEwen notes, 'cases of nervous breakdown amongst nurses on active service are remarkably few',[14] but her research has shown much evidence to the contrary. Similarly, as Santanu Das has observed, an article in *The Lancet* argued that war trauma or shell shock can affect civilians and even cows, but excludes the nurse, so that 'neither soldier nor civilian, she is not granted a place even in this medical "no man's land". Entrusted with the repair of minds and bodies the war has ravaged, she is thought to be immune to war trauma.'[15] McEwen attributes this exclusion in large part to the professional context: 'It was not good for the professional image of nurses to appear to be breaking down under the strain of warfare.'[16] At times this stamina was 'imposed' by senior staff. One nurse records that '[t]he matron of no. 12 was not at all sympathetic if a sister took sick … she informed me that we should not go off duty unless we fainted at our posts.'[17] For some individuals, the work itself was a continual reminder of the greater burden carried by the patient. In *A Diary Without Dates*, Enid Bagnold describes the sense of 'shame' she carries in the face of her patients' physical pain: 'To stand up straight on one's feet, strong, easy, without the surging of any physical sensation, by a bedside whose covers are flung here and there by the quivering nerves beneath it … there is a sort of shame in such strength.'[18] The experience thus reinforced the unwillingness of the nurse to admit, even to herself, to a response that was other than stoic, such that many nursing accounts refer to psychological breakdown of nurses only obliquely.

It is therefore unusual to find women, like American senior nurse Julia Stimson, who openly acknowledge a breaking-point not only for her staff but for herself. Writing home from a French hospital in 1917, she connects what she has seen with the psychological distress she and her nurses attempt to hold at bay: 'These frightful sights would work havoc with one's brain … what will we think when we get through with it all. How are we going to stand the mental strain?'[19] Stimson's concern is unusually prescient in recognising that the full psychological weight of the experience may well emerge only in the aftermath of war. Returning in the late 1920s to her experience as a VAD [Voluntary Aid Detachment] nurse, Vera Brittain employs 'sight' as a metaphor to draw attention to the tension between the psychological necessity of dissociation in the immediate term, and the post-trauma inability to shut out intrusive memories of the wounded and dead, a feature of traumatic witness:

most of us … possessed a kind of psychological shutter which we firmly closed down upon our recollection of the daily agony, whenever there was time to think. We never dreamed that in the years of renewed sensitiveness after the War, the convenient shutter would simply refuse to operate.[20]

Stimson reveals that emotional response is not confined to female nurses: 'It isn't only the women that are affected by these things, the men [doctors] don't weep often, but they come near to it. And they get just as edgey.'[21] Accounts by male doctors in the First World War are even less likely than those by women to represent their own breakdown, in part perhaps because the cultural context does not give them permission. In her analysis of First World War narratives and war trauma, Robinett notes how constructions of masculinity dictated that 'men were expected to be models of self-discipline, emotional and intellectual discretion, charac-terized by the suppression of any display of emotion and a determin-ation not to give way to "womanish wailings". Nervous collapse among males was believed to be the result of a failure of the will.'[22] In *A War of Nerves*, Ben Shephard points out that these expectations were reinforced by suspicion of introspection and any examining of emotion. Individuals were encouraged to learn 'not the indulgence but forgetfulness of their feelings, not the observation but the renunciation of self, not introspec-tion, but useful action.'[23] Such prescriptions existed alongside conditions of unprecedented psychological stress and overwhelming administrative tasks. However accustomed as both regular army and civilian doctors were to performing surgery and dealing with 'critical wounds', 'in no area of medicine was pre-war knowledge sufficient preparation for the prob-lems that arose between 1914 and 1918'.[24] The overwhelming numbers of wounded and sick, the severity of gunshot and shrapnel wounds, the rampant nature of sepsis and severe infections, the lack of equipment and often cramped and dirty conditions of the casualty clearing station, or working under fire in dressing stations, meant there was a vast gulf to cross. There was also the moral dilemma of making decisions about who to save and who to treat. 'Officers had to accept these limitations on their sense of duty to the sick, wounded and dying.'[25]

While a range of discourses demanded that male doctors conceal emo-tion, another idealised the nurse and the nursing context. The nurse role was informed by the image of the ministering angel tending the wounded soldier, prominent in popular culture, from posters and postcards to novel dustjackets and magazine features, all of which conveyed a com-pletely unrealistic picture of actual work. Such idealisation was imposed on nursing as a profession not only from outside, but from within the profession itself, and through the nurse-narrator's internalisation of such discourses. In his preface to Luard's second collection of diary-letters detailing her nursing experience in France and Belgium, *Unknown Warriors* (1930), which admits the reader to a world of death, exhaustion and psychological and physical strain, Field Marshal Viscount Allenby, while acknowledging the 'crushing burden' that fell on the nurses, and clearly writing with the intention of acknowledging the difficulty of their work, represents the experience through an idealised and gendered vision: 'I remember well those days and nights of bitter fighting, and how crushing was the burden which fell upon the gentle women who tended our wounded. I look back, still, with admiration on the amazing endurance and self-sacrificing devotion of those Nursing Sisters in their work of mercy.'[26] Appropriately nurturing and self-abnegating, this is a discourse that excluded breakdown.

As we note in the Introduction, paying particular attention to what can be said or not said and the language used are thus important in considering the way these texts represent trauma and breakdown. A more general reading of First World War texts reveals that even if the psychological response to the war experience was not defined by individuals as 'shell shock', related definitions such as 'nervous debility' and 'neurasthenia' were certainly recognised in wartime culture, especially at the front, with neurasthenia sometimes being used interchangeably with shell shock to define combat-induced breakdown.[27] To understand the meanings carried by these terms, we need to be alert not only to their use in wartime diagnoses, but also to the extent to which alternative or euphemistic terms were employed to avoid the stigma of naming breakdown. Thus Young notes that '[n]eurasthenia could be weakness without stigma, and the doctors who wrote about war neuroses in the medical journals … promoted this view'. But at the same time he comments that '[d]octors recognized the moral ambiguity attached to "neurasthenia" and routinely diagnosed the affected officers as suffering from "exhaustion", a somatic term, as long as these men returned to their units immediately following brief treatment'.[28] Similarly, '[n]ervous exhaustion was an acceptable compromise formation, implying neurological routes into the body for psychical damage. The generic terms traumatic or war neurosis existed in the same space'.[29] It is not surprising then, that the texts we examine employ terms that retain these ambiguities and compromises so that physical and mental exhaustion are often presented as interdependent. Moreover, while stress is acknowledged by doctors and nurses, individuals may be unwilling to acknowledge their own 'nervous exhaustion'. Thus C. McKerrow, a medical officer attached to the 10th Northumberland Fusiliers, is direct in referring to 'nerves', and a letter to his wife emphasises the psychological pressure of the work, although he does not include himself in the 'nerves' narrative: 'ten months as MO to a battalion in the trenches [his current length of time] is quite an unusual spell. Their nerves generally require a rest before then. A lot of MOs are giving up their Commissions. Should hate to do that' (11 February 1916).[30] When individuals do acknowledge the psychological stress, 'strain' is a particularly common term used to indicate an affective response without directly stigmatising it as breakdown. Medical officer George Gask's account, which combines his wartime journal entries with later commentary, acknowledges the weight of the strain medical officers were under, in terms of both their surgical work and the task of administration that made them directly responsible for the treatment of thousands of soldiers in unimaginably difficult conditions. As Gask implies below, complete collapse of the unit was at times held precariously at bay by the efforts of constantly exhausted staff. Recounting the Battle of the Somme he notes:

> My memory of what happened on those first six days of July is very vague. In a letter of July 7th I find it stated 'my mind seems very blank about it, and perhaps it is best so'. It was day and night work, with brief intervals for food and sleep. There was no need to urge people to work – medical officers and men, they had to be watched to see that they did not overwork. And become useless. It is thought we had about 2,000 cases through our hospital on July 1st. … My clearest recollection is a sort of nightmare of going into the crowded tents at night trying to pick out the worst wounded by the light of an electric torch. Poor McPherson, the CO, was like a lost soul, wandering up and down the camp – he was not a good administrator, and he nearly cracked under the strain, and he would not go to bed and rest. I believe the hospital must have broken down if it had not been for the wonderful way in which every man, medical officer and sister worked like Trojans.[31]

While Gask asserts his memories are 'vague', the evocation of vast numbers of wounded and the unrelenting work communicates the intensity of the experience. His 'clearest recollection' is, by his own admission, not clear, but rather a 'nightmare' of searching the 'crowded tents' 'by the light of an electric torch' for the most badly injured cases. It invites connections both with the more literary evocations of Barbusse's novel *Le Feu* (1916) and the underworld of Owen's 'Strange Meeting', and a historical comparison with an earlier wartime hospital, Scutari, and the most famous figure in wartime medical history, Florence Nightingale, her kerosene lamp replaced by its modern electric version, though Gask's narrative is one of chaos rather than imposed order. Although the 'blank' in Gask's memory might be interpreted by a twenty-first-century reader as indicative of a traumatic witnessing, his 'perhaps it is best so' reads as a welcome forgetting. Given that he is writing this looking back, he implies that the inability to remember contributes to resilience rather than indicating the 'gap' in memory characteristic of trauma as defined by Caruth and others. Instead it brings us closer to Hunt's hypothesis that 'avoidance can be a very successful long-term coping strategy'.[32] In addition, Gask's emphasis on the ability of medical personnel to sustain work under these conditions is an affirmative to set against McPherson's breakdown. Where the physical needs of the wounded supersede the emotional needs of their carers, resilience is crucially important.

The tension between breakdown and resilience is a constant feature of medical personnel writings. The 'strain' under which 'poor McPherson' 'nearly cracked' also afflicts Julia Stimson's nurses:

> Our hospital is very full and we have many very bad cases. My nurses are beginning to show the effect of the emotional *strain*. Their nerves are a bit on edge, and I find that when they lose for a few days time-off-duty, as they all have been doing, they are not standing the *strain* and loss as well as they did the last time we were so busy. I have had about a dozen of them weeping. The continuous rainy damp weather, the accumulating emotional *strain* and the real hard work are having an effect on them that is bothering me. There is a convalescent hospital for Sisters at E. to which I can send one or two at a time for a short rest.[33] [our italics]

'Strain' is not the only word that repeatedly marks Stimson's prose. 'Weeping' is a consistent feature. Of herself, she admits, 'Naturally I cannot do any weeping as I have to be wept upon, but there are times when it would be such a comfort to be braced myself'. Thus she reveals the tension between her position of responsibility that demands steadfastness and control, and her own potential breakdown and need for support: 'I would have given a good deal myself to have had someone like Mother to weep on.'[34] The phrase '[t]here are times' simultaneously hides and reveals her own 'strain', even as her overall narrative focuses on the nurses in her charge.

J. Breckenridge Bayne, an American doctor in Romania, looking back on his war experience from the vantage point of 1944, likewise represents the nurses' work as a constant struggle between endurance and break-down. They 'saw only suffering and pain. Everywhere they were con-fronted by torn and mutilated bodies. Often the sights were so repugnant that I wondered at their ability to endure them.'[35] Yet this endurance often gave out through sheer physical or emotional exhaustion:

> One by one the girls who were making such great efforts to carry on would finally have to give up but not until they had literally dropped in their tracks. Some of them would be on the verge of hysteria, others just com-pletely exhausted. However, with a day or two for rest they would be back at it again.[36]

For doctors and nurses, relieving the stress was crucial if they were to sustain their work over the longer term. Looking back on his experiences after the war, George Gask draws attention to the need for a specific strat-egy to maintain his emotional equilibrium, employing a kind of 'mind over matter' approach, in response to 'strain', that word again repeated:

> We were now all beginning to get tired and feel the *strain* of the Summer's work, yet the hammering at the Passchendaele ridges still went on and we were to have another pretty hard two months work before things eased. The *strain* showed clearly in the rising sick returns of the Unit, we had many ill-nesses both among officers, nurses and men. One had to use one's brain to keep well, to interest oneself in some way or another; to me literature was a great resource and I was very thankful my wife kept me well supplied.[37] [our italics]

In addition to using 'one's brain to keep well', Gask advocated phys-ical exercise as another coping mechanism: 'Even during the hard fight-ing I always tried to get about 20 minutes or half an hour's walk after breakfast to keep fit.' In representing exercise and reading literature as means of maintaining control, and seeing these tactics as his respon-sibility, Gask upholds the contemporary ideology of mind–body fit-ness as appropriate to his role as a doctor. In reflecting on these after the fact, he implies that they were important in preventing the 'strain' from being overwhelming. His stoic stance is reflected in his account: he allows statistics, numbers of wounded and hours worked to indicate the 'strain' that he acknowledges almost brought the unit to a state of col-lapse, rather than graphic description. But his emphasis is on the need for endurance since without it the medical system of care would have collapsed; crucially, the stoic ability to withstand the 'strain' kept the hospital running.

Rest, though often accepted only on the point of collapse, as Bayne indicates above, could also be key in heading off complete breakdown, as Alice Essington-Nelson's account of nursing at Lady Gifford's rest home for nurses near Boulogne demonstrates:

> They sleep sometimes for nearly 24 hrs. Some of them come just *dead* tired and others have small septic wounds and others again have had their nerves shattered, one of those latter when she came just cried if you spoke to her but we nursed her up and in three weeks she was as fit as ever. ... [S]he told me what had finished her was the night after Neuve Chappelle when 45 *terrible* cases had come into her bit of ward and 15 had died before morning ... her weary body and tired nerves then gave way; however, she is back at her post now and her matron told me she was one of her best nurses.[38] [original emphasis]

These 'shattered nerves' suggest what would now be diagnosed as 'acute stress reaction', a 'normal' and immediate response to physical and mental exhaustion and traumatic witnessing.[39] It is often manifest in persistent, unbidden, repetitious images where the memory of what has been witnessed assails the subject not long after the event, as Vera Brittain describes, but in the immediate term.[40] Male ambulance driver Leslie Buswell explicitly describes how 'Sometimes when I get into my bed or am trying to get a few hours' sleep ... the horrors of blood – broken arms, mutilated trunks, and ripped-open faces, etc. – haunt me'.[41] Yet most writers eschew such descriptions, preferring to indicate their presence without actually naming them. In moving between his immediate experience recorded in his diary and his later commentary, Gask brings together the psychological burden that involves both the confrontation with the daily horror and its later recollection. He recalls how in his therapeutic walking, 'a ridge parallel with the Ancre [t]o me was a *via sacra* along which I tried to brace myself to bear the burden of another day. The remembrance of that path and the railway line near Poperinghe, where I used to exercise in 1917, is burnt deep into my mind.'[42] Gask's emphasis on the need to 'brace' himself, the same term used by Stimson, suggests, as her writing does, the fine line between resilience and breakdown and the consciousness of the need to exert one's will to avoid breakdown. The extent to which the walks he recalls long after the fact are embedded with the memory of his experience so that they still remain a *via sacra* 'burnt deep', makes them bear a painful but unspoken narrative, in contrast with the 'convenient psychological shutter' that prevents him remembering fully the earlier scene. Clearly, not only does the *via sacra* stand in his mind for what he does not describe but suggests, but the physical image of bracing for the burden carries the weight he intended; moreover, it has branded him indelibly: 'burnt deep into my mind'. Similarly, the indelible nature of the small details that made up this accumulation of traumatic seeing is recounted by Gask's medical colleague, Geoffrey Keynes, as he describes in his memoir years later one particular incident when he witnesses the horrific destruction of a direct shell burst, and attempts to treat shattered individuals. He explains that 'the pattern of war is shaped in the individual mind by [such] small individual experiences, and I can see these things as clearly today as if they had just happened'.[43] In neither case, however, do we have an indication of a traumatic repression of experience; rather, as Keynes indicates, the memory serves its purpose only too well.

In the immediacy of the event, however, some individuals' writing indicates how silence can help contain such images – not writing about them in detail is a refusal to admit them to memory.[44] For K. Luard a kind of willed avoidance is necessary if she is to do her job. In the immediate context of treating the wounded on an ambulance train, her response to the experience is unrecorded, an absence: 'Couldn't write last night: the only thing was to try and forget it all. It has been an absolute hell of a journey – there is no other word for it.'[45] Likewise, in an unpublished diary of nursing on a hospital ship taking the wounded from Gallipoli, Miss M. Brown breaks off a daily entry with: 'The sights one sees are too terrible to write about' (8 June 1915). Again, anchored off Anzac Cove, she records of a single day in August, '[w]e dressed nearly 1000 … the whole thing is too ghastly to write about'(8 August 1915).[46] While the act of writing may at times be therapeutic, it also involves reliving an experience that in the interests of practical professionalism is best left unsaid, since reliving through writing stands in the way of the suppression necessary to do the job.

The conscious necessity of suppressing emotions, or the unconscious repression of emotion that is a response to the task at hand, may appear in these writings as forms of silence. Yet another form of silence, while similarly manifest as the appearance of a calm professional exterior, may indicate a response to trauma defined by the psychological state of dissociation as much as an expression of the conscious will. The constant witnessing of trauma, often in the context of a threat to one's own life, for example when under fire, can result in a sense of unreality that allows the medic to sustain a necessary detachment in spite of the conditions and is a common response amongst medical personnel, as one doctor quoted by McManners describes:

An extra screen seemed to come down in front of my emotions, shielding me. … As the day went on, I detached my self from what was happening. I felt as if somebody else was doing the job, and I was watching from a distance. This is a common psychiatric defence mechanism. I was outwardly functioning in the same way, but my emotions were dissociated from my functioning ability (in order to cope) and I became an automaton.[47]

The working environment for doctors on the front lines was such that the need to attend to the injured could provide a welcome distraction. Many medical officers were killed as they went as close as possible to the front to treat wounded, or were shelled when they set up aid posts near artillery batteries to the rear. American Doctor Grover Carter, later killed at Le Cateau on 16 October 1918 while dressing a wounded officer, describes in his diary the experience being shelled near Poperinge on 15 May 1918:

Went to 'C' Battery about 10 am. Place was immediately shelled, two hit about 8 or 10 yds from me. Was hit all over by clods of earth. Was expecting to be wounded any minute. Got in shell hole for 30 min. Went to 'B' Battery and it was shelled also. Was chased all over the place. Kept falling on ground when heard shells coming and running between times. Real hot day, too. Went out of action at 4 pm.[48]

Even though Carter uses brief matter-of-fact statements, the tension of the experience is reflected in the terseness of each description and in the way that, although he is recounting the experience later, his staccato narrative still reflects the frantic nature of the experience in the present. It is noteworthy, too, that Carter refers to his going 'out of action' which places him in the same position, and thus danger, as the combatants. A similar sense of being with the combatants (though even more vulnerable as they paused to treat the wounded rather than taking cover) runs through many medical officers' accounts. Treating and evacuating the wounded at Gallipoli, MO Norman Tattersall recounts in his diary entry of 9 August 1915:

Have had another 24 hours of Hell. Cleared about 800 wounded from the pier since last night but cannot cope with the ever increasing stream. Have now worked 62 hours without a break, and only water and biscuits – no sleep – am getting tired. The stretcher bearers are magnificent – the wounded have to be carried down about 2 miles in the blazing heat – over rough ground – and under direct and indirect fire all the way. Many of them have been doing it for nearly 70 hours now without a break and still go on – exhausted – and bleeding feet – Sniped at and cannot snipe back – they are heroes to a man.

> The snipers have been at us on the pier again today. One stretcher bearer was helping me to get a stretcher on to a boat when they got him in the neck. He died in about 5 minutes. Three others have been wounded on the pier today. I wonder if they will get me. It is pure luck.[49]

Notably, Tattersall passes over his own endurance to focus on the heroism of the stretcher-bearers. As nurses downplay their own exhaustion in the face of the suffering of the patients they treat, so here it seems that Tattersall's switching of the focus from himself to the stretcher-bearers is both a way of downplaying his own obvious heroism and, perhaps, a way of surviving emotionally. In so far as the stretcher-bearers are in worse circumstances than he is, turning his gaze away from himself and onto them he can avoid sinking into the emotional despair that is suggested by the opening lines of the entry. Removing the focus from his own hardship is thus, one might suggest, a strategy for resilience. Similarly, his claim that being wounded or killed is 'pure luck' shows him adopting a combatant fatalism that may offer a means of coping with the stress of the environment.

In the immediacy of treating the wounded in the front lines, McKerrow sees the work itself as the important diversion that helps him avoid the strain while at the same time acknowledging the 'trying' nature of his work. He writes to his wife 'It is a queer thing that, as soon as one gets some work to do amongst the wounded, one ceases even to notice the shelling. It is a blessing because, otherwise, the doctor's life in the trenches would be undoubtedly trying. I am glad that I have a fairly healthy nervous system' (30 January 1916).[50]

Concentration on the work can thus distract from the fear that might otherwise be a response to the shelling; the demands of the work itself can create a kind of dissociation that protects from its emotional impact. Olive Dent records the contrast between her emotional response, 'an acuteness of mental suffering hitherto unparalleled in life', and its split from her external self which is 'one strange, curious self … busily concerned with sterilizer and instruments, dishes and lotions'.[51] This experience of dissociation is explored more fully by Mary Borden in *The Forbidden Zone* (1929) which includes 'fragments' written at the front and stories composed after the war. In the story 'Blind', Borden is able to explore such experience reflecting back after the fact, employing a strategy by which she moves from the objective to the subjective representation of her experience. The detached professional focus on the men in her care acts as a shield, it seems, that protects her psyche from comprehending what she is actually doing and the emotional stress that it causes her. This distancing mechanism removes her from herself, so that she is no longer a feeling subject, but emotionally numbed and objectified to the point where she watches herself from outside: 'I think that woman, myself, must have been in a trance … Her feet are lumps of fire, her face is clammy, her apron is splashed with blood; but she moves ceaselessly about with bright burning eyes and handles the dreadful wreckage as if in a dream. She does not seem to notice the wounds or the blood.'[52] So long as this dissociation allows her to stand outside herself and become the object, nurse, she can perform as nurse, but an abrupt move back into her subjective self precipitates a breakdown, leaving her incapable of performing her duties. Psychological survival and the ability to behave professionally, she implies, are only possible in this state of detachment in which she can stand outside herself. When an incident forces the humanity of the wounded on her and she can no longer view them only as bodies to be treated, her 'trance', the protective objective distance, is shattered and along with it her psyche: 'I was awake now, and I seemed to be breaking to pieces.'[53] Borden's exploration of this personal experience points to an important aspect of reading these accounts that alerts us to the tension between 'feeling' and its incompatibility with doing the job. When the proximity of breakdown threatens the nurse's ability to carry out her work, then the only option is avoidance.

At the very practical level, Nurse Katherine Ferguson emphasises the need for a professional hardening in the interests of patient care. Looking back on her wartime experience many years later, she comments on her reaction to her ward of fifty seriously injured filling with more and more patients:

> The MO's must have been busy in the Theatre all night and only one looked in once or twice. He was American and could not bear the sight and wept a bit. He could have helped me by feeling some pulses. After some years of Warfare I suppose I was a hardened wretch but it seems necessary to be so.[54]

These accounts thus show how the conditions under which medical personnel work can have contradictory effects in that they may lead to breakdown on the one hand, but on the other can reinforce the need for endurance; this last includes a heightened sense of purpose and satisfaction in the ability to confront what is most terrible and survive. Thus in an interview long after the war, when Nurse Hitchens is asked about her emotional response to treating terrible injury, she acknowledges that the work did result in breakdown for some nurses, but that her medical interest and satisfaction in her nursing work prevented her own collapse:

> [T]he friend who went with me and my cousin to Rouen broke down. She was haunted by the wounds. She was haunted by the suffering but I always said that I felt they were a challenge and I was so interested in the various techniques of doing the dressings and nursing and keeping the patients happy and comfortable that the fact [*sic*] I didn't lie awake at night and think of the sufferings and I didn't shudder when I thought of the war wounds that I had seen or the amputations, all these things.[55]

Canadian Sophie Hoerner is unusually candid about the paradox that defines her experience: she can at once express her extreme distress at the sights she witnesses and at the same time affirm that she is well and happy. On 8 June 1915 she writes to a friend 'Oh dear, if you could see the dreadful smash-ups of these splendid fellows. It's awful and I cry many, many times. I can't get used to it. It's so dreadful.' On 10 June, 'I had to cry the other day in the service tent at one awful case I saw, – a young man that had to lose both arms, had a thigh wound, and head … I am well and happy, and am so glad I am here.' Again on 2 July she writes 'The patients are so ill in my ward and suffer so terribly that before afternoon came I thought I should scream myself. I am seeing the grimness of war now and it's awful … every patient with more than one wound, so terrible I can't describe them … but I'm glad I'm here and I am happy.'[56]

Resilience, particularly as it is manifest through the individual's sense of satisfaction in aiding the wounded and sick, is thus also a key theme of these accounts. As we note in the Introduction, the concept of resilience is as important as breakdown to this discussion – the two are interdependent – especially, it must be understood as more than a manifestation of the 'stiff upper lip', while at the same time we need to be alert to the cultural constructions of appropriate response to war conditions that, as we have seen, applauded stoic endurance and stigmatised breakdown.

Within the context of 1914–18, in particular, constructions of endurance and resilience were central to how individuals perceived their roles during the war, even though this changed in the late 1920s as the narrative of disillusionment become dominant in war memoirs that were being published at the time. It is arguable that such constructions in themselves aided in the resilience evident in some of these writings. Christine Hallett's explication of the cultural context for the combatants' 'cheerful stoicism' and 'emotional containment' applies equally to their carers:

[I]t [stoicism and containment] can be viewed as one of the great struc-
tural cultural forces governing the social behaviour of the time. It can be
argued that these men suffered more because their stoicism would not
allow them to voice any sense of anguish – or indeed of protest. Yet it could
also be argued that stoicism permitted anguish and outrage to be released
in a slower and more controlled way – a way that was valued by early
twentieth-century society.[57]

Keeping in mind the relationship between public discourses and the
individual's private representation of his or her experience, it is important that we recognise the extent to which both narratives of resilience and
breakdown are constructed within cultural contexts that give or with-
draw permission to certain representations of that experience. Thus, for
example, published collections of nurses' letters home may have been
written with the express purpose of eliciting support for the Red Cross,
or trying to maintain morale and support for 'the cause' more generally. Moreover, they were also subject to censorship. As Sophie Hoerner
writes to a friend: 'I wish I was allowed to write all I see and hear'
(4 June 1915). Post-war publications, especially works that appeared in
the late 1920s and early 1930s, on the other hand, were written or published (in the case of letters or diaries written during the war) in response
to and fed a post-war mood of reassessment and disillusionment. In the
first instance, therefore, women may focus on the self-sacrificing nature
of the men they nurse, and on their own contribution to the war effort,
hence constructing a narrative of resilience as a necessary response; in
the second instance writers found a readership for the anger and hopelessness recorded in private wartime diaries, or, reflecting back on their
war experience, now had permission to perceive it in terms of a massive
waste of lives and thus could construct their memoirs accordingly. Lack
of official censorship post-war may also have made it easier for writers
to include comments that could not have been published during the war,
especially evidence of breakdown.

The distinction between what could and could not be said is emphasised by Kate Finzi's declaration in her 1916 memoir *Eighteen Months in
the War Zone*: 'If there are many omissions it must be noted that a War
Diary published during war time is of necessity much expurgated to meet
the demands of the censor.'[58] Yet Finzi's memoir is unstinting in its details
of the horrors of war. She openly discusses injury, but the purpose is to
instil support, to celebrate resilience, as well as to speak for the dead: '*They
are all gone. I alone am left to tell the tale*' [original italics]. Echoing the
Messenger in the Book of Job, she communicates the emotional burden

she takes on as witness to the pain of others, rather than to her own: 'The sigh of the wind came through a broken pane. Was it imagination, or did it bear with it faintly from afar the oft-heard cry: "Christ help us!"'[59] Here Finzi's experience is not so much 'unclaimed', as Caruth would call it, but camouflaged or screened. For Finzi, her screen or camouflage is the patriotic rhetoric that marks her text, and can obscure a more complex reading especially of her more lyrical and poignant passages. Thus she offers graphic accounts of mutilation to bring her audience to an understanding of what she has witnessed:

> Have *you* seen faces blown beyond recognition – faces eyeless, noseless, jawless, and heads that were only half heads?
>
> …
>
> Have *you* seen forever nameless enemy corpses washed and carried out to the mortuary, and enemy though they were, because of their youth, wished that you could tell their mothers you had done your best?
>
> …
>
> When *you* have seen this … and not before, will you know what modern warfare means.[60] [original italics]

At the same time she ends her account with an emphasis on the importance of dying for a cause: 'Yet surely the warrior spirits will arise and strengthen us, whispering: "Let us not have died in vain. We laid down our lives for the Old Country. For the love of God Carry on, as we had hoped to do." '[61]

It is not just absence imposed by censorship then, that is noteworthy in writing published during the war, but what is present in the form of a rhetorical impulse to impose an affirmative narrative of stoicism on the trauma story, particularly one which reassures both writer and reader that the horrific circumstances being witnessed are politically and morally necessary. Leslie Buswell's 1917 memoir characteristically attests to the interdependence of potential breakdown with determined resilience: 'it has been good to be here in the presence of high courage and to have learned a little in our youth of the values of life and death.'[62] Similarly high-minded sentiments are juxtaposed with graphic descriptions of wartime nursing in Olive Dent's 1917 memoir, *A VAD in France*. When a young nurse, exhausted, overwhelmed, and nearly hysterical by the strain of nursing men after 'a big push', exclaims 'What a useless waste!' another nurse admonishes her, saying

> I am too tired to sleep, too tired to do anything but lie and look up at the wooden roof of the hut, too tired to do anything but think, think, think, too

tired to shut out of sight and mind the passionate appeal of two dying eyes, and a low faint whisper of 'Sister, am I going to die?'

But, oh, how glad I am to have lived through this day! With the stinging acute pain of all its experiences raw on me, I say it has been a privilege to undergo these sensations.[63]

Likewise Elizabeth Walker Black in *Hospital Heroes* (1919), written before the end of the war, affirms '[t]hat the blessés make it all worth while and chase away the "cafard", that slough of despond when you feel you don't like to be out there at all and yet would hate not to be there. Luxuries seem contemptible when men are dying. ... There is regeneration in knowing that you can meet the worst and survive.'[64] While at one point she questions the whole effort – 'It seemed so futile, all this struggling and misery in order that one army of frozen men could take away some snowy, uncomfortable holes in the ground away from another army, equally wretched'[65] – dogged endurance offers a form of affirmation at the same time: 'It is hard, but you somehow stumble along, "fed up" but "sticking it". Living on the edge of eternity this way raises one's working efficiency to a higher rate. ... You must stay and work and comfort and cheer and help all you can until the light comes.'[66]

Towards the end of the war it seems that she has only the idealised image itself left to support her: 'I would stagger back at the end of my twenty-four hours to report, with an apron and often a face spattered with blood and mud, and yet a spirit radiant and unweary with the thrill of service.'[67] When the traumatic experience is juxtaposed with an idealism that offers meaning in the immediate term, the response must be considered in the context of the time in which it was written. Responding from within a world of injury and death with no prospect of an ending, accounts like Dent's and Black's are important to our understanding of the subjective experience; they reveal the extent to which the rhetoric of sacrifice and service appears to have imposed much-needed meaning that enabled individuals to 'carry on'. The emotional strain of wartime medical care is held in check by seeing the horror as part of a 'greater good': their work and the larger cause of the war itself. Such belief in this 'greater good', as well as in the individual's ideal of service, can become a survival strategy, a private therapeutic act that exists alongside the more overt political act of witness to soldiers' injury, suffering and death. Caring for the wounded with 'a spirit radiant with service' is more than empty idealism. It is a means of psychological survival.

This idealism offers a means of psychological survival in the immediate term, but one that may fail to support the individual in the war's
aftermath. While doctors such as Gask maintain a narrative of resilience post-war, other writers returning to their experience document
graphically the lasting psychological effects of their war service. Thus an
exchange between two nurses near the end of the war in Lesley Smith's
Four Years Out of Life (1932) is very different from the elevated tone of
Dent's conversation above. Here a nurse voices what has been omitted
from the accounts published during the war: the psychological burden
she must carry as a result of her war experience without an alternative
affirmative narrative offered by her companion:

> It's not just that I've lost my nerve at the moment, I've lost it permanently.
> I am not frightened about to-day or to-morrow, I am frightened to turn
> every corner – mentally and physically – I am afraid to go through a door
> or to open a letter or to waken in the morning … I am afraid that, if I open
> the door, I shall find a maniac crawling along the floor; if I think, I shall
> remember a dying man fallen out of bed … I used to think that unreason
> and mania and crawling fear were outside of real life and had no relation to
> it … there is only a thin crust of make belief between sanity and madness,
> between ease of mind and uncontrolled horror.[68]

Smith's use of dashes suggests a further unspoken narrative that exists
alongside the fear she voices: anxieties that cannot be articulated because
they have not yet materialised. The repetition of key words and phrases
underscores the trauma: to open either a door or a letter, to allow oneself
to 'see' what is hidden is dangerous. 'Crawling', 'mania', 'maniac' reinforce
the fear of madness, this 'uncontrolled horror'. This admission of breakdown post-war allows for no possibility of redeeming values that could
mitigate the sense of complete hopelessness and despair. Yet it must
also be noted that it comes from within the safety of post-war survival
and thus must be placed in contextual contrast to the wartime writings
which, as we have seen, were more likely to include alternative narratives
of resilience that would allow the writers to sustain their own morale
and that of others. Thus the rhetoric of sacrifice and service offered an
ideology that provided emotional support, yet at the same time it often
stood in the way of medical personnel claiming a place at the centre of
that narrative, or encouraged them to remain silent about their own suffering. The stripping away of an affirmative rhetoric after the war allowed
individuals like Smith and Borden to articulate a traumatic legacy that is
only glimpsed in writings written and published during the war. As we
have shown, however, breakdown and resilience are not experienced as

oppositional states, but exist on a continuum, and as part of a range of responses to wartime medical practice.

To understand how trauma is represented in these works, however unwillingly or obliquely, as well as the attendant resilience, we therefore need to be sensitive to the diversity of responses and contexts that include both the wartime need for a stoic idealism and the profound disillusionment of its aftermath. Examining the way these individuals express an experience that would by any measure be defined as traumatic, allows us to uncover the emotional impact of war on these medical men and women. Far from being silenced by trauma, they offer a range of narratives through which they confront it. At the same time, it is only by paying close attention to the way that experience is articulated, particularly their unwillingness to place themselves at the centre of their narratives and to claim their pain, that we can disembed both the emotional toll of their work and their extraordinary resilience from these texts. The complexities, ambiguities and contradictions in these writings at once affirm the reality of the experience as traumatic and contest the idea that such experience is inevitably dominated and silenced by that trauma.

Notes

1 An earlier version of this chapter appeared as Carol Acton and Jane Potter, ' "These Frightful Sights Would Work Havoc with One's Brain": Subjective Experience, Trauma, and Resilience in First World War Writings by Medical Personnel', *Literature and Medicine* 30: 1 (Spring 2012): 61–85.

2 For a thorough discussion of the position of the 'shell-shocked' soldier in a cultural, economic and political context during and after the war see Reid, *Broken Men*.

3 For information on this campaign see www.shotatdawn.info/index.html. A moving contemporary work that explores breakdown in combat and contests labels of cowardice is A. P. Herbert, *The Secret Battle* (London: Methuen, 1919).

4 Erich Maria Remarque, *All Quiet on the Western Front* (St Albans: Triad/ Mayflower Books, 1977; Putnam & Co., 1929), p. 173.

5 Harvey Cushing, *From a Surgeon's Journal: 1915–1918* (Boston: Little, Brown and Co, 1941), preface.

6 Robinett, 'Narrative Shape', 291.

7 Hugh McManners, *The Scars of War* (London: HarperCollins, 1993), 371.

8 As we will see in later chapters, this is consistently a feature of medical accounts.

9 K. E. Luard, *Diary of a Nursing Sister on the Western Front 1914–1915* (Edinburgh and London: Blackwood & Sons, 1915), p. 90.

10 Geoffrey Keynes, *The Gates of Memory* (Oxford: Clarendon Press, 1981), p. 128.

11 McManners, *Scars of War*, p. 301.

12 Ian R. Whitehead, *Doctors in the Great War* (Barnsley: Leo Cooper, 1999), p. 189.

13 Marjorie Barron Norris, *Sister Heroines: The Roseate Glow of Wartime Nursing, 1914–1918* (Alberta: Bunker to Bunker Publishing, 2002); Yvonne McEwen, *It's a Long Way to Tipperary: British and Irish Nurses in the Great War* (Dunfermline: Cualann Press, 2006); Eileen Crofton, *The Women of Royaumont: A Scottish Women's Hospital on the Western Front* (East Linton: Tuckwell Press, 1997); Christine Hallett, *Containing Trauma: Nursing Work in the First World War* (Manchester: Manchester University Press, 2009).

14 McEwen, *It's a Long Way*, p. 98.

15 Santanu Das, *Touch and Intimacy in the First World War* (Cambridge: Cambridge University Press, 2005), p. 195.

16 McEwen, *It's a Long Way*, p. 99.

17 Mary Knocker, unpublished memoir, 'Through Shadows and Sunshine 1914–18', papers of Mary Ethel Cory Knocker (later Love) (1883–1970), Wellcome Library and Archives, London(CMAC/GC/258).

18 Enid Bagnold, *A Diary Without Dates* (London: Virago 1978; Heinemann, 1918), p. 22. Although Bagnold was working at a London hospital rather than at the front, her comment is representative of the tone of many of the writers under discussion.

19 Julia Stimson, *Finding Themselves: The Letters of an American Army Chief Nurse in a British Hospital in France* (New York: Macmillan, 1918), p. 84.

20 Brittain, *Testament of Youth*, p. 384. The suggestion of intrusive images does not seem to indicate what would now be defined as 'flashbacks', but rather the inability to prevent unbidden memories of the war intruding into the post-war context. Brittain has said that she did not suffer from these, but knew that they persisted for many war nurses.

21 Stimson, *Finding Themselves*, p. 93.

22 Robinett, 'Narrative Shape', p. 304.

23 Shephard, *War of Nerves*, p. 19.

24 Whitehead, *Doctors in the Great War*, p. 154.

25 Whitehead, *Doctors in the Great War*, p. 156.

26 Luard, *Unknown Warriors*, p. vii.

27 For an important discussion of the complexity behind what they term 'war syndromes', which examines the diagnoses of various physical and psychological reactions to war service, see Jones and Wessely 'War Syndromes'. For an historical overview of symptoms and diagnoses, see also their article 'A Paradigm Shift'.

28 Allan Young, *Harmony of Illusions: Inventing Post-Traumatic Stress Disorder* (Princeton, NJ: Princeton University Press, 1995), pp. 62–3.

29 Luckhurst, *Trauma Question*, p. 53.

30 C. McKerrow, Unpublished diary, Liddle Collection (GS 1020), Brotherton Library, University of Leeds. McKerrow was fatally wounded in December 1916.

31 George Gask, *A Surgeon in France: The Memoirs of Professor George E. Gask CMG, DSO, FRCS 1914–18* (Liskeard: Liskeard Books, 2002), p. 17.

32 Hunt, *Memory*, p. 65.

33 Stimson, *Finding Themselves*, p. 92.

34 Stimson, *Finding Themselves*, p. 92.

35 Breckenridge Bayne, *Bugs and Bullets* (New York: Richard R. Smith, 1944), p. 76.

36 Breckenridge Bayne, *Bugs and Bullets*, pp. 82–3.

37 Gask, *A Surgeon in France*, p. 53.

38 Alice Essington-Nelson, Personal Papers, Department of Documents, Imperial War Museum, London (86/48/1).

39 Scurfield and Platoni, *War Trauma*.

40 As Dr Vaughn DeCoster, a medical social worker in Iraq, affirms in an interview: 'As far as post-traumatic stress, the reality is [for] most people over there you're not post anything … The stress, the nightmares, it's a way of processing some pretty horrific things.' Vaughn DeCoster, Vaughn DeCoster Collection (AFC/2001/001/60195), Veterans History Project, American Folklife Center, Library of Congress, Washington, DC, interview transcript, p. 5.

41 Leslie Buswell, *Ambulance No. 10: Personal Letters from the Front* (London and Boston: Constable & Co., 1917), p. 98.

42 Gask, *A Surgeon in France*, pp. 27–8.

43 Keynes, *The Gates of Memory*, p. 138.

44 For further discussion on the concept of emotional containment see Hallett, *Containing Trauma*.

45 Luard, *Diary of a Nursing Sister*, p. 88.

46 M. Brown, Personal Papers, Department of Documents, Imperial War Museum, London (88/7/1).

47 McManners, *Scars of War*, pp. 283–4.

48 Grover Carter, 'Diary', Carter Grover Collection (AFC/2001/001/44233), Veterans History Project, American Folklife Center, Library of Congress, Washington, DC.

49 Norman Tattersall, 'Gallipoli Diary', Personal Papers, Department of Documents, Imperial War Museum (98/24/1).

50 McKerrow, Unpublished diary.

51 Olive Dent, *A VAD in France* (London: Grant Richards, 1917), p. 334. VAD refers to her nursing position as a member of the Voluntary Aid Detachment.

52 Mary Borden, *The Forbidden Zone* (London: Heinemann, 1929), p. 151.

53 Borden, *The Forbidden Zone*, p. 159.

54 Katherine Ferguson, 'War Experiences', Liddle Collection (WO, 134), Brotherton Library, University of Leeds, p. 8. Discussing wartime accounts written by both trained nurses and VADs, Christine Hallett notes: '[A]lthough this tendency to "shut down" emotionally in the face of suffering is a recurring theme in the writings of both nurses and VADs, the latter were much more likely to comment on it in their diaries. It may be that most trained nurses ... had learned to detach themselves from their emotional responses at an early stage in their careers; hence they no longer saw it as a focus for interest or reflection'. Christine Hallett, 'Portrayals of Suffering: Perceptions of Trauma in the Writings of First World War Nurses and Volunteers', *Canadian Bulletin of Medical History* 27: 1 (2010): 65–84; p. 71.

55 Nurse Hitchens, Liddle Collection (First World War Women's Recollections/Tape trans. 548), Brotherton Library, University of Leeds.

56 Nursing Sister Sophie Hoerner Fonds, Library and Archives Canada (R2495-0-7-E).

57 Hallett, *Containing Trauma*, p. 175.

58 Kate Finzi, *Eighteen Months in the War Zone* (London: Cassell & Co., 1916), p. 260.

59 Finzi, *Eighteen Months*, p. 205.

60 Finzi, *Eighteen Months*, pp. 228–9.

61 Finzi, *Eighteen Months*, pp. 251–2.

62 Buswell, *Ambulance No. 10*, p. 103.

63 Dent, *A VAD in France*, p. 339.

64 Elizabeth Walker Black, *Hospital Heroes* (New York: Charles Scribner's Sons, 1919), pp. 16–17.

65 Black, *Hospital Heroes*, p. 124.

66 Black, *Hospital Heroes*, p. 126.

67 Black, *Hospital Heroes*, p. 219.

68 Lesley Smith, *Four Years Out of Life* (Glasgow: Phillip Allen, 1932), p. 284.

2

'Over there': American confidence and the narrative of resilience in the Great War

One of the best-known First World War American ambulance drivers, Ernest Hemingway, asserted in his 1929 novel *A Farewell to Arms* that

> There were many words that you could not stand to hear and finally only the names of places had dignity. Certain numbers were the same way and certain dates and these with the names of places were all you could say and have them mean anything. Abstract words such as glory, honor, courage, or hallow were obscene beside the names of rivers, the numbers of regiments and the dates.[1]

The sparseness of Hemingway's response to his experiences in the war, spoken through his character Frederic Henry and stripped bare of sentimentality, is the characteristic voice of what Gertrude Stein called 'the lost generation'.[2] Others of Hemingway's generation, including E. E. Cummings, John dos Passos and Malcolm Cowley also served as ambulance drivers and also refashioned their war experiences in their writings of the 1920s and 1930s. Women writers, too, have entered the canon of American war literature, if not the canon of American literature more generally: Ellen La Motte and Mary Borden, who nursed in France, wrote equally experimental and stark accounts of their experiences of the places, rivers and dates that were forever associated with their treatment of the wounded. Numerous accounts by lesser-known and indeed largely forgotten ambulance drivers and nurses, usually in the form of a memoir or a collection of letters, were published between 1914 and 1919, for although the United States did not officially enter the war on the side of the Allies until April 1917, hundreds of young – and indeed not-so-young – Americans volunteered for service in the British and French forces, the Red Cross and American-sponsored aid organisations. These accounts served to enlighten a distant American public – 'distant' both in geography and in mind[3] – and also to encourage financial support for the various aid associations. The role of such accounts as pro-war, pro-Allies propaganda should not be underestimated. Indeed, in the years before America's declaration of war, they formed part of the unofficial means by which the country became convinced of the need for its involvement in this European conflict.[4] But, crucially, the memoirs and collections of letters considered in this chapter also bear witness to the suffering of the fighting men as well as to the resilience of the authors themselves. The up-beat image of the American home front in the First World War, as projected by the great majority of wartime (as opposed to post-war) fiction, newsreels and the now-iconic recruitment posters, is only one facet of what is a complex and contradictory society at war,[5] but in 1917, the ambulance driver C. de Florez was still able to declare that 'History will record glorious names, glorious deeds, la Marne, la Somme, l'Aisne, but none more glorious than Verdun where German Kultur shattered itself against French valour'.[6]

When President Woodrow Wilson delivered his address to the joint session of Congress on 2 April 1917, he positioned the United States as 'one of the champions of mankind', a beacon of light for the world, in the face of 'selfish and autocratic power', which still has resonance today.[7] Declaring that 'The world must be made safe for democracy', Wilson articulated a particularly 'American' response to the 'war to end all war', one that resounded in popular culture, particularly in song. George M. Cohan's 'Over There', with its lyrics, 'Send the word, send the word over there – / That the Yanks are coming, / The Yanks are coming' became a rallying cry.[8] Naïve in its assuredness, evangelical in its outlook, the United States occupied a unique position between 1914 and 1918: first as a seemingly detached spectator and second as a crusading participant.

The ambulance drivers and nurses considered in this chapter not only confronted the paradox affecting all medical personnel in wartime – what Margaret Higonnet highlights as 'underlying contradiction of military medicine, which subverts the Hippocratic oath "Do no harm"' – the imperative to rescue and heal men in their care so that they can be sent back to the fighting.[9] Mary Borden characterised this paradox as 'The Conspiracy' in her 1929 memoir, *The Forbidden Zone*. Likening the wounded whose 'feeble whining' sounds like an animal and whose smell is that of 'a corpse' to so many pieces of laundry and frayed items of clothing that require mending 'again and again as many times as they will stand it', Borden notes healers' complicity in the suffering:

And we send our men to war again and again, just as long as they will stand
it. ...

We send our men up to the broken road between the brushes of barbed
wire and they come back to us, one by one, two by two in ambulances, and
lying on stretchers. When these men can no longer 'stand it' and they die,
'then we throw them into the ground'.[10]

Ambulance drivers and nurses also confronted a paradox unique to
them as Americans, one distinguished by moral outrage and detachment
on the one hand (America as 'a city on a hill') and a moral investment
and active participation on the other (America as a world police, the
armed 'champions of mankind'). The shifting nature of American volunteers' position with regards to their country's involvement added a further level of paradox: before April 1917, these men and women were in
the war, but not of it – they were not citizens of an official combatant
nation. They could and did judge the conflict in multiple ways that varied from the feeling of superiority that such chaos was not of their making to a disdain for the inaction of their American government. After
April 1917 they were faced with the unsettling reality that the terrible
suffering of the men – American troops in particular – was the result
of recruitment efforts in which they themselves were complicit. Nursing
and other memoirs published before the United States joined the Allies
attempted to coerce, if not to shame, a desultory citizenry into action,
while those published after aimed to strengthen the resolve of a nation
that, through its president, claimed to seek 'no conquest, no dominion'.
The medical volunteers' sense of their political and national selves, fil-
tered down through their writing, was the product of an education that
'assigned a redemptive role to the United States, fighting evil to create a
new international order'.[11] Thus, while they do not shirk from graphic
descriptions of wounds, the feelings of helplessness buoyed by a sense
of duty, the devotion to the soldiers in their care, and, in the aftermath,
a sense of loss, isolation and sadness, the memoirs considered here are
distinctly American, their authors viewing themselves (whatever their
age) as the offspring of a new and bright nation, distinct from the Old
World, whose redemptive mission made them witnesses to and actors in
a global conflict. Thus their own trauma generated by these experiences
is negotiated by them within a different set of expectations. They were
missionaries as well as patriots, crusaders, who in the words of the song
'Good-bye Broadway, Hello France' (1917), 'will pay our debt to France'.[12]
Carrying on was particularly important; losing face was more than just
failing the fighting men or failing to live up to their example of courage

and dignified suffering, as we assert in Chapter 1. It was also tied up with the hype about the 'grit' of America's sons – and indeed daughters – 'of liberty'.

In 1914 America was able to view the situation in Europe from a distance but even so, it was not immune to the arguments for and against its participation in this foreign conflict. Well-known literary figures, especially female literary figures, published accounts early on in the war describing what they saw either as much-maligned 'war tourists' or as inhabitants of France, including Mary Roberts Rinehart (*Kings, Queens and Pawns*, 1915), Mildred Aldrich (*A Hilltop on the Marne*, 1915), and Edith Wharton (*Fighting France*, 1915).[13] Gertrude Atherton, in her memoir *Life in the War Zone* (1916), was scathing about 'self-righteous citizens, who have grown fat on the European war', 'a certain type of smug American, who, without experience or imagination, has refused to believe in the attendant horrors of war'. She felt they should 'be encouraged to visit these deliberately wrecked towns' and to 'take a motor-trip through the ruined district a year hence and spend an hour or two with the survivors'.[14] No doubt such an exhortation would have irritated the military men who wanted to keep such spectators out of the warzone.

American aid organisations, such as the American Hospital at Neuilly-sur-Seine, a suburb of Paris, were more pragmatic in their approach. Eliciting funds and volunteers from the United States, they found themselves providing much-needed support to the French. The US neutrality agreement did not forbid non-combatant involvement or recruitment, 'so Americans began to flood the volunteer movement'.[15] One hundred and fifty nurses and forty-five surgeons were sent to France by the American Red Cross in the first five months of the war. Harvard University sent 110 skilled, experienced doctors and nurses to a new camp hospital in July 1915 and many young men from other American universities, including Cornell, joined ambulance corps overseas, not only the American Ambulance Service but also the American Red Cross Ambulance and the Norton-Harjes Ambulance Corps.[16] It took enormous courage to undertake such work. Division Surgeon Richard Derby in his memoir, '*Wade in, Sanitary!*' (1919) paid tribute to ambulance drivers and their orderlies:

> There were no braver or more devoted men in our forces, and I include in this category not only the men driving ambulances with our troops, but those driving for the French and Italians and those who drove for the French before we entered the war. And I am speaking of the orderly who

accompanied each driver as well as the driver himself. After dark it was possible to bring the ambulances much closer to the line than during daylight, although shell-swept roads, under plain observation from enemy balloons, did not in the least daunt these men. Their one idea was to keep their cars rolling, and roll they did, in and out of shell holes, over or around fallen trees, around death corners sprayed by Austrian eighty-eights. The work of the ambulance drivers in the forward area required brave, cool, and daring men, and such men did the work.[17]

As for women, the 'exodus of American girls' and 'the passionate desire on the part of the women of one people to go to the help of the men of another people', was particularly surprising, yet pleasing to Margaret Deland.[18]

Events such as the execution of Edith Cavell in 1915 galvanised American outrage. In an effort to memorialise this victim of German barbarity, a committee in Boston was formed to appoint a special 'Edith Cavell Memorial Nurse' to serve with the British Army in France. Forty-one-year-old Alice Fitzgerald, who had been working for most of her life to promote her profession, was appointed. On 19 February 1916, she sailed for England and was eventually attached to the Queen Alexandra's Imperial Military Nursing Service at Boulogne. Fitzgerald felt particularly duty-bound as an American to show she could work hard and withstand the hellish conditions, especially when she was transferred to a casualty clearing station.[19] The novelist Marie van Vorst was also keen to show her ability to cope with distressing work she had to perform as a frontline nurse with the American Ambulance and to overcome any suggestion that she was merely a war tourist. Her memoir *War Letters by an American Woman* (1916) describes how, to her own 'tremendous surprise', she assists in dressings 'without feeling the slightest atom of nausea, and carried away pile after pile of that loathsome, infected linen ... several times I felt, not like fainting, but like weeping my heart out'.[20] Courage, therefore, lay in controlling one's emotions, not one's physical revulsion.

'*Mademoiselle Miss*' (1916) was published in order to elicit supplies and other financial support from those back home. The anonymous author's 'unique and inexpressible life' is vividly portrayed in what is a relatively short text of 100 pages.[21] Not surprisingly for a book meant to encourage charity from America, numerous passages are devoted to illustrating the dire need for 'platinum needles, big and little', cotton and gauze, rubber gloves, ether, 'dear little wash-clothes and hot water bags and rings, and oil-cloth and malted milk': 'I lack everything ... cuvettes, glass jars, cups, oilcloth, syringes, needles, all in fact lacking but the pharmacy. *Ether is a memory here. Please* send the needles and all the other things'[22] [original italics]. She often describes nearly weeping at the sight of new parcels, 'fresh blessings from our golden shores', and also 'growing patriotic, to a degree I never knew in former days ... a wee thrill that is quite peculiar, and makes me think that some day I may be a better American'.[23] In praising 'all the generous donors' she echoes her male counterparts whose memoirs make sure to note those who have helped them. Robert Whitney Imbrie lists by name those who have paid for the ambulances he drives, first, Mr Cleveland H. Dodge of New York City who supplied 'Old Number Nine', then Mr Edward Moore of Philadelphia who supplied 'New Number Nine', which provided a model for all subsequent ambulances: 'After looking it over I felt it must almost be a pleasure to be wounded to have the privilege of riding in such a car'.[24]

In the years before 1917, both male and female volunteers expressed their dismay at their country's 'fence-sitting'. Katherine Foote declared:

> Wilson's last pipe-dream exasperates ... me. Why doesn't he come over and see what he is talking about? He writes as if we were still dealing with the world as it was before the war. We are not – it's gone, over, and before the United States tries to make any further progress, that fact must be registered once for all. We find here a very appreciative, sympathetic and intelligent interest as regards the situation at home. They are tolerant and anxious to make every allowance for the difficulty of our position. It is felt, however, that Wilson must be under German influence ... and there is even a canard that the present Mrs Wilson is a Boche![25]

Her angry assessment of wavering US support is not atypical, though it is perhaps one of the more vociferous. Thus, when America does join the Allies in April 1917, she is ebullient. Seeing the Stars and Stripes hanging in St Paul's Cathedral 'fills her with joy that the great and glorious days of the new birth of our nation have come' and an article in the *Daily Telegraph* entitled 'America at War' makes 'proud reading nowadays'. When 'the band of the Royal Welsh Fusiliers struck up "The Star-Spangled Banner," there was tremendous applause, and you can't think what a feeling it gave me'.[26] When at last 'the papers here give one a splendid idea of what America is doing, – her efforts and accomplishment' she hopes 'everyone at home realizes what we are up against'.[27] But not all were convinced that America knew what she faced. The anonymous 'college man' whose letter was collected in *Camion Letters* (1917), asserted that 'America is absurdly ignorant of the part she is expected to play in this great war. It is a tremendous and grim thing, and the sooner America realizes it, the better. France has fought a wonderful fight and it is now time for a fresh entry into the conflict.'[28] Frederic R. Courdert similarly argued that 'The American people, long isolated from European affairs, might not have understood that this was not a mere European conflict, but transcended the boundaries of time and space as the latest and greatest phase of the eternal struggle between that which is highest and that which is lowest in man.'[29] For Margaret Deland, up until the moment of Wilson's declaration, 'American knowledge of what war means had been Academic'. Now, 'everybody is in the Cast of the Terrible Show – nobody is a Spectator.'[30] America had now to face 'the supreme test of our nation … We must all speak, act and serve together!'[31] James M. Beck displayed an evangelical spirit in language not entirely unfamiliar in the early twenty-first century, when he declared that 'It is essential that America should go into this war with a feeling of heroic joy in again battling for the noblest principles of liberty and justice … The very soul of America is to be tested.'[32]

William Yorke Stevenson is joyous about such a test, declaring that 'America at last is doing her full share, and She is doing it well AND THOROUGHLY', while James Wilson Gailey, who would be killed at Chemin des Dames when his ambulance was struck by a shell, enthused early on in his service:

> Make no mistake about that. It's the real thing at last. I can't tell you how glad I feel. I am now really and truly in the war. All the realities of a terrible warfare have been opened before my eyes. For three years I have read about it in a careless, rather unsympathetic manner, but my heart never beat faster for it then. Now I am interested heart and soul.[33]

The first mobilisation of nurses stationed at the United States Quarantine Hospital, Island No. 3, Ellis Island, New York, occurred in June 1917. A further 250 nurses from United States Army General Hospital No. 1, Williamsbridge, New York City were mobilized on 8 September 1917, followed by others from stations at Hoboken, NJ, and the Colony Club, Madison Avenue, New York City.[34] Of the many male ambulance drivers, some joined combat units with the American Expeditionary Forces (AEF), though others stayed on to serve with French medical units or with the American Field Service, which the American Ambulance had been renamed.

The memoirs of female nurses and male ambulance drivers share common topics and pre-occupations from baptisms of fire to the struggle to hold one's nerve. Devastating wounds, unimaginable suffering and immersion in work as an emotional shield mark out these testimonials. For some, the initiation is relatively gentle, as when Maud Mortimer is introduced to her 'principal field of activity', the '*salle d'attente* – the portal of the hospital'. The wounded arrive, heralded by a whistle, 'huddled', 'inarticulate bundles of pain and misery with stone-cold feet and chattering teeth'. She rather matter-of-factly describes the process of undressing the men, whose 'boots and puttees are caked with mud and their clothes stiff with blood and dirt', laying them on beds, cataloguing their belongings and noting their 'names, their wives' names, their addresses, and the numbers of their regiments'. The contents of their pockets

> are emptied into coloured cotton treasure-bags. These follow them to their wards and are hung at the head of their beds. It is in these bags that they keep their most precious trophy of all – their splinters of shell – when the surgeon is fortunate enough to extract them and they lucky enough to survive the ordeal.[35]

'Mademoiselle Miss' is more dramatically ushered into the experience of war near the front lines:

> But oh, I can't express what it means to hear the guns for the first time! It is a sensation so vast and lonely and crowded and cosmic all at once that one seems born into a new phase of existence where the old ways of feeling things do not answer any longer.[36]

Robert Whitney Imbrie, who joined the American Ambulance in 1915, recalled how, when first hearing the 'rumble of the guns and knowing I should be out there from whence came that rumble', he 'speculated on just what my sensations would be and wondered whether my nerve would hold when confronted with the conditions I had come to seek'.[37] His baptism of fire came with a twenty-four-hour shift that began with him crossing the Aisne with his group of cars:

> the Germans shelling the bridge with 150's, I think. They had the exact range, as regards distance, but the shells were falling about a hundred yards to one side, throwing up great geysers of water as they struck the river. On reaching the other side I stopped and watched them come in. They came four to the minute.

He muses that he wasn't so much frightened by his first experience of shells, as curious, but as time went on, and I saw the awful, destructive power of shell fire, when I had seen buildings leveled and men torn to bloody shreds, the realization of their terribleness became mine and with it came a terror of that horrible soul-melting shriek. And now after a year and a half of war, during which I have been scores of times under fire and have lived for weeks at a time in a daily bombarded city, I am no more reconciled to shell fire than at first. If anything, the sensation is worse and personally I do not believe there is such a thing as becoming 'used' to it.[38]

Indeed, as Philip Dana Orcutt testifies,

The first ordeal by fire is easiest. It is then but a new and interest-ing sensation and experience. Later, after one has seen the effect and had some close calls, it is more of a nervous strain. The whine of a shell is very high-pitched, and after a time the sound wears distinctly on the nerves. It is a curious fact that, in spite of the philosophy developed, the longer a man has been under shell-fire the harder it is for him to stand it. By no means would he think of showing it, but he would not deny the fact. It is only the philosophy and callousness developed which keep the men from breaking down, and in many cases the strain on the nerves becomes so great that men do collapse under it. This is one of the forms of so-called 'shell-shock'. The car loaded with blessés, we start back, driving more slowly this time, as precious lives are in our care and jolts must be avoided wherever possible.[39]

Philip Sidney Rice, who had wanted to serve in the Spanish-American War but was rejected on the grounds of his 'weight and heart action', knew he would not be accepted into the forces in the First World War, so volun-teered for the American Ambulance. He 'did not want to miss the chance of in some measure giving his personal services for the cause against the Hun'.[40] His maturity (he was over forty) was both a help and a hindrance. He seems to have had the will to endure, but his mind and body reacted otherwise. To begin with he was 'in good condition and had not yet suf-fered from great fatigue or undue nervous strain'. He could sleep anytime and in any place. But as time went on, he became 'so fatigued and my nerves were so shaken from the continual strain that I could not sleep at all'. His baptism of fire occurs on his first night duty at the front, at the 'wrecked town of Sillery', where he collects two men, 'suffering very great agony but I could see no marks of blood':

I understood at once – they were victims of poison gas. This time there was no need to drive slowly back again to the town of Ludes to the hospital. It was broad daylight when I reached there. A sleepy stretcher bearer came out carrying a lantern, which was not needed. The two men were lifted out of the car and lowered to the ground. They were writhing in agony – one of them rolled off his stretcher into the gutter and died at my feet.[41]

Just as Kate Finzi, discussed in Chapter 1, questioned 'What do *you* know of War?' and, in an attempt to bring the reader closer to the reality, catalogued the gruesome nature of wounds and suffering, so too do American nurses and ambulance drivers. Imbrie addresses the 'gentlemen' of leisure who 'have shot rapids, great game and billiards, who have crossed the Painted Desert … who have killed moose in New Brunswick and time in Monte Carlo' and 'recommends'

> night driving without lights over unfamiliar shell-pitted roads, cluttered with traffic, within easy range of the enemy … Your car, which in daylight never seems very powerful has now become a very Juggernaut of force … Throttle down as you may, the speed seems terrific. You find yourself with your head thrust over the wheel, your eyes staring ahead with an intensity which makes them ache – staring ahead into nothing. … the *brancardier* by your side rasps our '*Vite, pour l'amour de Dieu, vite; ils peuvent nous voir*' … Then in a narrow mud-gutted lane in front of a dug-out you back and fill and finally turn, your bloody load is eased in and you creep back the way you have come, save that now every bump and jolt seems to tear your flesh as you think of those poor, stricken chaps in behind. Yes, there is something of tenseness in lightless night driving under such conditions. Try it, gentlemen.[42]

But while many ambulance men's memoirs recount instances of the gratitude of the French soldiers and non-combatants who cheer them with '*Vive l'Amérique!*', Ellen La Motte provides an alternative reaction:

> Two ambulance men came in, Americans in khaki, ruddy, well fed, careless. They lifted the stretcher quickly, skilfully. Marius opened his angry eyes and fixed them furiously.
>
> '*Sales étrangers!*' he screamed. 'What are *you* here for? To see me, with my bowels running on the ground? Did you come for me ten hours ago, when I needed you? My head in mud, my blood warm under me? Ah, not you! There was danger then – you only come for me when it is safe!'
>
> They shoved him into the ambulance, buckling down the brown canvas curtains by the light of a lantern. One cranked the motor, then both clambered to the seat in front, laughing. They drove swiftly but carefully through the darkness, carrying no lights. Inside, the man continued his imprecations, but they could not hear him.
>
> 'Strangers! Sightseers!' he sobbed in misery. 'Driving a motor, when it is I who should drive the motor! Have I not conducted a Paris taxi for these past ten years? Do I not know how to drive, to manage an engine? What are

they here for – France? No, only themselves! To write a book – to say what they have done – when it was safe!'[43]

These two ruddy-faced Americans could have been any of the men considered in this chapter and Marius mocks the very books which form the basis of its analysis. The passage highlights the very prejudices that ambulance men and doctors were consistently working against: the idea that they were merely body-snatchers, opportunistic collectors of tales from a safe distance. It was an attitude that surely was not unique and one which pushed some to the point of breakdown, as will be considered below.

Those who received these wounded were confronted with the full horror of the effects of shells and heavy artillery on the body. One French soldier, 'nineteen, not more', is described by surgeon James Robb Church. The corners of his mouth are 'pulled down into a piteous droop' from 'pain and constant suffering':

> On his left leg and thigh he has four wounds varying from four to six inches; on the right leg, the ends of all his toes are shot away and on the same thigh, underneath, a wound about fourteen inches long, open and showing the muscles and fascia. If you want to know what such a wound looks like, go buy a beefsteak big enough for a family of four and lay in on the back of your thigh and then try and realize that it is a tender, quivering area. He has two other wounds that I cannot describe. Each morning the surgeons pull gauze out of and push gauze into all those eight wounds and sponge and dress them.[44]

Throughout, he notes how the young man 'does not whimper' but bears his torture with 'pathetic dignity'.

Nurses had similar horrors to speak of. Katherine Foote, whose 1919 memoir *Letters from Two Hospitals* was published under the pseudonym 'An American VAD', asserted that no amount of reading or imagination, no amount of training, however professional, and could have prepared America's daughters for what they would be up against: 'One cannot describe it; one must see it to feel it. … Apart from the suffering, one's principal impression is that one has never seen so much mud caked on to human beings!'[45] Seeing a train empty itself of its wounded – grimy, dishevelled, abject – at Amiens, Maud Mortimer similarly asserts: 'Around this driftwood of war is certainly no trace of the glamour [of war].'[46] The enthusiasm Shirley Millard felt as her and her contemporaries' 'hearts thumped to the tune of *Over There*,' would be quickly dispelled. Yet, the lilt of *Tipperary, Madelon,* and *Roses of Picardy* heated my enthusiasm to fever pitch … I wanted to help save France from the marauding enemy. Banners streamed in my blood. Drums beat in my brain. Bugles sounded in my ears. I wanted to go overseas. … [K]nitting and selling Liberty Bonds [were] not enough for me. My imagination caught fire. I visualized myself driving an ambulance along the line of battle, aiding and comforting the wounded, or kneeling beside dying men in shell-torn No Man's Land. Or better still, gliding silently among hospital cots, placing a cool hand on fevered brows, lifting bound heads to moisten pain-parched lips with water. Reading to quiet men with bandaged eyes. Gently dressing a broken arm or leg. Or bearing the weight of a heroic convalescent as he took his first steps with a crutch.[47]

And, like other nurses, including Vera Brittain before her, Millard imagined being able to nurse her boyfriend Ted, 'oh, very slightly wounded … Gassed a bit, perhaps. Or with a sprained ankle. He would open his eyes and find me bending over him, my white veil brushing his cheek.'[48] Such effervescent romantic ruminations starkly contrast with what she actually faces, her diary days later recording simply: 'Terribly busy. It is all so different than I imagined. No time to write.'[49] Looking back (her book combines diary transcripts with post-war recollection), Millard argued that 'There was no need to write. The memory remains indelible.'[50] The picture-postcard images of Florence Nightingales of the Western Front are unable to depict the gravity of the suffering. Three thousand five hundred cots are 'filled with wounded'. The quiet ward of imagination, where she fancies herself floating as a latter-day Lady with the Lamp, is replaced by:

> [C]onfusion, disorder and excitement … chaos. Nurses, doctors, orderlies, beds everywhere; yet not nearly enough to take care of the influx of wounded. … Hundreds upon hundreds of wounded poured in like a rushing torrent. No matter what we did, how hard we worked, it did not seem to be fast enough or hard enough. More came. It took me several days to steel my emotions against the stabbing cries of pain. The crowded, twisted bodies, the screams and groans, made me think of the old engravings in Dante's *Inferno.* More came, and still more.[51]

A cool hand on a fevered brow and the gentle dressing of a broken arm or leg are unwanted when 'blood- and mud-soaked bandages' are removed to 'find an arm hanging by a tendon'. 'Gashes from bayonets. Flesh torn by shrapnel. Faces half shot away. Eyes seared by gas' make a mockery of the tune that inexplicably 'runs inanely through my head: "Roses are blooming in Picardy".'[52]

Foote too describes 'hideous shell wound[s] of the arm and hand', 'dreadful' head wounds, stumps of legs, all of whose dressings 'torture', resulting in 'terrible agony'. One man's wound, 'after many fomentations and a fresh incision, has yielded up a piece of shrapnel about half an inch thick and a little less in length'.[53] 'Mademoiselle Miss' tells her family:

> I think you would sicken with fright if you could see the operations that a poor nurse is called upon to perform – the putting in of drains, the washing of wounds so huge and ghastly as to make one marvel at the endurance that is the man's, the digging about for bits of shrapnel.[54]

Maud Mortimer is even more unsparing in her depictions of the suffering she attempts to alleviate. Her memoir *A Green Tent in Flanders* (1917) employs straightforward, unembellished prose. One man 'has had a bad time with his knee. It seemed nothing at first but, after two operations, the articulation of the knee had to be opened. With forceps I hold the desolate flap while the pus is cleaned away and disinfectants poured on the wound.'[55] Another has:

> [A] bad case of gas gangrene, and the doctors pass the fatal verdict: '*Faut te couper la jambe.*' He refuses at first then consents; it is his only thread of chance. DePrecy amputates the leg at the hip joint, a staggering operation. The beauty of the mutilated body lying on the table and the severed leg carried away to be dissected is almost intolerable.[56]

And another young soldier has 'a bullet through the spleen and kidney, half-flayed, with stomach, liver, and part of his intestines laid impudently bare, drains in the abdominal cavity and in his back'.[57] In the chapter entitled 'The Eye' we are told about Mongodin, the soldier of whom all you could see was his eye, which had a 'brave smile':

> His wound was just above the left temple – a triangular-shaped hole almost an inch wide on its upper side. The projectile had passed behind the left eye … had opened way down behind the nose, and lodged rather forward in the roof of the mouth. It made his head seem like an empty hole … The hour of his daily dressings was one for which I grew to time my visits to his ward. His nurse would allow me to pass her what she needed and, while the ordeal lasted, to engage the eye in conversation. The ordeal consisted partly in the excruciating change of *meches* and drains and in pouring through the gaping triangular temple wound streams of peroxide which would flow down behind the damaged left eye, behind the nose, and be caught by Mongodin himself, sitting up against his bed-rest, in a little white enamel kidney-dish which he would hold, without so much as wincing or even giving vent to

any of those strange animal-like sounds for which the time being stood him instead of speech.[58]

La Motte writes a similarly arresting description of a soldier's eye, that of the thirty-nine-year-old former gardener, Little Rochard:

> The piece of shell in his skull had made one eye blind. There had been a haemorrhage into the eyeball, which was all red and sunken, and the eyelid would not close over it, so the red eye stared and stared into space. And the other eye drooped and drooped, and the white showed, and the eyelid drooped till nothing but the white showed, and that showed that he was dying. But the blind, red eye stared beyond. It stared fixedly, unwinkingly, into space. So always the nurse watched the dull, white eye, which showed the approach of death.
>
> No one in the ward was fond of Rochard. He had been there only a few hours. He meant nothing to any one there ... there were many people there to wait upon him, but there was no one there to love him. There was no one there to see beyond the horror of the red, blind eye, of the dull, white eye, of the vile, gangrene smell. And it seemed as if the red, staring eye was looking for something the hospital could not give. And it seemed as if the white, glazed eye was indifferent to everything the hospital could give. ... He sank into a stupor about ten o'clock in the morning, and was unconscious from then till the time the nurse went to lunch. She went to lunch reluctantly, but it is necessary to eat ... After a short time she came back from lunch, and hurried to see Rochard, hurried behind the flamboyant, red, cheerful screens that shut him off from the rest of the ward. Rochard was dead.
>
> At the other end of the ward sat the two orderlies, drinking wine.[59]

The pathos of Rochard's condition is compounded by the emphasis on his being unloved, while the emphasis on the 'smell' of his wounds reinforces how his memory lingers in a visceral way, for nobody could 'forget about that smell'. Like Mortimer's Mongodin, his eyes see all but his body is helpless and on his death the final insult is La Motte's sentence 'At the other end of the ward sat the two orderlies, drinking wine', though it also reinforces the ordinariness of such gruesome suffering.

Higonnet's assessment of La Motte's text is equally applicable to Mortimer's: 'Unlike many wartime reminiscences that collect senti-mentalized portraits of wounded soldiers these pages were not token bits abstracted for propagandistic or nostalgic purposes.'[60] Such graphic description was no doubt part of an almost prurient attraction for readers of these memoirs, and may have tacitly served the needs of propaganda for American involvement in this war against the barbaric Axis. But more importantly they reflect the author's need to release and to bear witness, 'the peculiar predicament of the First World War nurses' that Santanu Das has identified. Das asserts, moreover, 'If physical wounding and pain cannot possibly be shared, the First World War nurses repeatedly dwell on acute body memories and body knowledge to establish a *physical continuum, a bodily bridge, as it were, over an ontological impossibility*: touch becomes the ground of both testimony and trauma' [original italics].[61]

Although Katherine Foote acknowledges that her twelve-hour day allows her little time for sleep and even less for 'more than a hasty scrawl', she asserts that

> Actually for the first time in my life I begin to feel as a normal being should, in spite of the blood and anguish in which I move. I really am *useful*, that is all, and too busy to remember myself, past, present, or future. While it's such a great, terrible, sweet, sad world to live in, [it is] always wonderful, and I would not be doing anything else but this.[62]

To be needed in and 'useful' to a cause larger than oneself is a sustaining force in the midst of the 'blood and anguish'.

That is not to say that the 'blood and anguish' did not take its toll – on men as well as women. Ambulance driver memoirs are surprisingly candid about 'strain', 'nerves', and the necessity for rest. Rice, who was awarded the Croix de Guerre for his service, is, as seen above, clear about the 'nerve wrecking Hell', seeing soldiers going mad, and his fellow drivers break down 'under the strain'. His nerves also were shattered after the 'shrieking blood-stained Hell in front of Verdun'. On leave in Paris, his sleep fitfully achieved, is haunted: 'I was once more back at Verdun. I could hear the aeroplanes whirring overhead – I could hear the bursting shells – I could see the dead horses on the crowded roads I could see the rats and filth, the desolation of the front.'[63] He recognises that his 'nerves seemed to be temporarily shattered' – and it is interesting he uses the word 'temporarily' because he is eager to return to the front and to his work. The closeness of such volunteers is attested to by the numerous references to each other in individual memoirs: Rice refers to Stevenson whose 'brainy, watchful, sympathetic leadership' held his ambulance group together;[64] Stevenson defends Rice against accusations of cowardice:

> Poor Rice went to pieces at about dinner-time; but when he overheard White calling him a quitter he went out and cranked his car and started up. The man was all gone; so when I heard he had disobeyed orders, I went to hunt him up around ten o'clock. I found him out near Sainte-Fismes, and

cursed him for disobeying and sent him back. I also jumped on White, who had no business to criticize a man who had worked until he broke down.[65]

Thus, there was recognition that overwork could lead to breakdown, and that breakdown was not the result of weakness in body or in mind. Resilience was achieved by recognising breakdown and allowing time for rest. One's training and one's dedication to the mission to 'make the world safe for democracy' could only go so far. Alice Fitzgerald, for one, began 'to lose all sense of compassion and feeling for her patients', who were becoming 'stretcher cases, not human beings'. As Victoria Holder noted, 'The physicians tried to excuse her from work, but she refused because she knew she was needed'.[66] In her book, Fitzgerald herself notes that when reflecting on the endurance of British Tommies to 'stand the pain like super-human-beings', 'it is best not to stop and think too much; one could never do the work'.[67] Back in London, she was diagnosed with 'a mild case of shell shock', and was close to a nervous breakdown. With rest, she recovered and was asked to train incoming British VADs at Boulogne. When the United States entered the war, she requested to be reassigned to the American Red Cross. At the ARC headquarters in Paris, she became friends with another American nurse, Julia Stimson, whose memoir *Finding Themselves* (1918), is discussed in Chapter 1.

The word 'strain', used so often by the writers considered in this chapter as in the previous one, also has resonance for Katherine Foote:

> Even with your big hearts and sympathy and imagination, you can hardly realize how terrible the strain is, nor how one longs for the end. … [O]nly there's nothing for us all to do now but sit tight and work and fight until we win, even if it take all our lives; so uneasiness can have no lasting place in one's mind.[68]

To 'win' is paramount, and she admits that 'if one did not have plenty of work to do, the contemplation of such suffering and the problems which the nations must deal with after the war would drive one mad'.[69] Foote repeats the phrase 'would drive one mad' in another passage when, after witnessing countless amputations, she exclaims: 'Oh, the appalling, futile horror of it all! It has to be, but the longer one is in it, the more one is oppressed by the terrible waste of everything, from life downward, and to think of it constantly would drive one mad'.[70] Such repetition reinforces the fear of succumbing to mental collapse. For these nurses, as opposed to their ambulance driver colleagues, work is the only antidote. 'Mademoiselle Miss', too, finds that relentless work sustains her:

> During the last week we have averaged 25 operations daily. One day we had 33, and if you have any conception of an operating-room where they are short of assistants, you may know the struggle, and the sense that one is saving bits from the wreckage, doesn't give one a chance to be mastered by the unutterable woe.[71]

Much like Rice, she finds leave in Paris almost too much to bear: 'I am ecstatic over getting back to work! Now that my Parisian fling is over, I might as well own that it was a terrific strain on my nerves. I discovered that a civilian life is unhealthy for me, and that I thrive under the banner of the Red Cross.'[72] Rose Peabody Parsons asserts similarly that 'it was slack times that were almost the hardest of all. When we were busy no one had time to think, and it was far better not to be able to wonder what it was all about.'[73] It was necessary to protect the psyche, but Mortimer wonders, '[D]o I grow cynical of decorations? The price, these young lives, and the dear, boyish recklessness of their inexperience, are distorting my values' and comments: 'How soon the priceless thin edge of deep emotion blunts.'[74] Fitzgerald admits to similar desensitisation: recognising that she could often only treat the worst cases, she does so in a matter-of-fact statement that tells volumes: 'The treatment was neither brutal nor indifferent. It was simply necessary.'[75]

When peace comes, Shirley Millard, though 'glad it is over' finds 'my heart is heavy as lead'. Her British counterpart Vera Brittain heard the guns in London heralding the Armistice 'crash with terrifying clearness', but 'like a sleeper who is determined to go on dreaming after being told to wake up, I went on automatically washing the dressing bowls in the annexe outside my hut'. Like Brittain's VAD colleagues, Millard's are determined she should celebrate: 'One of the girls came looking for me. They have opened the champagne for the staff in the dining hall. I told her to get out. Can't seem to pull myself together.'[76] 'Numb [and] bewildered', she is, like Brittain, an automaton. Moreover, she

> felt a sudden shyness about returning home. I dreaded the curious eyes and eager questions. They would make a fuss. I knew that from the letters and clippings I had received. I shrank from the prospect of honors I neither wanted nor deserved. How could they know what *real* bravery, *real* heroism, was? I had seen it and wanted no chatter about it over teacups and cocktail glasses.[77] [original italics]

Going home, though welcome for many nurses, was also traumatic and bewildering, far removed from the life they considered normal for so long, as Mortimer attests:

A wire calls me home. Through a maze of conflicting emotions I look back along the days. Civilian life seems as far from me as a skin long ago sloughed off. After my breezy corner of a green shack, in this tiny world of keen living, how self-centered, and cluttered with artificial values that other life will seem.[78]

William Yorke Stevenson reflected that on his return home, 'Life seems so banal after one has been a part, however humble, of history in the making. As I write, I know that if I had my way, I should be back there washing my old "Tin Lizzie" in some muddy horsepond, right now.'[79]

The psychological aftermath was to be revisited in the years after the war in countless ways, for some, like Millard, through publication, 'a simple record of the dark caravan that winds endlessly through the memory of my youth.'[80] Although Philip Sidney Rice was far from young during his service, he too writes wistfully of his experiences, which were also filled with much horror and 'the monotonous song of death': 'I wonder if I shall answer that voice which whispers to me as I walk along the crowded streets, which whispers as I lie awake at night, which whispers in my sleep and says to me – "Come back." '[81]

The war never left its participants. And many hoped that their publications would 'perpetuate the vision' that inspired them, as Adam Piette Andrew asserted in his introduction to a 1921 memorial volume documenting the 'brief lives' of the young men of the American Field Service:

> If there is anything in this volume to awaken solemn and mournful thought, it must not be regret for the lives that have ended and for youths that are gone ... of blighted hopes, or loss, or unfufillment. It is really the story of dreams that have come true, of careers that have been completed without disappointment ... The men had the good fortune to depart gloriously at the pinnacle of their career ... facing eternity in the morning of their lives, gallantly offered life's noon time and its evening upon the altar of their country.[82]

Such purple prose and high-minded sentiment sits in stark contrast to Rose Peabody Parsons's reflections in her 1923 article for the *Atlantic Monthly*:

> Memories of the war crop up. We suppress them. Books and articles dealing with the war we simply won't buy. We have had quite enough of unpleasantness. Yet we don't enjoy ourselves. ... We think of those who bravely died. We think, too, of our dead selves who once vowed that these others should not have died in vain.[83]

It may be that she is referring to such texts as Andrew's as she prefigures the stark assessment of Hemingway and positions herself – if unselfconsciously – as part of what would become known as the Lost Generation, those who served and came of age in the Great War, many of whom were shattered by it. The patriotic confidence in America's mission 'over there', the ideals of a 'young' nation coming to 'old' Europe's aid underpins the mechanisms by which this generation of aid workers and healers coped with the blood and anguish with which they were faced and their own trauma. Their narratives do not ignore the 'strain', the 'nerve-wrecking Hell' of war; rather, they consistently use such language to name their own and others' personal trauma, and indeed, they are forthright in naming the trauma of fellow drivers and nurses. While they may break down at times, or come close to doing so, the ambulance drivers and nurses demonstrate in their narratives resolve and resilience in spite of, or even in opposition to, the graphic descriptions that attempt to bring the reader to the heart of what they witnessed. As Parsons's comments demonstrate, however, resilience was not the same as triumphalism. As La Motte presciently argued in the introduction to her memoir published in 1916:

> After this war, there will be many other wars, and in the intervals there will be peace. So it will alternate for many generations. By examining the things cast up in the backwash, we can gauge the progress of humanity. When clean little lives, when clean little souls boil up in the backwash, they will consolidate, after the final war, into a peace that shall endure. But not till then.[84]

The basic numbers of over 322,000 American casualties in the First World War, nearly 117,000 of whom died, could be considered insignificant, in comparison to the millions lost by Germany, France and Britain. But for those who pulled them from the battlefields or treated them in hospital, each individual was not insignificant. And when added to the thousands of men from other nations that came their way in the years before America's entry into the war, the volume of human suffering which confronted the male and female volunteers considered in this chapter was enormous. The American national memory of the First World War is dominated by the literature of the Lost Generation, by popular song, images of Doughboys parading down Fifth Avenue, Hollywood films such as *Sergeant York* (itself an important propaganda tool in the Second World War), and numerous recruiting posters now sold as decorative art. But it should also be informed by the kinds of narratives considered here. Digitisation by the Library of Congress allows public online access to these books that for decades lay on its shelves, consulted by only the most tenacious academic. The relevance of these texts to the narratives of later conflicts, especially the Vietnam War, is evident throughout our following chapters, for although separated in time by decades, these memoirs of America's first world crusade can help to illuminate its later efforts 'to fulfil its global mission',[85] and what that means for those healers who, like their predecessors, would be 'shaken with that same vibration of the shock and hideousness of it all'.[86]

Notes

1 Ernest Hemingway, *A Farewell to Arms* (New York, Scribner's, 1929), p. 196.

2 In *A Moveable Feast* (1964), Ernest Hemingway recorded Stein as saying 'That is what you are. That's what you all are ... all of you young people who served in the war. You are a lost generation.'

3 Fiction served similar ends. Mary R. Ryder demonstrates how Edith Wharton's *The Marne* and Dorothy Canfield Fisher's *Home Fires in France* 'promoted American virtues while chastising American shortcomings ... [in] the last historical moment in which Americans believed themselves capable of saving the world'. M. Rydon, '"Dear, Tender-Hearted, Uncomprehending America": Dorothy Canfield Fisher's and Edith Wharton's Fictional Responses to the First World War', in P. J. Quinn and S. Trout, eds., *The Literature of the Great War Reconsidered: Beyond Modern Memory* (Basingstoke: Palgrave, 2001), p. 144.

4 A review of the US government's official propaganda organisation, the Committee on Public Information, is provided by Krystina Benson, in 'Archival Analysis of the Committee on Public Information: The Relationship between Propaganda, Journalism and Popular Culture', *International Journal of Technology, Knowledge and Society* 6: 4 (2010): 151–64.

5 Susan Zeiger, *In Uncle Sam's Service: Women Workers with the American Expeditionary Force, 1917–1919* (Ithaca, NY: Cornell University Press, 1999), 142. The experiences of African-American women, in particular, have only recently received attention. Over a thousand African-American nurses who were registered with the Red Cross were rejected for service with the army, although some eventually were allowed to nurse wounded soldiers from the segregated black regiments when these returned stateside. *Two Colored Women with the AEF* (1920) was an early effort to chronicle not only the service of approximately 150,000 African-American soldiers who served in France, but that of the sixteen African-American women who were attached to the YMCA canteens. But more scholarly

work remains to be done. See A. W. Hunton and K. M. Johnson, *Two Colored Women with the American Expeditionary Forces* (Brooklyn, NY: Brooklyn Eagle Press, 1920). Recent studies about African-American soldiers include A. Lentz-Smith, *Freedom Struggles: African Americans and World War I* (Cambridge, Mass.: Harvard University Press, 2009). J. M. Beck, *The War and Humanity: A Further Discussion of the Ethics of the World War and the Attitude and Duty of the United States* (New York and London: G. P. Putnam's Sons/The Knickerbocker Press, 1917), p. xvii.

6 C. de Florez, *'No. 6': A Few Pages from the Diary of an Ambulance Driver* (New York: E. P. Dutton & Co., 1918), p. 141.

7 *President Wilson's Great Speeches and Other History Making Documents* (Chicago: Stanton & Van Vliet Co., 1919), p. 29. For an analysis of debates surrounding the 'war on terror' and the wars in Iraq and Afghanistan, see L. E. Ambrosius, 'Woodrow Wilson and George W. Bush: Historical Comparisons of Ends and Means in Their Foreign Policies', *Diplomatic History* 30: 3(2006): 509–43. George Bateson, *Steps to an Ecology of Mind: Collected Essays in Anthropology, Psychiatry, Evolution and Epistemology* (Northvale, NJ and London: Jason Aronson Inc., 1987), p. 206.

8 George M. Cohan, 'Over There' (New York: Leo Feist, 1917).

9 Margaret Higonnet, 'Cubist Vision in Nursing Accounts', in Alison S. Fell and Christine E. Hallett (eds), *First World War Nursing: New Perspectives* (New York and London: Routledge, 2013), p. 161.

10 Borden, *The Forbidden Zone*, p. 118.

11 Ambrosius, 'Woodrow Wilson', p. 509.

12 C. Francis Reisner and Benny Davis (words), Billy Baskette (music), 'Good-Bye Broadway, Hello France' (New York: Leo Feist, Inc., 1917).

13 'Thank you for "The Hill-Top on the Marne". It is a good experience, spiritedly sketched, and I like the lady's pluck. It was diverting to read English again after so long.' *'Mademoiselle Miss': Letters from an American Girl Serving with the Rank of Lieutenant in a French Army Hospital at the Front* (Boston: W. A. Butterfield, 1916), p. 94.

14 Gertrude Atherton, *Life in the War Zone* (New York: New York Times, 1916), p. 16.

15 V. L. Holder, 'From Hand-Maiden to Right Hand: World War I – The Mud and the Blood', *AORN Journal* 80: 4 (2004): 652–65; p. 657.

16 Holder, 'From Hand-Maiden to Right Hand', p. 658.

17 Richard Derby, *'Wade in, Sanitary!' The Story of a Division Surgeon in France* (New York and London: G. P. Putnam's Sons/The Knickerbocker Press, 1919), p. 61.

18 Margaret Deland, *Small Things* (New York: D. Appleton & Co., 1919), p. 8.

19 Holder, 'From Hand-Maiden to Right Hand', p. 659.

20 Marie van Vorst, *War Letters of an American Woman* (New York: John Lane Co. and London: John Lane, The Bodley Head, 1916), p. 62.

21 *'Mademoiselle Miss'*, p. 29.

22 *'Mademoiselle Miss'*, pp. 29, 91, 28.

23 *'Mademoiselle Miss'*, p. 59.

24 Robert Whitney Imbrie, *Behind the Wheel of a War Ambulance* (New York: Robert McBride & Co., 1918), pp. 14, 72.

25 An American VAD [Katherine Foote], *Letters from Two Hospitals* (Boston: Atlantic Monthly Press, 1919), p. 9.

26 Foote, *Letters from Two Hospitals*, pp. 62, 65, 68.

27 Foote, *Letters from Two Hospitals*, p. 98.

28 *Camion Letters: From American College Men Volunteers of the American Field Service in France, 1917* (New York: Henry Holt & Co., 1918), p. 38.

29 Frederic R. Coudert, preface to de Florez, *'No. 6'*, pp. xii–xiii.

30 Deland, *Small Things*, pp. 28, 30.

31 Address of the President to his Fellow Countrymen, 16 April 1917, *President Wilson's Great Speeches*, p. 37.

32 Beck, *The War and Humanity*, p. xvii.

33 James Wilson Gailey in James William Davenport Seymour, *AFS Memorial Volume: American Field Service in France* (Boston: AFS, 1921), p. 29.

34 J. C. Stimson, 'The Army Nurse Corps', in *The Medical Department of the United States Army in the World War*, vol. XIII, part two (Washington, DC: US Government Printing Office, 1927), pp. 287–351, at pp. 307, 309.

35 Maud Mortimer, *A Green Tent in Flanders* (Garden City, NY: Doubleday, Page and Co., 1917), p. 85.

36 *'Mademoiselle Miss'*, p. 12.

37 Imbrie, *Behind the Wheel*, p. 23.

38 Imbrie, *Behind the Wheel*, pp. 39–40.

39 Philip Dana Orcutt, *The White Road of Mystery: The Note-Book of an American Ambulancier* (New York: John Lane and London: John Lane, The Bodley Head, 1918), pp. 121–2.

40 Rice, *An Ambulance Driver in France*, p. 5.

41 Rice, *An Ambulance Driver in France*, p. 39.

42 Imbrie, *Behind the Wheel*, pp. 40–1.

43 Ellen N. La Motte, *The Backwash of War: The Human Wreckage of the Battlefield as Witnessed by an American Hospital Nurse* (New York: The Knickerbocker Press, 1916), pp. 20–1.

44 James Robb Church, *The Doctor's Part: What Happens to the Wounded in War* (New York and London: D. Appleton and Company, 1918), p. 37.

45 Foote, *Letters from Two Hospitals*, p. 1.

46 Mortimer, *A Green Tent in Flanders*, p. 320.

47 Shirley Millard, *I Saw Them Die: Diary and Recollections* (New York: Harcourt, Brace and Company, 1936), p. 3.

48 Millard, *I Saw Them Die*, p. 4.
49 Millard, *I Saw Them Die*, p. 10.
50 Millard, *I Saw Them Die*, p. 10.
51 Millard, *I Saw Them Die*, pp. 11–12.
52 Millard, *I Saw Them Die*, p. 14.
53 Foote, *Letters from Two Hospitals*, p. 80.
54 'Mademoiselle Miss', p. 33.
55 Mortimer, *A Green Tent in Flanders*, p. 142.
56 Mortimer, *A Green Tent in Flanders*, pp. 144–5.
57 Mortimer, *A Green Tent in Flanders*, p. 149.
58 Mortimer, *A Green Tent in Flanders*, pp. 186–9.
59 La Motte, *The Backwash of War*, p. 57.
60 Margaret Higonnet, *Nurses at the Front: Writing the Wounds of the Great War* (Boston: Northeastern University Press, 2001), p. xvii.
61 Santanu Das, '"The Impotence of Sympathy": Touch and Trauma in the Memoirs of First World War Nurses', *Textual Practice* 19: 2 (2005): 239–62; pp. 244, 257.
62 Foote, *Letters from Two Hospitals*, p. 28.
63 Rice, *An Ambulance Driver in France*, p. 93.
64 Rice, *An Ambulance Driver in France*, p. 89.
65 William Yorke Stevenson, *From 'Poilu' to 'Yank'* (Boston and New York: Houghton Mifflin Co., 1918), pp. 158–9.
66 Holder, 'From Hand-Maiden to Right Hand', p. 660.
67 A. L. F. Fitzgerald, the Edith Cavell nurse from Massachusetts, *A Record of One Year's Personal Service with the British Expeditionary Force in France, Boulogne: The Somme, 1916–1917*, with an account of the imprisonment, trial and death of Edith Cavell (Boston: W. A. Butterfield, 1917), p. 5.
68 Foote, *Letters from Two Hospitals*, p. 47.
69 Foote, *Letters from Two Hospitals*, p. 7.
70 Foote, *Letters from Two Hospitals*, p. 63.
71 'Mademoiselle Miss', p. 21.
72 'Mademoiselle Miss', p. 94.
73 R. Peabody Parsons, 'Have We Kept the Faith?', *Atlantic Monthly* (August 1923): 666–72; p. 670.
74 Mortimer, *A Green Tent in Flanders*, pp. 112, 127.
75 I. Noble, *Nurse Around the World: Alice Fitzgerald* (New York: Messner, 1964), p. 68.
76 Millard, *I Saw Them Die*, p. 110. Brittain recalled:

on Armistice day not even a lonely survivor drowning in black waves of memory could be left alone with her thoughts. A moment after the guns had subsided into sudden, palpitating silence, the other VAD from my ward dashed excitedly into the annex.

'Brittain! Brittain! Did you hear the maroons? It's over – it's all over! Do let's come out and see what's happening!' (*Testament of Youth* (1933/2004), p. 421).

77 Millard, *I Saw Them Die*, p. 111.
78 Mortimer, *A Green Tent in Flanders*, p. 239.
79 Stevenson, *From 'Poilu' to 'Yank'*, p. 6.
80 Millard, *I Saw Them Die*, p. 115.
81 Rice, *An Ambulance Driver in France*, p. 109.
82 Andrew, preface, to Stevenson, *From 'Poilu' to 'Yank'*, pp. xi–xii.
83 Parsons, 'Have We Kept the Faith?', pp. 666, 672.
84 La Motte, *The Backwash of War*, p. vi.
85 'Appealing to the old American hope of "freedom just around the corner", both Wilson and Bush proclaimed American ideals to justify their new foreign policies. Whether in 1917 or 2001 or 2003, they led the nation into war, promising to protect traditional values and institutions at home and to expand these abroad, thereby making freedom and democracy the foundation for world peace. ... They assigned a redemptive role to the United States, committing it to fight evil and create a new international order. After World War I, Wilson failed to make the world safe for democracy. His experience suggests that fighting wars to spread democracy and thereby attain perpetual peace is more likely to result in unanticipated costs and unintended consequences.' Ambrosius, 'Woodrow Wilson', pp. 542–3.
86 Parsons, 'Have We Kept the Faith?', p. 672.

3

'You damn well just got on with your job': medical personnel and the invasion of Europe in the Second World War

The resilience that allows medical personnel to endure wartime conditions while witnessing unimaginable pain and suffering, and the concurrent potential for breakdown, are inescapably elements of First World War narratives. The same need for endurance is echoed in the words of one Second World War nurse who recalled of her experience, 'Post-traumatic stress had not been invented. It's still double Dutch to me. You damn well just got on with your job.'[1] Yet there is a marked contrast between narratives of these two wars in the way traumatic experience of and responses to breakdown and resilience are negotiated. The tension between stoic endurance and the enormous psychological stress borne by medical personnel in the First World War is, as we have seen, integral to their accounts of their war experience. No matter how obliquely at times, the emotions that attended treating wounded in the warzone were acknowledged by men and women alike. Even while breakdown was often represented euphemistically as exhaustion – mental and physical – to avoid the stigma of a 'nervous' breakdown, it was also acknowledged as an inevitable consequence of the work for some individuals, and always a force to be struggled against. While the ideal was endurance, a part of the necessary sacrifice of the self to the needs of the wounded, the work and the environment are often depicted as almost unendurable and the psychological strain that was a consequence of this work does find its way into these accounts.

The Second World War, similarly, stressed the need for a stoic endurance, but, as suggested in the direct statement of the nurse quoted above, it was attended by a cultural context that denied emotion to a much greater degree than that acknowledged in the First World War narratives discussed in Chapters 1 and 2. The reaction of the nurse against the concept of post-traumatic stress alerts us to a cultural climate that, even

long after the war, was unwilling to acknowledge the psychological consequences of working in the wartime medical arena. The statement carries with it the idea that such an acknowledgement is incompatible with
'getting on with the job'. J. Westren, a VAD nurse on the British Home
Front, sums up this environment, not just of her work, but of the cultural
climate in Britain during the war: 'We didn't emote.'[2] As in all wars, the
importance of medical personnel enduring the traumatic environment in
which they worked was crucial for the maintenance of patient care under
enormously adverse conditions, yet the public emphasis on silent endurance, on both the home and battle fronts, on not showing or articulating
emotional distress, appears to have been much greater than in the First
World War, in spite of a better understanding of combatant breakdown,
often called 'battle fatigue'.[3] As Sheldon writes of Elizabeth Bowen's work
for the War Ministry: '[h]er accounts of the bombing of London and the
preparations for the expected invasion by Germany stress the pluck and
resourcefulness of the public: blood and death are noticeably absent.'[4]

Yet, of course, the lack of overt expression did not preclude emotional
response, but meant that its public demonstration was less acceptable. In
the interests of morale, emotional responses to the devastation of war were
thus given even less space in the cultural arena than in the First World
War, amongst medical personnel at the front as well as in the populations
at home. The private space of personal narratives may thus become the
only site within which deep emotion can be expressed and these accounts
are thus more likely to reveal evidence of breakdown existing alongside
resilience than we find in the public wartime narrative.[5]

While the narrative of endurance, the home front maxim of 'Britain
can take it', was deemed to be necessary for morale, it silenced voices
that would have admitted the possibility and actuality of breakdown,
or of lesser degrees of emotional stress. In her wartime essay, 'They that
Mourn' (1942), Vera Brittain points particularly to the difference between
the First World War and the present one in terms of the permission or
refusal to express emotion:

> one purpose of modern war propaganda is to conceal personal suffering as
> effectively as it hides the horrors of every war-time 'incident'.
>
> ...
>
> Let us hope that there are many future artists and writers ... who will one
> day make real the meaning of this War in human terms. They alone have the
> power to show us the lost homes, the broken families, the sorrowful wives, the
> terrified children, who are pawns in the huge political chess-game of total war.
>
> ...

Once, even in the last War, sorrow was honoured as an emotion deserving of consideration. This respect was extended to the mourners of 'the other side'.

...

Here, as in Germany, they that mourn must today find their own consolation. They will discover it, perhaps, when they are permitted to speak again, in making their pain real to our defective imagination.[6]

As Brittain implies, and as our work demonstrates, the silenced emotion is revealed in subjective stories and exists in tension with the prevailing culture of silent stoicism. Discussing the lack of expression of grief, arguably the most profound and commonly experienced wartime emotion, in women's wartime writing, Hartley suggests that 'women seem to have felt the pressure of male codes of behaviour, to the extent of being unable or unwilling to show grief openly'.[7] One can extend this to other forms of emotion, particularly the expression of emotional distress or breakdown. The writer Margaret Kennedy remarks on how this silencing operates on the level of personal interactions: 'We are all keeping a check on our emotions. ... One tries to short-circuit emotion rather than to share it. The "genial current of the soul" is damned up, and we fall back on bromides and bright little jokes.'[8] Westren similarly writes that 'I know inescapably that life now for everyone wore two masks, one the merriment we pretended, and beneath it the tragedy that we all knew was actually present'.[9] Pressure to maintain such stoic silence thus comes from within as well as without. As Summerfield asserts, 'drawing on the available cultural constructions we contribute to them'.[10] Accordingly, Blythe reminds us, writers exchanging letters between home and front were equally directed to avoid writing anything that might distress the addressee, encouraging a culture of silence around painful emotions.[11]

The tension between an acknowledgement of distress and breakdown and the need to steel oneself against it runs throughout the medical personnel narratives as it does in all the wars under discussion. Yet in the face of public silencing, their often graphic depictions of death and wounding and the distress that caused for care-givers tells the absent war story of what Sheldon calls 'blood and death'. While writers such as Brittain and Westren are speaking from the home front, they echo the general silencing of emotions and the 'keep cheerful' mentality that was encouraged both at home and in the forces, in Britain and in the United States once they entered the war.[12] Medical personnel accounts are particularly well placed to present the 'real meaning of the war in human terms' that Vera Brittain asks for, since it is in these writings that we find the enormous psychological and physical costs of that enterprise, not just for the combatants, but for those who cared for them when sick or wounded. Indeed, the tension between 'getting on with the job' and reacting to that 'job' is vividly evoked by Nurse Marie Stedman in her description of her post D-Day nursing:

> We just had to get on with it, no matter what we felt. ... I was in the 3rd Ambulance Clearing Station and 75th BGH [British General Hospital]. No one ever came to see how we were coping with all the stress then and no one ever came to see us later. But we were young, though sensitive nevertheless. We were so near to the front line that I remember one day waving to the boys standing up in the turrets of their tanks. They were so glad to see us and so cheery. I was still on duty shortly afterwards when those same young lads were brought into Reception, half their faces blown away. Bodies burnt to a frazzle, some lay dying quietly, other screaming with pain.[13]

Typically, Marie Stedman does not claim her pain and stress, but offers a depiction of the context that carries it, notably through the pain of others.

In spite of such representation, the need to perpetuate the stoic narrative has been so insistent that it has persisted into twenty-first-century constructions of the medical experience of the war. The admiration for the British Army nurses of the Second World War, and their endurance in unimaginably difficult conditions told in Nicola Tyrer's *Sisters in Arms*, for example, is constructed in terms of their ability to endure uncomplainingly. She quotes surgeon Sir Frederick Treves: 'They did a service during those distressful days which none but nurses could have rendered and they set to all ... an example of unselfishness, self-sacrifice and indefatigable devotion to duty.'[14] While Tyrer's inclusion of comments from some nurses does allow for a sense of the emotional strain they had to carry, her account leaves no space for breakdown, or for an alternative to the 'Britain can take it' narrative. Such an approach arguably devalues that experience by denying the legitimacy of the individual story that does not fit the narrative. Yet, as in the First World War, it is in the willingness of these men and women to seek to endure in spite of almost overwhelming 'strain' that is crucial to our understanding of their experience.[15]

The accounts by medical personnel under consideration often challenge the dominant paradigm and return both suffering and emotional stress to the story, but at the same time it is arguable that the culture of silence during and after the war did contribute to the dearth of such writings to come out of this war. In contrast to the numbers of accounts, especially by nurses, to be published both during and after the First World War, the Second World War offers us very few. When nurses and doctors did write their accounts they have tended to come long after the war, or have remained unpublished in archives. Of the works under discussion in this chapter Lucilla Andrews's home front account *No Time For Romance* was not published until 1977; Brenda McBryde's *A Nurse's War* appeared in 1979; June Wandrey's *Bedpan Commando* in 1989 and Mildred McGregor's *World War Two: Front Line Nurse* as late as 2007; Mary Morris's 'A Nurse's War Time Diary' remained unpublished until 2014. Of the doctors, Stuart Mawson's *Arnhem Doctor* (1981), Brendan Phibbs's *The Other Side of Time* (1987), and Zachary Friedenberg's *Hospital at War* (2004) were products of their retirement or old age. An exception is Lieutenant Colonel J. C. Watts's *Surgeon at War*, published in 1955.[16]

Mark Harrison points out in *Medicine and Victory* (2004),[17] that 'though the importance of medicine was generally acknowledged in wartime, it has been strangely ignored ever since. ... It is hard to think of any other aspect of military life that has been so poorly served. But the invisibility of medicine in the historical record belies its true significance and masks some of the army's greatest achievements.'[18] While Harrison returns medicine to the history of the war, however, the 'human' stories that make up the medical experience are noticeably absent. The lack of historical interest in the medical war, and in the stories of those who made that history, along with the time lags and the much smaller output, suggest both a reluctance to speak and, perhaps, a lack of public receptivity. This is in contrast to the First World War, where individuals appear to have needed to confront and draw meaning from revisiting their war experiences, resulting in a plethora of published accounts during the war and then, after a ten-year gap, in the climate of disillusionment in the late 1920s and early 1930s.[19] The difference between a ten-year gap and one of more than thirty years in the cases of Phibbs, Mawson, McBryde and Andrews, or of more than sixty for Wandrey, McGregor and Friedenberg, for example, is noteworthy and may be explained in part by McBryde's telling comments in an interview after the publication of her book: 'we pulled down shutters after the war. We didn't want to think about it. ... But war should not be forgotten ... I am so glad I have written it. I feel relieved.'[20] It took American nurse Mildred McGregor even longer to lift the shutters on her experience, bringing together her diary entries and recollections with other accounts by nurses and doctors as part of a writing workshop. She ends by acknowledging that '[i]n retrospect, I believe we block from our minds the destruction of war and remember the pleasurable experiences.[21] Clearly, however, in piecing together her account, she confronted the memories of destruction that had been repressed or excluded from conscious recollection, articulating at this late stage much of the sorrow she had avoided for so many years.

Cynthia Toman's analysis of the Second World War Canadian nurse experience suggests that such pulling down of shutters and selective recollection are, in part, the result of a cultural construction of the war, not only during it, but in its aftermath and the way it is popularly remembered. Toman argues that silencing occurred both during and after the war because of the cultural and historical context within which the nurses worked: 'The literature has perpetuated historical silences regarding military women in general and nurses in particular.' She quotes one nurse: 'As Nursing sister Mary Bray wrote about her submission to one anthology, for example: "We were asked to recall the fun times but indeed there were more sadness and horror of what the war was all about." '[22] The desire to forget that McBryde acknowledges, along with the need to rebuild lives interrupted by the war, also seem to have contributed to the post-war silence. Both Mawson and Phibbs cite the heavy medical workload that preoccupied them after the war until retirement, when they were prompted to return to diaries and notes written during the war. Mawson notes that he did write a private account of his experience immediately after the war and that his memoir 'has been compiled from notes and a narrative put together soon after, in 1945, and from old newspaper cuttings, photographs and, of course, from memory.'[23] Phibbs tells us that 'for thirty-five years [his stories] waited, locked in a box … until the noise of life receded enough to let me hear what the box had been muttering down there in the dark all those years.'[24] The distance both Mawson and Phibbs needed before returning to their 'stories' further suggests a cultural discomfort with speaking publicly of the terrible nature of what was coming to be defined as 'the good war' as well as the need to suppress or at least avoid dwelling on, the emotional response at the individual level.

In addition to these forms of silence, we also argue that the stoic narrative is itself a form of silencing and one that pervades, in different ways, the popular memory of the war in Britain and the United States. For the United States it can be summed up in the title of Tom Brokaw's book, *The Greatest Generation* and in Britain through the 'Britain can take it' Blitz experience narrative. As already noted, choosing to remember the war experience of nurses through the stoic narrative, as Tyrer does, for example, is to silence voices that do not fit. In the same way that Brittain interrogated the tone of wartime propaganda and silencing as a form of politics between 1939 and 1945, long after the war this kind of privileging of one form of remembering over others is an act of erasure that takes place in a cultural and political context; as Kirmeyer asserts, '[a]s remembering is a social act, so, too is forgetting'.[25] Articulating alternative stories is thus not only political, but a reminder of the importance of the subjective narrative to which Brittain pointed as the source of the war story that was not being heard. As she suggests, personal stories of suffering offer an antidote to the state-sanctioned version of the war. The way these accounts of wartime medical experience tell the war story at the time, or remember it later, is thus arguably political in the 'uncovering' in which these individuals participate, illicit in itself because these accounts rely on a forbidden practice – the keeping of a diary on active service – but also in their uncovering of the damage war inflicts on the body and on the minds of its participants, including those whose job is to ameliorate the suffering. Our analysis of these texts thus interrogates those ideologies that serve the dominant narrative of wartime stoicism in the service of a just war, and uncovers the subjective pain that is at the core of the narratives.

Like Marie Stedman's account above, the pain obscured by the stoic veneer further emerges in an interview with British Queen Alexandra nurse Joan Eileen Nicolson which emphasises the extent to which the directive to 'get on with the job' must be understood in the context of the enormous stress of the environment. Nursing at 106 British General Hospital, she particularly remarks on the tension that arises when the individual is confronted by the demand for stoicism while at the same time registering the shock of being plunged into treating the horrific wounds of the casualties. She recalled working 'round the clock for many weeks – you felt the world had gone mad'. She was 'utterly exhausted; deeply shocked' but 'because you were young you just got on with it (as matron said)'.[26] So while medical personnel necessarily sustained a professional stance in order to perform their job, this clearly did not preclude emotion or its expression. As American nurse Audrey Albertson admitted about her experience during the Battle of the Bulge: 'I cried after soldiers died, I still cry, during training we were told not to get emotionally involved, but it was impossible not to be emotionally involved – everybody, including doctors, cried when soldiers died – so often so young – 17, 18, 19'.[27] Albertson's crying is not suggestive of traumatic breakdown, but instead provides a necessary release of feeling and an acknowledgement both of the emotion that attended the work, and of the impossibility of keeping an emotional distance. But this extends beyond the war for in one short phrase, she testifies to the long-term emotional repercussions of her work that have not historically been acknowledged: 'I still cry.'

Accounts from the immediate experience reflect the conflict between private feeling and the public face. Yet the emotion is expressed only in private or revealed long after the war. June Wandrey ends a letter to her family from Sicily in 1943 after describing the death of a patient:

> Many of us shed tears in private. Otherwise, we try to be cheerful and reassuring.
>   I've seen surgeons work for hours to save a young soldier's life, but despite it they died on the operating table. Some doctors even collapsed across the patient, broke down, cried. There are many dedicated people here giving their all. Very tired, June.[28]

While crying here is a response to the overwhelming emotion of witnessing death and being helpless to save the badly wounded, crying as a response to the larger situation could be seen as pointless in the face of the enormity of the war. Mary Morris writes on 11 October 1944 that she 'could cry for all of them, but what good would it do'. Wandrey. writing again to her family from 'somewhere in miserable France' in September 1944, suggests that being past the point of crying makes the emotional strain more difficult to carry: 'what do you do, Mother and Daddy, when you run out of tears?'[29] Later in the letter she implies that even to write is too painful as it would force her to express the details of a 'misery' she would prefer to suppress: 'If you don't hear from me as often as before it's because I'm surrounded by so much misery, I'd rather not write.'[30]

The end of the war, or even years later, no longer needing to maintain a stoic endurance allowed some nurses to express the emotion they had held back for so long:

> We were all so relieved that the war was over, after what we'd been through the last three years. I couldn't find enough words to express how I felt. I had said many times that when the war ended, I would cry for all the soldiers who had such terrible wounds and who had died. One night a friend came from another unit. We drank some wine and that night I cried for the men.[31]

In this instance the expression of emotion must wait until the need to maintain a professional stoic detachment is no longer needed. In the context of accounts by the medical personnel under discussion here, however, which reveal the conditions under which they lived and worked, it is noteworthy for its foregrounding of the nurse's distress as being for the soldiers rather than for herself. While Diane Fessler above begins by including herself, 'after what we'd been through' her focus turns to the wounded. This change in direction away from the individual and towards the many who are deemed to suffer more emphasises the difficulty of articulating her own pain. Her immediate focus on the wounded is a way of finding a site on which she can focus the emotion. Her crying is explicitly represented as being for 'the men', but her comment that begins with 'we' indicates that the crying includes her own pain, if obliquely. It appears that her emotional response is only legitimate if it is presented as being for the soldiers she nursed, not for herself. This recalls the dilemma we have seen in First World War medical personnel accounts where there is a constant tension between the legitimacy of the emotional response of the individual doctor or nurse in the face of much greater suffering and the need to uphold a professional stoicism when confronted with that suffering. Arguably such tension tends to result in the kind of deflection we see above. It reflects the degree to which the war experience for these men and women is interdependent with that of the men they care for, but also indicates their internalisation of a hierarchy of suffering: having witnessed the terrible pain of others they are often unwilling to claim any pain for themselves. Particularly, for nurses and doctors, the emotional stress is often directly related to their inability to offer care to their patients, as we have seen in Wandrey's letter home.

American doctor Zachary Friedenberg, with the 95th Evacuation Hospital during the landings at Salerno in September 1943, writes as recently as 2004 that 'I often dream about that eventful night [11 September] and its horrors'.[32] In charge of 'about forty mortally wounded' soldiers and civilians, Friedenberg describes the emotional strain on the physician:

> The patients were on litters in two rows with an aisle in the center of the cavernous tent lit by two electric light bulbs. Everyone was in the shadows. There were no faces, only voices. '*Mio Bambino ... mamma mia ...* the Lord is my Shepherd ... Mother of Mercy ... *Mein Gott ...* Doc, do something, I can't breathe!' The cries for help that I could not give have haunted me ever after.[33] [original italics and ellipses]

While nurses were primarily, though not always, working at a remove from the battle front, doctors such as Phibbs and Mawson were positioned with their troops in the fighting line. Mawson's account of the Battle of Arnhem takes us into the immediacy of the environment where as a doctor he must confront what stoic endurance really means not just in the face of treating terribly injured men, but also in the face of the threat to one's own life. Here he offers a meditation both for himself and his reader on the doctor's position in combat which focuses particularly on the relationship between his professional duty to his patients and the psychological toll this exacts:

> A doctor in every action is always relatively protected from the naked atmosphere of aggression that envelops visible antagonists. ... The doctor's vision is focused downwards on immobile, sanguinous objects lying beneath his hands while only his ears range over the battlefield. He may be more comfortable in body [than the combatant] but hardly more so in spirit. He can do little or nothing to influence events, cannot resort to violent action to relieve his feelings and must submit utterly to the discipline of his profession, allowing himself to serve as a one-way channel through which succour and healing may be brought to the wounded, without counting the cost to himself or considering his own position. If the enemy choose to kill him, he must submit to that, even if it should be unintentional. If his own side abandons the field to fight another day, he must submit to the needs of the wounded and be abandoned with them. Let it not be wondered at, if the fabric sometimes cracks, rather that in the main it holds tolerably together.[34]

The use of the third person here on the one hand indicates Mawson's desire to be objective and to speak not just for himself but to the general condition of the doctor in a warzone. However, the objective stance may also imply a necessary distancing both from the extreme stress of his own experience and from the potential for breakdown. While Mawson acknowledges breakdown, like doctors in the First World War his representation here and in his more subjective evocation of treating patients stresses the remarkable ability of medical personnel to endure, though at the same time recognising the potential for the 'fabric' to 'crack'. Mawson's need for an indirect approach in this last sentence suggests an unwillingness to focus further on the potential for breakdown. At the same time, he recognises in the same chapter that the doctor's stress derives in part from his need to confront the internal struggle wherein his desire to remove himself to a safe place conflicts with his reason for being there: his duty as a doctor. Such tension is present throughout *Arnhem Doctor* and persists in his account of being a prisoner of war in Germany, *Doctor after Arnhem*. Individual vulnerability, and the fear that attends it, are central to the subjectivity of Mawson's accounts. For both him and Phibbs, 'getting on with it' is not a question just of maintaining an outer control that allows them to tend the badly wounded under extreme conditions, but of constantly trying to find reserves of endurance when the whole environment conspires to undermine or destroy psychic defences.

The degree to which medical personnel needed that endurance even in hospitals at a remove from the fighting, is described from the perspective of an outside observer, the entertainer Joyce Grenfell. Writing a journal account of her visit to a hospital in Naples in March 1944, Grenfell says:

> Oh God, the sights I've seen today. We haven't *touched* the war till today. Bed after bed filled with mutilated men, heads, faces, bodies. It's the most inhuman, ghastly, bloody, hellish thing in the world. I couldn't think or work or even feel in the end. It was quite numbing. ... The nurses are at it every minute and seem so calm and encouraging. I take my hat off to them. It's a terrific job and they are doing it beautifully here.
>
> ...
>
> I *must* forget all this or I shan't be any good but in another way I must remember it for the effort I, as an individual must make to see that there are never any more wars.
>
> ...
>
> I have *got* to get it all clear in my mind or I'll be no good at all and that's what I'm here for. ... The nurses here, 65, are welcoming and friendly, but even so I feel we are more of a nuisance than a value here. They are *so* busy and so admirable in their apparent inexhaustibleness. It must be awful to be in a ward and watch your friends suffer so; and die. I must stop this. It's *no good*.[35] [original italics]

Grenfell's view is of considerable importance in directing our attention to the emotional repercussions of witnessing such suffering. Most notably it is in seeing these wounded that she feels she has just now 'touched' the war. She moves back and forth between confrontation with what it means and avoidance of that meaning. As an outsider, Grenfell has the luxury of deliberation. The 'inexhaustible nurses' or doctors who treat the wounded, cannot either deliberate or leave, as Mawson points out so directly, but must wrestle with their own emotions *in situ*, and, as Friedenberg has shown, for the rest of their lives. At times the pressure of treating the wounded does become overwhelming. American nurse Elizabeth Hopkins recounts the suicide of a doctor in charge of triage at an aid station in North Africa: 'There was one tent that was the evaluation tent, evaluated who got care right away, who could wait. Number one had to have immediate care. Number two could [wait? word unclear]. The doctor in charge committed suicide when it was all over.'[36] Taylor, similarly, recounts two accounts of breakdown by doctors in Normandy in July 1944: 'A medical officer of a Durham Light Infantry battalion had to be relieved by the MO of Number 149 Field Ambulance Station owing to extreme fatigue' and at Number 75 BGH one doctor 'seized a scalpel, cut his brachial artery and shot himself. … In cold, official words the subsequent court of enquiry found that he "expired in five minutes" and that he took his life when the balance of his mind was disturbed on account of both physical and mental fatigue following extreme pressure of work under Active Service conditions.'[37] The other side of such breakdown is when the recurring trauma leads to what psychologists would now refer to as 'psychic numbing'. American doctor Frank Ellis writes that

> once the unit became engaged in fighting, we were so busy caring for wounded there was little time to worry about personal injury … seeing the physical destruction of buildings, dead animals and humans – the utter devastation of our surrounding – it should hardly be surprising that one became cynical. This loss of the sense of perhaps becoming 'the next one' may have been the result of an emotionally protective shield against losing one's mind completely.[38]

Having nursed on several war fronts since the spring of 1943, by January 1945 June Wandrey admits to an extreme sense of physical and mental exhaustion and retreat from feeling in a letter home: 'Most everything has lost its meaning. Sometimes I'm absolutely numb. Life here is so cheap.'[39]

As we have seen in the First World War accounts, writing could be a way of containing and coping with such emotional strain. For doctors and nurses who in civilian life operate under a code of silence, forbidden to breach patient confidentiality, to record and later to make that recording public (including the donation of diaries and letters to an archive) confounds the issue, even more so in wartime service when the private recording of events in diaries may be forbidden. Thus, while articulating the experience was often psychologically necessary to the recording individual, to keep them, therefore, and to speak from them can be considered subversive. Like First World War medical memoirs, there is a direct correlation between the need to write and the uncovering of war as an activity whose main concern is, as Scarry puts it, 'injury' and 'injuring'.[40] In the Second World War the stories told by medical personnel not only tell their experience and that of the wounded, but in doing so disrupt the more comfortable Allied narrative of victory over an evil Nazi machine. Bearing witness to their own trauma and that of those they care for is integral to the transgressive element of these accounts.

For Phibbs working on the front lines, and Morris in relative safety in various hospitals, writing becomes the means by which they forge resilience to set against the surrounding chaos. Phibbs explains his motives for journal-writing as a way of ordering the tense and unpredictable nature of existence, opening his chapter 'Herrlisheim: Diary of a Battle' with this rationale:

> This is a journal I kept during the battle of Herrlisheim, to try to record three weeks of the heaviest, bloodiest fighting in our division's history.
>
> One might reasonably ask how I had time or inclination to keep a journal, but the truth is that boredom is one of the sensations that dominates any modern battlefield hard on the heels of fear and loneliness. Between eruptions of violence stretch vast deserts of empty time when there is literally nothing to do. Idleness during combat is not the happy idleness of flower-picking; rather, it is often tense, fearful, and the fascination of trying to transmute sensations and events into words often filled one's mind with a grateful surge of activity.[41]

Whether in the immediate instance or long after the war then, the diary or memoir offers a site within which such extreme experience can be contained and controlled. Phibbs further tells us that his compulsion to record came out of a need, in the first instance, for a distraction from fear:

> In battalion aid stations a few hundred yards behind the line, in armoured columns when we medics were jammed between tanks and guns, I wrote in diaries, on the backs of requisitions and report forms, and even, as the best revenge, on the empty side of Nazi propaganda sheets ... Writing was an infinitely better use of thought than brooding about future mutilation.[42]

Even if, as Judy Long writes, 'the audience is no more than the self ... [it is] still a self that participates in the interrogation of experience that buffers and anchors the subject in her [or his] daily rigors'.[43] The diary offers what she calls a 'private and protected means of expression'.[44] Writing a diary is a conversation with the self – in wartime a way of imposing order on the external chaos and of negotiating emotional reactions to it, as we have seen in First World War accounts. More practically, that conversation with the self aided resilience in offering moments of privacy in a life lived entirely amongst others. Blythe's comments on letter-writing during the war, that it was 'both a sane task and an acceptable retreat into privacy', can usefully be extended to include diary writing.[45]

While Phibbs writes to record and contain, for Mary Morris the diary is a space outside the control of the censor where she can express her sometimes contradictory thoughts about the war and her situation. Almost daily she uses her diary to work through her interactions with the wounded and with wartime conditions, both at the level of her nursing and more broadly in her response to what she witnesses outside the hospital. Whereas during her nursing in England her diary records immediate personal responses (even when she is caught in London bombings) and specific details of her work, in France and Belgium its scope enlarges to become a site wherein she can consider and negotiate contradictory responses to the war, ones that may challenge what she thinks she should feel. After two months of nursing in Normandy she writes: '[w]hat an awful waste of life and property all this is and so much destruction and yet there is a feeling of constant chance and excitement. I should, I know, hate it all – and the human suffering is appalling – but I must admit to enjoying the excitement' (16 August 1944). The diary is crucial as an outlet from the extreme emotional and physical constraint, including a denial of all privacy, that is necessary in their work. Phibbs writes out of a need to control thoughts of what is to come, while Morris uses it as a vehicle for recording what should not be revealed publicly, including her patients' stories of the chaos at Arnhem. She remarks, after recording these experiences, that she '[s]hould not be writing this diary. It is against regulations. … I probably write this because I resent having my private letters censored!'(6 October 1944). Yet the forbidden act allows her to bear witness to the soldiers' experience and especially the breakdown of military order that could not be part of official accounts at the time. This is a further defiance of the forms of silencing that, in excluding individual voices from the larger narrative, can maintain a story that fits the narrative a higher command would prefer to make public.

The importance of the diary to the individual is exemplified in Nurse Mildred McGregor's inclusion in her book *World War Two: Frontline Nurse* of another nurse's memory of her experience during the Battle of the Bulge. When the nurse's mobile surgical unit is briefly captured by the Germans and she must surrender at gunpoint, she recalls that her first response is not fear but '[t]he thought that was going through my head was: what if they capture my diary? Diaries were forbidden in the combat zone but most of us kept one anyway. Mine was tucked away in my bedding roll … We had ten minutes to gather our belongings. That finished all chances of retrieving the diary.'[46] This account suggests that its capture or destruction would be a loss of the memories it contained and thus a loss of self along with the story of her war experience. Moreover, the physical space, the page, a place to write and record in private, is now lost, and with it, the privacy and the place to negotiate the experience. Implied here also is the important relationship between recording and remembering. It was often impossible to remember more than the overwhelming nature of the work, as days were blurred by exhaustion, lack of sleep and the need to treat the injured rapidly which allowed for no real communication between patient and nurse.

A particular dilemma in such remembering, and thus in communicating the war experience, particularly as a form of witness, is that in conveying the overwhelming nature of the casualties the individual suffering may be lost. The contrast between Morris's forbidden diary-keeping as a site wherein she can record the minutiae of daily events and comment on individual patients, and McBryde's inability to remember specifics long after the war is important in our reading of these two works and points to the difference between the war story as told in a diary and the construction of a memoir years later. Morris uses her diary to manage the emotional pain that confronts her every day; McBryde, lifting the 'shutters' many years later, is confronted by multiple memories merging into an almost overwhelming impression of suffering. Nursing in the resuscitation ward during the battle for Caen she remembers: 'Again and again they came, through the day and night, men with different faces, different names but the same terrible injuries: the lieutenant needing amputation of both shattered legs, the tank commander baked like a potato in his burning tank, the sergeant with the piece of mortar lodged in his carotid artery.'[47] From the distance of almost forty years, McBryde can allow herself to remember the horror of these images and the attendant human suffering. Yet even from this distance she does not seem able to look closely enough to move beyond defining men by their wounds. The dilemma is one of proximity and distance: how closely can she bear to look and how does that determine what she can disclose to the reader. Moreover, communicating the experience is hampered by the practice of nursing itself; as we have noted before, faced with these 'terrible injuries', adequate patient care depended upon the nurse maintaining a professional distance which involved avoiding as far as possible both the memories and their attendant emotions. There was no time for breakdown, but it constantly hovers at the edges of the text, articulated so poignantly, if sometimes indirectly, by the writers under discussion.

McGregor's very similar articulation of exhaustion suggests that her work prevented her from confronting the nature of the existence she had to endure. Of her first months nursing in Normandy, she writes, 'I don't remember much about those days. We hardly had time to think, no time for anything other than operations on those terrible wounds and the sleep of exhaustion. No time to reflect on any other type of existence other than war. We had become like robots.'[48] And again: 'We nurses operated eighteen-hour stretches in the beginning, and I remember one thirty-six hour stretch, after which we stumbled to our tents and collapsed into profound exhaustive sleep. There was no time to think. We became like robots during the next several months.'[49] McGregor's repetition of words like 'exhaustion', 'exhaustive', 'robot' and the phrase 'no time to think' reinforces both the mind-numbing work that she endured, and also the legacy of distress that could not adequately be expressed or even consciously confronted at the time. Like McBryde, she emphasises the impossibility of remembering the details of the experience, except for a very particular noteworthy event. She also stresses the connection between the exhaustive work, lack of time for writing and thus recording the events in detail and loss of accurate memory: 'there was a period when there was no time or thought of writing or remembering letters received nor memory of many of the happenings.'[50]

The tension between emotion and the retreat from it also points to the tension between remembering and forgetting. Returning to her recollection of her robotic existence, McGregor also reveals moments when emotion threatens such distance. Nursing a specific casualty she recalls, 'My heart ached, raced, and skipped beats, sobs held back in my throat. I blinked away the tears. There was no time to cry.'[51] Remembering years later allows her to pause and consider that particular moment and to articulate the attendant anger and helplessness, using italics to indicate feelings which were present but necessarily had to be repressed at the time: '*What a dreadful waste of lives. Machines were tearing men to pieces. We could never keep up or undo the damage even if we had a hundred times the help*'[52] [original italics]. To have acknowledged such feelings in the midst of war would have been to allow the absurdity and hopelessness of the situation to overwhelm her ability to cope. In a Veteran's History Project interview McGregor is asked 'did you become numb?' and she answers 'Yes – you turned off all feeling – you had to be a zombie to perform'. At the same time, however, in an apparent contradiction, she acknowledges, 'I remember the tears', though does not elaborate.[53] It was not possible to think about the larger moral context when faced with the exhausting work. However, long after the war, speaking to the trauma that could not be acknowledged at the time, she can critique the absurdity of killing and her helplessness in the face of it and, by implication, of the war itself, no matter what its justification.

As these accounts tell us, most men and women did 'get on with it', but such endurance demanded enormous emotional and physical courage and, as Albertson has argued, did not preclude an emotional response. Mawson's immediate account and recollections by nurses attest to this. The same tension between emotion and endurance reveals the connections between these individuals' experiences and looks back to those of medical personnel in the First World War as well as forward to accounts from the war in Vietnam and contemporary experiences in Iraq. The uncovering of emotion in the context of the sick and wounded, rather than a dispassionate recounting of their medical practice, gives these subjective accounts their poignancy and energy. At the same time it reinforces the human experience that these writings capture – not only that of the doctors and nurses themselves, but also of the soldiers they care for. The experience that confronted nurses in particular on their arrival in Normandy in the aftermath of the D-Day landings is described by Morris, McGregor and McBryde, not only through the facts of their work but, as highlighted above, through the subjective reactions that cling to the recounting of their experience.

Brenda McBryde, landing in Normandy in late June 1944, describes her initiation into front-line nursing as she hurriedly cuts away the uniforms of her first convoy of wounded to reveal and treat the wounds underneath: 'This battle was being *translated* to us in a grim toll of casualties … most of their proud uniform, stiff with blood and caked with mud, had to be cut from them. We sliced the tough boots with razors to release shattered feet' [our italics].[54] For McBryde and her fellow QA nurses, the most immediate and concrete evidence of this *translation* is the transformation of men from soldiers – anonymous members of fighting units for whom injury is only further anonymity in the casualty statistics – to men as vulnerable wounded human beings. It is this interdependence of medical personnel and wounded soldier that makes human the 'grim toll of casualties' as they are physically translated in being moved to the hospital or mobile surgical units where they are treated and, at the same time, evokes their 'translation' by McBryde as she writes them into her war story, acting as intermediary between the experience and the reader. Her memoir, like the other life-writings under consideration, is a form of witness that deciphers the immediate and physical experience of caring for the wounded and sick in a warzone into a language that allows the reader to share her gaze. Her very concrete description of the physical act of stripping off those uniforms, central to her account of that first confrontation with battle casualties in large numbers, is what draws the reader into her world and, while she does not state her feelings directly, allows her reader to realise its impact on her.

The practical and concrete act of stripping off the uniform leaves an equally forceful impression on another QA nurse, Mary Morris, whose specific recording of a similar experience after months of nursing in a Normandy tent hospital and in Belgium suggests that its impact derives not just from the sensory contact with war in the form of the injured body, but also from its symbolic power: 'We had to cut the battledress off their bodies and the stench of blood and vomit was overwhelming'(20 February 1945). By the end of McBryde's first day, what she describes as the 'tattered uniforms' are just so much waste material for the incinerator: 'Hard one stripes and pips and crowns, sewn on by proud Mums, wives and girl-friends: the leaping black boar of XXX Corps, the blue and red flash of 21 Army group. It was all the same now. The field incinerator smoked all night.'[55] The physical strength required by nurses is here set in opposition with the vulnerability of those whose uniforms are being stripped or cut off. In particular, the physically strenuous cutting and slicing cast off the popular idealised image of the wartime nurse as ministering angel: nursing in a warzone demands physical and mental toughness. What is unstated but implied here is the symbolic resonance of the act of stripping away the uniform and its burning in the incinerator. Nursing at a casualty clearing station in southern England and taking in wounded from the Normandy invasion, Lena Chivers makes a similar observation on the men's discarded uniforms: 'The pile of dirty uniforms lay in the corner like the discarded costumes of a crowd of players.'[56] The soldier, then, this might suggest, is a performer, but the superficiality of his role is revealed only by those whose work is 'off stage', particularly the nurse whose job of stripping off the uniform is what allows her to see and thus reveal the real war, injury, underneath. The nurse's gaze goes beyond revealing injury to uncover the man who inhabits the wounded vulnerable body. Having nursed badly wounded, sick and dying soldiers on the home front, Lucilla Andrews recorded her reaction to reading the war news in the newspapers:

> When reading the newspaper war reports, I wished I had never nursed sol-diers and could think impersonally of armies as fighting machines labelled with numbers. When I read … I saw the faces of the soldiers I had nursed, met, seen marching, faces that belonged not to 'soldiers' but to men in sol-diers' uniforms. I remembered how men looked when wounded, the feel and smell of fresh-spilled blood on skin and khaki, the sounds men made when in pain, the solid, stiffening silence when men died.[57]

As noted earlier, bringing together emotion and representations of the wounded is subversive both in rejecting cultural norms of stoic silence and in undermining constructions of war itself; here it not only reveals injury, but through such an uncovering redefines soldiers as not soldiers but 'men in soldiers' uniforms'. Necessarily, medical personnel are particularly placed to reveal the concept of soldier, and thus of ally and enemy, to be an artificial construction, maintained only by the superficial wearing of a uniform. Once the soldier is wounded, that uniform is cast off, distinctions of rank or national allegiance are removed, revealing the vulnerability of the body and of the soldier himself. If, in the context of the front-line hospital or the aid station, the uniforms that construct soldiers are rendered meaningless, what does carry meaning for the nurses or doctors and for their reading audience, is the man who owns the vulnerable body beneath, a vulnerability that had been temporarily disguised by 'proud uniforms' and 'tough boots'. Equally, it is that recognition that breaks down the emotional barriers medical personnel are encouraged to put in place to protect their own psyches. The nurses' and doctors' compulsion to record their experience, both during the war in a diary or afterwards in a memoir – or both – lies, we suggest, not only in their need to articulate, both to themselves and to an imagined audience, the very physical experience of cutting off the uniform to reveal hidden damage, but in the symbolic power of the image to bring both teller and listener face to face with Scarry's assertion that 'the main purpose and outcome of war is injuring',[58] in the most immediate human terms.

In spite of the potential for the breaking down of defences, in an uncontrollable environment individuals at times find control through exercising a professional training that demands detachment. While McBryde records the potential for being overwhelmed physically and emotionally by the work, describing her response to the men whose uniforms she must cut off, she can also find resilience in her ability to perform effectively as a nurse within the larger context of the chaos of a world at war. The need to 'get on with the job' becomes a source of inner strength:

> In the trauma of that first day everything I had learnt during four hard years of training suddenly made sense. My hands had a sure and certain skill and my brain was unflustered as I replaced dressings over gaping wounds, gave injections of morphia and the new wonder drug, penicillin, charted blood pressures. That tent, full of men reeking of blood, was where I was needed. These men with the nauseous sweet smell of shock were my fulfilment, since they could no longer help themselves.[59]

Yet while McBryde gains a sense of control in practising her nursing care, the vulnerability that defines the wounded and the burden placed on medical personnel to care for them can carry an enormous weight of responsibility beyond that of providing adequate medical care, as we have seen in Friedenberg's haunting dreams of the Salerno landing and in accounts of doctors' suicides. Phibbs captures the powerlessness that attends his role as doctor; even as he remains physically whole and is able to provide medical care, he is unable to protect the wounded from the real threat which is the uncontrolled nature of the war that still intrudes on hospital or aid station. In an extended entry dated 'January 6th 1945 Five pm', he evokes the intense psychological strain not only of the war and its threat of death, but also of the relationship between healer and sufferer and his need to bear witness to the distress of those in his care:

> Five pm: Infantry Aid Station. Thoughts after two hours of frantic work, sitting still now, staring at bloody hands. The wounded are instruments, singing pain. A monster strums steel claws across them. This is a general monster, with three stars on its shoulders. It loves consistency and order, and it clacks its beak and nods its head in time, happy, approving, as the proper resonances of agony fill the room, each man tuned by the pegs of childhood and culture, by heroes and scoldings and shaming, each with his own fixed pitch of despair or fear.
>
> ...
>
> Finale: When sounds have quieted a little with morphine and splinting for some and death for others, shellbursts make the walls dance and send flakes of ceiling down; sounds rise again, edged now with terror, screaming seagulls, grunting of bears, squealing of spitted rabbits, the last defences of brave men ripped away, all down to the simple crying of terrified children: 'Oh God, Doc, don't let them hurt me anymore.' 'Jesus, I can't take any more.' 'Don't let them, don't let them.' Men whose courage carried them past terror and pain have in this world of kindness and care let down their defences briefly; now they find themselves totally helpless, crying, clinging, agonized, bleeding children, pitifully dependent on us, their physicians, and we're responsible for them; we are supposed to keep harm from them; and we can stop their bleeding and their pain some of the time, but we can't stop this dark, roaring insanity that keeps hunting them down to inflict pain on pain, an insanity that won't give up even when they're whimpering remnants on litters, and a voice inside my head is screaming stop, stop you fucking lunatics, for Christ's sake and the world's sake stop![60]

By the end of his entry Phibbs's emotional response has merged with that of the men in his care; like them he is crying 'stop!' His bearing witness to their helpless agony allows him simultaneously to represent his own helplessness – the inability to effect the important change – not saving lives by dressing wounds, but saving the world from this terrifying madness in which they are collectively trapped. Confronted with this nightmare, the directive to 'get on with it' seems entirely inadequate in offering an understanding of the weight of such a burden.

What that directive really meant in terms of physical and mental endurance is further articulated by Mawson in his account of an aid station during the Battle of Arnhem. Describing 20 and 21 September 1944, he, like Phibbs, integrates the experience of doctor and wounded, while at the same time drawing attention to the doctor's separateness:

> [Into] the harbour of this island [the aid station] was spewed the wreckage, human jetsam cast up helplessly by the tide of war, the doctors picking over it like beachcombers to salvage what might conceivably be used again in the currency of life.
>
> It was a nightmare, and in the grotesqueness of nightmares it was possible, by stepping out of the room onto the landing and closing the door, to find instant relative calm and normality. For the doctors and others, to whom this avenue of escape was always, theoretically, open, the duty of remaining within the room to care for the wounded, often entailing exposure of their persons in silhouette against gaping windows, was a severe and exhausting discipline. For the wounded, some of whom actually received fresh wounds from shell splinters or flying glass as they lay helpless on the floor, it was sheer, unrelieved hell.[61]
>
> ...
>
> Simmons and I crawled round from case to case, as we carried out our duties with an automatic administration of our hands, set smiles on our faces, minds numb and withdrawn, closing our senses against noises, sights and smells in an inwards struggle to disregard the circumstances. Throughout the hospital, in the rooms which were exposed, the same scenes were repeated. Outside erupting chaos, inside a brotherhood of suffering and service. Wounded, nurses, orderlies, administrators, padres, doctors all face to face with the same crashing world, all digging down into their deepest sources of endurance and miraculously finding something that answered their purpose.[62]

In these passages Mawson articulates both the doctor's distinction from his patients – he can move – but also the helplessness which binds him helplessly to the same condition. Yet it is his physical wholeness that places on him the obligation of bearing witness to their condition, and also allows him to explore what 'getting on with it' means: a 'severe and exhausting discipline' that requires 'digging down into [the] deepest sources of endurance'. Both Phibbs and Mawson show that any representation of stoic endurance without an understanding of its emotional cost and the exhausting struggle against breakdown is a misrepresentation and undervalues the experience itself. The writing here reveals the emotional stress Mawson is under. While the last passage begins in the first person, 'Simmons and I', he ends with the third person collective: 'Wounded, nurses … doctors all face to face with the same crashing world … all digging down', indicating an emotional removal from the situation as his memory of it becomes increasingly unbearable. Or perhaps Mawson is taking refuge in the collective experience. While at the beginning there is an isolation, 'Simmons and I', the only two doctors carrying the burden of their task, by the end of the passage he finds a source of endurance in the knowledge that he is not alone in seeking his 'deepest sources'.

In these accounts by Mawson and Phibbs, the individual doctor is positioned alongside the collective wounded. In another account, Phibbs moves in to focus on his response to the immediate individual experience of a wounded 'boy'. Here he offers us a witnessing that goes beyond more general representations of the patients not only to focus on an individual case, but to expose the travesty and indignity war exacts on that individual at the moment of death, as his brains, the site of the self, are laid open to public view:

> A wounded man was lying across an aid man's knees. His face was streaming red and I foolishly concentrated on it, mopping blood with an aid packet, looking for the lacerations, ignoring the frantic stammering of the aid man. Finally he connected words. 'He ain't got no back on his head, major. It's all tore off at the back.' As we turned the boy over his brains slid out on my lap and he died with a couple of agonal gurgles.
>
> [S]eeing somebody killed for the first time, actually seeing the body's parts sundered, sent reason squalling into outrage. Since when were people allowed to get away with murder? Before I could shout it at the colonel the question crumpled under the appalling swift answer from subterranean knowledge. Since forever. Since the first primates pulled themselves into clans and began social killing. The truth reared on its hindquarters, waving the bloody claws that only soldiers see, roaring what's learned on the killing grounds, that murder is what is expected, enforced, required, legal, proper, rewarded. Someone, somewhere, was being patted on the back by appropriate authority for tearing the bones off a boy's brain. To refuse to commit murder, to disclaim any part as an accomplice, is to suffer the punishment of one's proper, God-invoking, white-papered, courtroom-bounded governance.
>
> The world changed forever.
>
> The colonel might be happy in his file drawer, but I was groping in the dimension of bloody anarchy.[63]

In reading such accounts we find that the act of witnessing, so compelling for Santanu Das in First World War nurses' writing, is equally relevant here: 'Touching the wounds of soldiers is the most intimate way of body-witnessing history, witnessing in and through exposed flesh.'[64] While under ideal circumstances it could be noted that medical personnel do not actually touch wounds because of the risk of infection, the conditions in war breach such medical protocol and by implication, reveal all concepts of order and control to be false. As we see in Phibbs's account above, brains spill out onto the doctor, challenging his initial medical response to staunch bleeding. It is as if the unseen wound, the hole in the man's head, remains hidden until it intrudes into the medical scenario, impressing on the would-be healer that his ministrations are useless. In this frantic moment he recognises the kind of absurdity the wound represents, that '[s]omeone, somewhere, was being patted on the back by appropriate authority for tearing the bones off a boy's brain'. The image suggests that, as maintaining a physically sterile distance is impossible, so it is impossible to maintain an emotional sterility. Both physically and emotionally, doctors and nurses experience war through their intimacy with the wounded combatant body. As Mawson has demonstrated, it is not only in treating wounds that the doctor is engaged in such an intimacy, but also in his actual position as doctor – he must stay with the wounded and care for them even if his own life is threatened by doing so. His own instinct for self-preservation must be made subservient to the needs of those he cares for. It is this intimacy within the larger terrifying anarchy that can precipitate breakdown, the avoidance of which, as Mawson tells us, requires a degree of resilience beyond a language that can articulate it.

The uncontrollable nature of the environment, at its most extreme for doctors like Phibbs and Mawson who were at the front with combat units, but which included the intermittent shelling of the tent hospitals behind the lines, meant confronting a profound chasm between the previous world and the one these individuals entered. Having received wounded and set up an aid station in an organised fashion according to military-medical protocol, Mawson records a casual exchange with his sergeant as marking the end of such order:

> I never forgot that brief exchange because it marked the end of all my thoughts of the action as an exercise or game. It was a bridge of words that led from a relatively bright landscape, where the architecture conformed to accepted rules and events were still understandable and manageable, to an abrupt dark kind of nether region where to grope about in apprehension

and bewilderment became the new pattern of existence; where the future was quite unpredictable, the past unreal and the present, because of the jagged uncertainty of life became a single pin-point of nerve-tight awareness.[65]

As a response to this collapsing of the familiar and the mental strain, 'nerve-tight awareness', that attends it as well as the front-line medical work itself, the act of recounting the experience, whether by writing or speaking, becomes a means by which the writer or speaker can try and control this 'new pattern of existence' in which he or she is both participant and witness. As already noted, these works alert us to the constant tension between the need for control and the possibility of breakdown. Revisiting the experience much later in memoir, recording it in diaries or notes at the time or in the immediate instance through talking it over with a friend or colleague, is thus an attempt to exert control over a situation that is ultimately out of their control.

McBryde finds a certain control in her nursing skills during her first encounter with wounded, but such control cannot be maintained in the face of the overwhelming and seemingly never-ending nature of the work. After a day of caring for mass casualties from Caen, she records the mutual understanding contained in a brief exchange with her nursing partner:

'I wish we'd been able to finish all the dressings' …
'There's tomorrow.'
'And the next day. Bloody war.'[66]

She then comments: 'To be able to talk like this with a friend made it all bearable. If we had stopped to think too deeply, we would have been drained by the tragedy of it all. We were young, and youth is very sensible of how much pathos it can take. Older women, I think, would not have survived without scars.'[67] As quoted earlier, of writing the memoir she records feeling 'relieved', suggesting a formerly unarticulated burden had been lifted that she had carried unknowingly for years afterwards. The memoir may become a form of conversation perhaps, an extended version of the exchange recorded above, arising out of a post-war need to speak the pain. Yet what is particularly notable in the above exchange is the lack of expressed emotion. Nor does McBryde explore the tension we find enacted in Mawson's and Phibbs's accounts. She implies that the stress conveyed is understood by both women and thus does not need articulation, but the conversation also suggests an unwillingness to broach the actual strain that was felt.

While McBryde gives her youth as a reason for resilience here and avoids visiting the actual events that lay behind the exchange above, at the same time her memoir shows us that her work involved an unacknowledged and hidden pain that is only permitted to manifest itself as anger:

> Throughout these weeks in July, our stretchers in Resus. [Resuscitation Ward] were never empty for long, but only a few of the faces remain with me. Most of the men brought in were too badly wounded to communicate. Individual characteristics became blurred in men wounded so critically. I remember the continuous challenge of falling blood pressures, and the terrible haemorrhages when blood dripped to the tarpaulin floor at a faster rate than we could pour it into a vein. I remember the tell-tale bubbly feeling of flesh that told of the presence of gas-gangrene, but I remember too the miracle of a grey face turning pink. Strangely, and mercifully, I have forgotten the deaths, though one bright face I do remember. He was brought into our tent with eyes wide open, looking about him still remembering to be polite.
>
> 'I've often wondered what you sisters got up to,' he said, with a brave, cheeky smile. Then a sudden look of surprise opened his eyes very wide and he was dead, still with the smile on his lips. A captain of the Coldstream Guards, the same age as myself, he was caught unawares by death. With part of a shell buried in his back, he had suddenly tweaked his spinal cord and, in one astonished moment, he was gone.
>
> I realised I needed a break from Resus. when I lost my self-control over a tin of peaches. ... One day, when an unknown MO ... helped himself to a tin of peaches from our precious store in Resus. I suddenly saw red.
>
> ...
>
> 'He's stolen a tin of peaches from my patients,' I proclaimed and instantly started to cry, with tears of rage against the wicked MO and tears of chagrin that I should cry.[68]

Bringing together the account of nursing the wounded, the memory of one individual and the loss of 'self-control' and tears here demonstrates the pain, but avoids confronting it directly, like her earlier conversational exchange. Embedded as her emotional pain is in the narrative, McBryde's organisation of the material offers us more information than the explicit account of the tin of peaches does, and it is in the movement from generalised experience of nursing the wounded, to a specific death, and then to her own emotional response, that we find the hidden layers of stress. The incident of the peaches undermines the validity of her own experience in the context of what has come before. Her collapse into tears is portrayed as being in defence of her patient's treat, rather than for herself even though she begins by intimating to the reader the real cause of her outburst: 'I realised I needed a break from Resus. When I lost my self control over a tin of peaches.' Yet, like the nurse quoted earlier whose emotion at the end of the war is focused on her patients, McBryde frames her breakdown in a narrative of concern for her patients so that even as she acknowledges the stress of nursing in the Resus. ward she articulates her emotion only through the description of an event that avoids her directly claiming the legitimacy of her pain.

McBryde's account paradoxically obscures and reveals the emotional stress of her work and points to the way such deflection, gaps and silences in these accounts can also indicate forms of avoidance which in themselves suggest pain. Furthermore, the censorship Morris refers to or the forbidding of diaries can leave gaps or silences in the narrative, while without a continuous record the specifics are lost from memory and, at the same time, memory is selective. McBryde is thankful that she does not remember the deaths and perhaps this is a necessary forgetting, such as that described by Gask in his First World War recollections, yet clearly at the time she was under enormous psychological strain. The memory, therefore, seems to have been transferred to and also contained in a much less harmful remembering, the tin of peaches.

Silence also exists where the experience itself is too painful to record. Omissions may occur because the circumstances themselves are emotionally wrenching and impossible to articulate and respond to fully, especially when recording is a re-experiencing of an event that is emotionally dangerous to dwell upon. On 5 July 1944, Morris describes the terrible burning deaths of young Canadian soldiers in a friendly fire incident: 'Their bodies were black, their experience horrific. We gave them morphia and more morphia and watched helplessly as they died. Such is the stupidity and futility of war.' She also takes the account from the general, 'a convoy of young Canadian casualties' to the particular: 'A young officer, Jock McCabe, one of the few able to speak, told me what happened' (5 July 1944). Yet although she describes the event in the immediate aftermath, she is unable to write in the diary in the days that follow. Since Morris writes almost daily, this gap is particularly noteworthy. Her next entry is on 9 July when she records only 'Felt too ill and tired to write this for a few days'. Once she begins writing again she focuses on recovery, perhaps in an attempt to turn her own recollections away from the deaths she had witnessed: 'Jock McCabe is a little better and reacting to Penicillin. The other boys with burns are not so good. The smell is terrible. We carry on with intravenous fluids' (9 July 1944).

Her pain, the space implies, comes from her patients, and even in her private diary she tends to foreground theirs rather than express her own. Like McBryde, her focus is on the patients. The important distinction, though, is that Morris's diary entries allow her to record and contemplate the details of her daily experience, especially in focusing on specific individuals in her care. Rather than the blur of remembered injuries that McBryde recalls long after the war, the diary allows her to retain specific memories that otherwise would have been lost over time. Especially, the intimate details demonstrate the extent to which her story and that of the wounded she treats are inseparable. At the same time, the particular gap in her diary entries also points to a lost story, a silence that comes directly out of her own pain and exhaustion. Here, as we've seen in McGregor's account, she has little time or energy to reflect on the war, yet for the most part Morris's diary does just that. In contrast with McBryde and McGregor who reiterate times when it is impossible to recollect a coherent narrative, but rather a memory of wounds and exhaustion that precludes any time to think, Morris's immediate recordings, even when they are very brief, offer us an account of her daily impressions that range from descriptions of her work and patients, to her own working through of the larger wartime conditions and the ethical questions they raise. The necessity of recording comes out of a need not only to bear witness, but also to confront the larger and contradictory nature of the war seen from her perspective as well as her own contradictory responses to it.

As a form through which she can impose some order on the experience, the diary narrative here offers ways of reordering the world of suffering Morris must exist in. Part of gaining control over events written here, then, is in how she constructs her own immediate world of her tent ward. Even as she documents graphically the violence war inflicts on the human body and mind, her diary entries also articulate the political and nursing control she takes over her ward – a position that she represents as standing against the larger external chaos. The two constructs of violent chaos and order are held in tension through her account of this period, unlike Mawson and Phibbs whose world of 'bloody anarchy' elides any sense that they can impose either medical or political control. Control for Morris comes not only from her ability to cope professionally, but, very importantly, in interrogating the situation that has brought her together with her patients. While Phibbs and Mawson can adopt a similar strategy in memoirs written long after the fact, in Morris's diary we witness her working through the situation on a daily basis. In doing so she extends the symbolism inherent in the stripping away of the uniform further than

McBryde, in not only revealing injury, but in telling the stories of her patients as individuals, whether ally or enemy, thus using the patients to collapse the military-political constructions of nation-states that create soldiers. When the concept of enemy other is deconstructed, the war is rendered futile and absurd, with Morris offering her 'international ward' as an alternative ideology. Arguably, this construction in her diary becomes an important site of resilience. Unlike McBryde, her satisfaction in using her nursing skills to help the wounded is tempered by her questioning of the war that has caused them to in the first place. Where she does find order and resilience is in negotiating her experiences so as to actively reconstruct a different world order as she tells her story, allowing her not just to voice her frustration with things as they are, but to reimagine them. At the most practical level, her management of her ward becomes an exercise in such reimagining.

Receiving her first patient at the 101st British General Hospital on 23 June 1944, Morris deliberately collapses popular conceptions of the enemy: 'Hans [a POW patient] is quite unlike the jack-booted Hun whom we had anticipated. He is polite and timid and makes me feel that he is one of the many "pawns" in this game of war. Propaganda is a big word in war-time. We deduce that "good propaganda" is whatever makes us hate the enemy.' The next day she records the complete lack of animosity between so-called enemies: 'This multi-national microcosm of a Europe at war is interesting and sad. A badly wounded Cockney says "thanks mate" to Hans as he gives him his tea and fixes his pillows. Why are they all tolerant of each other inside this canvas tent, and killing each other outside?' (24 June 1944). Less than a month later, this specific narrative has become generally representative of her hospital environment. Taking control of her large ward she organises a co-operative system of patient care that relies for its efficiency on subverting wartime structure and hierarchy through 'the lovely spirit of warm friendliness between all of us. Here "pulling rank" is not "on". They are all patients and rank and nationality do not count. I suppose this makes us neutral territory' (4 July 1944). She repeats this narrative again in January 1945: 'We have an international ward once again, no barriers even of language, just the unwritten language of human caring' (6 January 1945). As in McBryde's memoir, here Morris's implied stripping away of the uniforms reveals the men beneath and removes distinction of ally and enemy. Like Phibbs and Mawson, it is this collapse of binaries within the hospital ward that points to the absurdity of war. Yet Morris goes beyond that to construct an alternative political and ideological structure.

While the tone of her diary entries are, for the most part, controlled and calm, even as she voices anger, other accounts use similar imagery to articulate a heightened emotion, both anger and sadness collapsing distinctions between ally and enemy that are almost unbearable in their poignancy. Mawson speaks from his position as a doctor within the killing zone:

> who would say that the act of killing is glorious, of bereaving, of maiming, of destroying other people's property? I thought, as I laid my hand on the handle of the ward door, that anyone interested in starting a war should come and spend an hour or two among the suffering wounded, observe German and British lying helpless side by side, indistinguishable in their bravery, paying the grisly price. I kicked the door open savagely.[69]

McBryde offers a similarly emotional account of the absurdity of war and the collapsing of difference between German and British when a ward of German POWs begin to sing 'Lili Marlene'

> in well-rehearsed harmonies that were a joy to hear. Then the moment enlarged to provide one of those memories that stay forever. From the adjacent British ward, came the same song, sung in English. The surprised Germans responded to the compliment with even more enthusiastic singing, and Soutie and I stood between the two wards listening to a performance that would have done justice to a male voice choir from men who, until recently, had been doing their level best to kill each other.
> 'Just shows how daft war is', said Soutie disgustedly.[70]

McBryde's choice of words here, 'the moment enlarged', suggests not only the enlargement of the singing, but an enlargement of the situation itself that looks forward to Soutie's comment on 'how daft war is'. As in Morris's diary, the confines of the wards offer an 'enlargement' of recognition and understanding, a moment that, like Mawson's much angrier account, reconfigures the politics of the war by foregrounding the common humanity visible in these men.

While these nurses and doctors record war in terms of injuring, the transgressive nature of their witness is manifest in how they choose to remember and what becomes central to their stories. Morris's reconceptualising of human interactions is both a real physical space, the ward, and a linguistic construction of it in her diary. Both can be read as political acts. While Morris consciously constructs the ideal of internationalism based on common humanity both in her hospital ward and on the pages of her diary, McBryde, less overtly and perhaps less consciously, offers a similar collapse of enemy and ally; her intimate narrative of a night spent caring for an 'enemy' soldier is given an equal place beside the allied in their war story. Especially significant is McBryde's retrieving of this badly wounded young German from the multiple injured from both sides she has nursed and whom, as she admits, she has been unable to remember as individuals, to enact how the 'body-witnessing history' that Das describes so eloquently transcends boundaries of ally and enemy:

> In the night that followed I stayed by the side of the desperately wounded man. ... I checked pulse and blood pressure, monitored transfusions, moistened his dry lips. His head tossed impatiently with the restlessness that tells of haemorrhage and his eyes ranged unseeing ... I spoke to him, in my bad German, hoping that it might help him to know he was not alone in his battle.[71]

Against all odds the patient survives the night and begins to recover: 'I held a feeding cup of water while he drank eagerly ... he looked at me and my uniform: "Danke", he said with an infinitesimal nod of his head.'[72] While Morris very deliberately uses the broad scope of her hospital ward as an international community to collapse the ideology of war, McBryde's attention to the physical needs of her patient is a form of witnessing that at once reflects the nurse's focus on the details of care and draws the reader into her intimate relationship with the soldier's body. Monitoring pulse and blood pressure, moistening dry lips, watching his restless head and eye movements bring the reader into this intimate physical relationship; we share her visual field, her touch, her desire to communicate that he might 'know he was not alone'. We share her relief at the man's survival and the poignancy of his thanks. McBryde of course also offers us an iconic nursing image: the nurse giving the enemy soldier a drink of water, but the way she ends her account reflects the nature of her work. One perfunctory sentence sums up his condition: 'He was on the evacuation list a week later and probably never went without a shirt again as long as he lived' – her writing essentially hurrying us away to the next task. That the event remained so embedded in her memory more than thirty years later suggests that returning to it gives her the time to reflect that she did not have originally. Its importance for her, the narrative suggests, lies not just in his miraculous recovery – the haemorrhage stopped on its own – but in its power as the interdependent story of a nurse and a badly wounded patient who is memorable not because he is ally or enemy, but because he is a man in a soldier's uniform who survives under her care. Her role in his recovery stands, to some extent, against the almost overwhelmingly sad experience that is war nursing. In this lies the kind of resilience necessary to endure, both during and after the war.

If the memoir is a public conversation between writer and reader, and writing the diary is a form of conversation between the self as writer and the self as audience, a place where the individual can both record and respond, the healer–sufferer narrative that is at the centre of both forms is a negotiation between that narrative and the larger Second World War story that has tended to exclude both of them. As already noted, once removed from combat, the soldier is just a casualty statistic. Morris's representation of her neutral hospital ward is transgressive in offering an alternative narrative wherein meaning is derived from 'the lovely spirit of warm friendliness' rather than from the image of the enemy that must be crushed through which the war is usually remembered. McBryde, less overtly, challenges concepts of enemy 'other' in choosing a wounded German to tell her most intimate nurse–patient story.

Yet while this collapsing of wartime binaries suggests a triumph of *inter arma caritas* (the motto of the Red Cross: in war, charity) – the ability of care-givers to create a world beyond war – a later entry in Morris's diary shows how such a conclusion may offer a too-easy resolution. Morris's account of the friendly fire incident discussed earlier shows her shock at the condition of the patients and anger and frustration at the absurdity of war, but it is clear that the event has been a mistake. However, in 1945 the arrival into her hospital of German POWs from a camp in Brussels who have literally been starved to death, shakes her composure and challenges her belief in the possibility of an internationalism that offers an alternative to war. Clearly, while German, British and other nationalities share a common humanity in the hospital, the inhumanity carries on outside even though the war in Europe is over. Here her diary becomes a site of witness and a space where she can reflect on the meaning of the event. Juxtaposing the physical condition of these men with the hospital as a place of caring becomes both literal and symbolic, reinforcing her imperative that the 'language of human caring' represented by her hospital ward must offer an alternative ideology to the larger inhumanity that characterises the conduct of war on both sides. This event elicits the strongest response against war in her diary – her emotions are of dismay, anger, frustration, as well as a larger concern over what this means in terms of the larger ethical mandate around which the war is constructed. Unable to prevent these young men from dying, her diary entry is a record of an event she is sure will never become public knowledge, precisely because it does not fit the 'good war' narrative. She describes it, conscious that her witness may be the only record to survive:

> We have been admitting German Prisoners from a camp here in Brussels. I am appalled by the condition of these prisoners in peace-time Europe. Starvation, filth and acute fevers are always hard to see and we all feel a sense of righteous indignation about the cruelty and sadism of the Germans in Belsen and Buchenwald,[73] but what are we to feel or say when prisoners come from our own POW camps suffering from the most advanced stages of starvation and smelling so badly that we have to wear double face masks? A young corporal who accompanied to-day's batch of prisoners tells me that they have been having 'an average of fifteen deaths per day for some time'. How long is this hate and cruelty and bestiality going to last? This 'little episode' will be covered up very nicely, nothing of it will reach the newspapers or the people at home. This has really shaken me. It is not very nice to see human beings reduced to the level of beasts. We must believe that this war was fought and won in order to preserve decency and humanity and sanity in the world. The condition of these poor German boys is too pitiable for words – despite all our efforts they are dying of starvation, and dysentery. They are too far gone for our help. They are just skin and bone – not enough elasticity in their veins to get a needle in for drip feeding. I feel ashamed and angry and depressed … Why has this happened six months after the end of the war – and who is responsible? It looks as if we too have our war criminals.

Even before this event Morris had claimed her generation as carrying the responsibility of seeing war did not happen again. She sustains her questioning of the war in its aftermath and this instance of POW starvation, when considered beside her recounting of the friendly fire incident, reinforces war as anarchic and chaotic. The humanity she finds in her hospital ward is still threatened by the inhumanity bred by the war.

Bearing witness, even at the private level of her diary, affirms a larger sense of social and political responsibility. In particular, her account challenges the idealisation of Allied wartime leaders that has become integral to the way the war has been and continues to be remembered. In June 1945, nursing on a psychiatric ward, she sees men who have been, she writes 'mentally shattered' and are thus forced to carry 'an excruciating aftermath'. 'I feel strongly that it is all of us who are young now, who must shape the world of the future for ourselves. I am tired of the Churchills and the Pattons of this war who enjoy the power it gives them. It is a game to them, these boys are the victims, heroes today, forgotten tomorrow' (5 June 1945 – BGH Brussels). As she refers to the German patients as 'pawns' on her arrival in Normandy almost a year earlier, so here she places the individual soldier as the one on whom the burden of war must fall. Her response is similar to Mawson's meditation on the British and German wounded lying side by side. The individuals whom the doctors and nurses care for seem forgotten by the leaders who use them in their games.

Morris writes of her psychiatric patients that '[p]eople are impatient of the mentally ill particularly in the army and think that they are "swinging the lead". The physically wounded can demonstrate their suffering, the mentally wounded are sad outcasts, whom nobody wants to know or care about' (4 July 1945). Her comments suggest that, in spite of some changes in attitude towards wartime breakdown amongst combatants in the military since the First World War, in general, even by the end of the war, signs of breakdown or stress were perceived as weakness or cowardice. It can be conjectured that medical personnel's proximity to combatant breakdown made them acutely aware of how it was perceived. Thus while their accounts, even long after the war, do present at times almost unendurable conditions, the emphasis is on resilience. While on the one hand this might suggest that their need to narrate themselves and their experiences from this perspective derives from cultural pressures as well as from their own need for psychological survival, it is equally important that we recognise its value. As we have noted in Chapter 1, the post-Vietnam War tendency to see breakdown as an 'appropriate' reaction to trauma has been contested. And in the Introduction we point to how Nigel Hunt's recent work on war and trauma describes a variety of responses to traumatic situations in war. In some instances individuals are traumatised, finding 'their memories emotionally unbearable'. Others 'manage to suppress their memories, whether through conscious or unconscious mechanisms'. Still others ' "work through" or cognitively process their responses, ultimately learning from what happens'. He affirms that many individuals have 'no difficult emotional memories or problems'.[74]

Morris's daily diary entries suggest that she 'works through' the traumatic nature of her nursing experience in a way that fits Hunt's definition of cognitive processing, ultimately coping in this way. Her diary ends with her marriage and the birth of her son and suggests no lasting negative psychological effects of her war service. Rather, she seems determined to contribute to a post-war world that will lead to improved socio-economic conditions. It is clear that those who, like McBryde, lifted the shutters on their war memories and wrote memoirs long after the war as did most of the individuals under discussion, also engaged in the cognitive processing identified by Hunt. The vivid nature of their accounts so long after the war does, however, suggest the indelible nature of the experience. Doctors like Friedenberg confess to being haunted by it still. At the same time, in pursuing careers and ultimately writing their accounts, they represent survival in war's aftermath. Drawing conclusions about the nature of breakdown and resilience is impossible since, for the most part, narratives of complete breakdown may, paradoxically, be present only in their absence, or in secondhand reporting, as we have seen here. At the same time, the kind of endurance we find in these accounts does affirm the possibility of resilience. Yet to understand what that ultimately means, we must read it in the context of the massive emotional burden carried by these men and women whose stories are still noticeably absent from the medical and military histories of the 'good' war.

Notes

1 Nurse Hilary Lewis in Eric Taylor, *Front-line Nurse: British Nurses in World War II* (London: Robert Hale, 1997), p. 113.

2 J. Westren, unpublished memoir, Private Papers, Department of Documents, Imperial War Museum London (91/4/1).

3 Shephard, *A War of Nerves*, pp. 183–234.

4 Sayre P. Sheldon (ed.), *Her War Story: Twentieth Century Women Write about War* (Carbondale and Edwardsville: Southern Illinois University Press, 1999), pp. 127–8.

5 In his discussion of psychiatry during the Second World, Ben Shephard points to conflicting attitudes towards breakdown at the front and at home (*War of Nerves*, p. 181):

Psychiatric policy towards civilians was being run by tough-minded veterans of the First World War, determined not in any way to encourage neurosis, whereas policy towards soldiers was run by younger, quasi-Freudian analysts from the Tavistock. The individual soldier was 'permitted to be a psychiatric casualty' but, one doctor noted sardonically, the 'non-combatant civilian is not permitted to be so diagnosed.'

6 *Humiliation with Honour* (1942) reprinted in Vera Brittain, *One Voice: Pacifist Writings from the Second World War* (London and New York: Continuum, 2005), pp. 62–3.

7 Jenny Hartley (ed.), *Hearts Undefeated: Women's Writing of the Second World War* (London: Virago: 1994), p. 7. We would include here not just grief at deaths at home or at the front, but other losses such as losing a home to air raids, the separation of children and parents due to evacuation and other forms of community and family disruption that entail loss. See also Joanna Burke, 'Disciplining the Emotions: Fear, Psychiatry and the Second World War' in Roger Cooter, Mark Harrison and Steve Sturdy (eds), *War Medicine and Modernity* (Stroud: Sutton Publishing, 1998).

8 Hartley, *Hearts Undefeated*, p. 66.

9 Westren, unpublished memoir, p. 31.

10 Penny Summerfield, *Reconstructing Women's Wartime Lives* (Manchester: Manchester University Press, 1998), p. 15.

11 Ronald Blythe, *Private Words: Letters and Diaries from the Second World War* (London: Penguin/Viking, 1991), p. 5.

12 This is particularly demonstrated in propaganda films of the time, such as *In Which We Serve, Millions Like Us* and *Mrs Miniver*.

13 Marie Stedman in Taylor, *Front-Line Nurse*, p. 112.

14 Nicola Tyrer, *Sisters in Arms: British Army Nurses Tell Their Story* (London: Phoenix, 2009), p. 4.

15 Hunt (*Memory*, pp. 105–6) comments usefully on the need for British remembrance of the war through a stoic attitude:

> During World War Two, the British displayed the stiff upper lip, the ability to stand firm against all adversity. Of course, at one level this was nonsense – people broke down, they failed to cope – but at another it was a necessary idea, a necessary collective ideal that helped the nation through the difficult years of the war; and after the war it became a collective memory. People looked back and thought that they 'pulled through' those years at least partly because they had a 'stiff upper lip'.

16 Lucilla Andrews, *No Time for Romance* (London: Corgi Books, 1978; Harrap & Sons, 1977); Brenda McBryde, *A Nurse's War* (New York: Universe Books, 1979); June Wandrey, *Bedpan Commando* (Holland, OH: Elmore Publishing Company, 1989); Mildred McGregor, *World War Two: Front Line Nurse* (Ann Arbor: University of Michigan Press, 2007); Mary Morris, 'A Nurse's War Time Diary', Personal Papers, Department of Documents, Imperial War Museum, London 80/38/1 (now published as *A Very Private Diary: A Nurse in Wartime*, ed. Carol Acton (London: Weidenfeld and Nicolson, 2014); this edition was not published at the time of writing so all citations are to the original typescript); Stuart Mawson, *Arnhem Doctor* (London: Orbis Publishing, 1981), Phibbs, *The Other Side of Time*; Zachary Friedenberg, *Hospital at War: The 95th Evacuation Hospital in World War*

II (College Station: Texas A&M Press, 2004); Lt. Col. J. C. Watts, *Surgeon at War* (London: Allen and Unwin Ltd., 1955).

17 Mark Harrison, *Medicine and Victory: British Military Medicine in the Second World War* (Oxford: Oxford University Press, 2004).

18 Harrison, *Medicine and Victory*, p. 1.

19 One could speculate that one reason for this may have been the hierarchies of suffering that became inherent to the memory of the war. The Holocaust made all other suffering insignificant. In the face of it, other stories seemed less relevant.

20 Brenda McBryde, interview in *The Age* (Wednesday 18 March 1981).

21 McGregor, *World War Two*, p. 450.

22 Cynthia Toman, *An Officer and a Lady: Canadian Military Nursing and the Second World War* (Toronto and Vancouver: UBC Press, 2007), p. 72.

23 Mawson, *Arnhem Doctor*, p. 6.

24 Phibbs, *Other Side of Time*, pp. 3–4.

25 Laurence Kirmeyer, 'Landscapes of Memory: Trauma, Narrative and Dissociation' in Paul Antze and Michael Lambek (eds), *Tense Past: Cultural Essays in Trauma and Memory* (New York and London: Routledge, 1996), p. 191.

26 Joan Eileen Nicolson, oral interview, Imperial War Museum, London (12075).

27 Audrey Albertson, Audrey Albertson Collection (AFC/2001/001/26868), Veterans History Project, American Folklife Center, Library of Congress, Washington, DC.

28 Wandrey, *Bedpan Commando*, p. 55.

29 Wandrey, *Bedpan Commando*, p. 152.

30 Wandrey, *Bedpan Commando*, p. 152.

31 Diane Burke Fessler, *No Time for Fear: Voices of American Military Nurses in World War II* (East Lansing: Michigan State University Press, 1996), p. 189.

32 Friedenberg, *Hospital at War*, p. 45.

33 Friedenberg, *Hospital at War*, p. 45.

34 Mawson, *Arnhem Doctor*, p. 98.

35 Joyce Grenfell, *The Time of My Life: Entertaining the Troops: Her Wartime Journals*, ed. James Roose-Evans (London: Hodder and Stoughton, 1989), pp. 65–6.

36 Elizabeth Hopkins, Elizabeth Hopkins Collection (AFC/2001/001/9639), Veterans History Project, American Folklife Center, Library of Congress, Washington, DC.

37 Taylor, *Front-line Nurse*, p. 113.

38 Frank R. Ellis, MD, 'Recollections of an Infantry Battalion Doctor' in Sewell (ed.), *Healers in World War II*, pp. 10–11.

39 Wandrey, *Bedpan Commando*, p. 173.

40 Elaine Scarry, *The Body in Pain; The Making and Unmaking of the World* (Oxford: Oxford University Press, 1985).

41 Phibbs, *Other Side of Time*, p. 117.

42 Phibbs, *Other Side of Time*, p. viii.

43 Judy Long, *Telling Women's Lives* (New York: New York University Press, 1999), p. 33.

44 Long, *Telling Women's Lives*, p. 31. For a psychological interpretation of the narrative process see Hunt, *Memory, War and Trauma*, p. 79.

45 Blythe, *Private Words*, p. 4.

46 McGregor, *World War Two*, p. 365.

47 McBryde, *A Nurse's War*, p. 108.

48 McGregor, *World War Two*, p. 310.

49 McGregor, *World War Two*, p. 263.

50 McGregor, *World War Two*, p. 283.

51 McGregor, *World War Two*, p. 329.

52 McGregor, *World War Two*, p. 329.

53 Mildred McGregor, Mildred McGregor Collection (AFC/2001/001/55277), Veterans History Project, American Folklife Center, Library of Congress, Washington, DC.

54 McBryde, *A Nurse's War*, p. 85.

55 McBryde, *A Nurse's War*, p. 89.

56 Hartley, *Hearts Undefeated*, p. 140.

57 Andrews, *No Time for Romance*, p. 202.

58 Scarry, *The Body in Pain*, p. 63.

59 McBryde, *A Nurse's War*, p. 85.

60 Phibbs, *Other Side of Time*, pp. 132–4.

61 Mawson, *Arnhem Doctor*, p. 81.

62 Mawson, *Arnhem Doctor*, p. 101.

63 Phibbs, *Other Side of Time*, pp. 83–4.

64 Das, *Touch and Intimacy*, p. 227.

65 Mawson, *Arnhem Doctor*, p. 54.

66 McBryde, *A Nurse's War*, pp. 98–9.

67 McBryde, *A Nurse's War*, p. 99.

68 McBryde, *A Nurse's War*, pp. 114–15.

69 Mawson, *Arnhem Doctor*, p. 112.

70 McBryde, *A Nurse's War*, p. 122.

71 McBryde, *A Nurse's War*, p. 137.

72 McBryde, *A Nurse's War*, p. 137.

73 Morris knew details of the camps from two nursing friends who had worked there, so she is not just writing from general hearsay.

74 Hunt, *Memory*, p. 8.

4

'It was a tough life and I did all I could to lighten the men's burden': British POW medics' memoirs of the Second World War

Medical personnel taken as prisoners of war were now no longer on the sidelines, bound up in the usual medic–combatant binary. They faced the same privations and brutality as those who witnessed and took part in the fighting. Hunger – or in the case of those in camps in the Far East – starvation, cruel, often sadistic guards and camp commandants, disease, sordid conditions were the common experience. This chapter will discuss the ways in which British medical personnel in both European and Far East camps articulated their experiences in published and unpublished memoirs written after their repatriation. It will consider how they differ in tone as the years between release and written responses lengthened. Memoirs written in the 1950s, for instance, are markedly different in tone and language from those written in the 1990s. And, as Hunt and McHale argue, 'The memories of World War II veterans are affected profoundly by the same influences that have led to society's constructions of World War II, through the media, books, television, and films.'[1] Moreover, 'Theirs was a generation not given to visible displays of emotion … the moral stigma that had been associated with "shell shock" during the Great War still lived on to some degree.'[2] The term 'shell shock' was replaced after 1942 by the term 'battle exhaustion',[3] but the services were no more welcoming of the idea, being suspicious of what might lead men to malinger or present a lack of moral fibre (LMF). And when individuals returned to civilian life, the War Office was not particularly interested 'so long as they weren't a drain on the public purse'.[4] Many psychological casualties could be explained away by pre-existing conditions, thus relieving the state of paying an appropriate war pension. 'It has been estimated that only about 30,000 pensions were granted to British Second World War veterans for psychoneurotic problems, less than half those awarded after the Great War.'[5] As Zeiss and Dickman argue,

Problems of delayed stress among POWs and veterans of WWII are much less studied than those of Vietnam veterans ... but [f]ormer POWs ... present a rich source of information with regard to PTSD because of the relative clarity of definition of the stressor ... and two naturally occurring subsets of POWs (those in European or Japanese POW camps).[6]

They identify 'two different levels of stressor': severity and duration, which varied 'significantly between European and Pacific POWs', the latter of whom experienced more severe treatment at the hands of their captors and were interned far longer than their European counterparts. Over 40 per cent of Pacific POWs died in captivity as opposed to 1.1 per cent who died in European camps, a fact that 'underscores the differential severity of treatment'.[7] Such variation of experience is clearly illustrated in the memoirs under discussion here.

Those in German camps, while deprived and at the mercy of often brutal guards, were held in accordance with the Geneva Convention: Germany recognised the special role of doctors and other medical personnel. Allan Hanson, captured in 1940, recalls how after being captured, a 'furious German officer' grabbed him 'by the throat':

> thrusting his revolver into my face and yelling I know not what. He flung me in the direction of a group of our men already rounded up. The rest of the men from the cellar and others soon joined us. It was clear then that we were being lined up along the edge of an open ditch with the Germans making great play the setting up of their heavy machine guns and training them in our direction. We were convinced we were going to be shot. ... Why were they waiting? A German Infantry Officer had arrived and was talking with the Panzer Commander. There was another tense wait. Then, almost in anticlimax, we were marched off. Clearly the panzer men were living up to their reputation and not taking prisoners but the Germany infantry had contrary orders. ... Perhaps they spared us because we were a medical unit. Earlier we had been ordered to camouflage ambulances and remove armbands because, we were told, the red crosses were being used as targets. Ironically our camouflage could have cost us our lives.[8]

Japan, however, though a signatory to the Geneva Convention, did not ratify the agreement. Moreover, culturally, it viewed surrender as failure and inflicted on its prisoners brutality of the worst kind. Richard Philps, captured in 1942, asserted that the Japanese 'did not see the need to conform with the normally accepted dictates of humanity because, if they were the winners, nobody could do much about it afterwards'.[9] And, as Aidan MacCarthy, who was imprisoned in Singapore and Japan, explained, 'we prisoners could only be losers' and the Japanese continually rubbed 'our noses in the squalor and degradation of our captivity':[10]

> One of the strictest codes of the Oriental way of life is the concept of 'Face' and 'Loss of Face'. ... 'Face' began to dominate the whole attitude of our captors towards us and it continued throughout our captivity. If for any reason the Commandant lost his temper, the results were like the ripples of a stone thrown in a pond. The Commandant slapped the sergeant. The sergeant slapped the nearest corporal. The corporal slapped the private. The private slapped the nearest Korean. The Korean then slapped the nearest POW. This system saved 'face' all the way down the line![11]

The Koreans, having been 'conquered and suppressed by the Japanese', were like 'prisoners in an open prison'.[12]

At the beginning of their captivity, things did not seem that dire. MacCarthy hailed from a small village in West Cork and qualified as a doctor from Cork Medical School at the end of 1938. He joined the RAF Medical Dental Branch just before the outbreak of war in September 1939 and was stationed at Bexhill: 'I was now desperate to get away from the woolly confines of this seaside suburbia – and involve myself in the struggle abroad. At this point, bad as it may sound, I was actually looking forward to the war.'[13] When first captured he describes how:

> The overall effect of our lazy life, unaffected by the guards, well-fed from our encounters at the fence, and washed by nature, put us in a dangerously euphoric state. Added to our complacency was our conviction that the war would be over as soon as our people recovered from the surprise attack and had begun to fight back. We were in for a rude shock. The front-line troops eventually left, and were replaced by less intelligent and certainly more brutal guards, interpreters and administrators. These were the 'average' Japanese and for us they meant trouble.[14]

Such initial 'innocence' is echoed by Richard Philps:

> In those early innocent days, we devised various activities for ourselves. We had language classes; we even arranged a concert party, partly because it was considered to be the done thing among prisoners in the First World War and we had some veterans of that war with us. It was all a novel experience: some kidded themselves (all of us to some extent, I suppose) that it was all a bit of a joke – and none of us had yet seen a Jap ... How very little did we know.[15]

Discipline became increasingly tightened and severe, as MacCarthy found out, making him 'all too aware of the brutal side of the Oriental nature'.[16]

MacCarthy's experiences and the candour with which he recounts them are not atypical. He endured 'a seemingly endless walk', a long march to a train and then a 'horrendous journey' of sixteen hours to Surabaja, East Java, then a two-mile march to the city to the Lyceum Camp, a former girls' day-school. Fifteen hundred men were kept there, while the other 2,000 were sent to Yarmaark Camp that was 'alive with rats' because it was built in the local open-air market.[17] These 'badly overcrowded' camps encouraged bacillary dysentery. The food supply was 'appalling', so much so that 'our conversation became obsessed with one subject – *food*' [original emphasis]. So-called 'dirty rice' contained maggots and earthworm eggs that 'hatched out in our stomachs', followed by the worm crawling up 'the passage from the stomach to the throat and then crawl[ing] into the nose or mouth. I have seen men playing bridge ask to be excused for a moment, remove a worm from his nose or mouth, and then return to the table. Nobody took any undue notice.'[18] The matter-of-fact description only compounds the reader's disgust. Philps, too, makes no apology for his tale not making 'pleasant reading', for the 'brutality and ill-treatment it describes' and the 'considerable amount of very squalid medical detail' he includes. Veracity is all-important: 'I have no choices: either the account is true, or it is useless and had better not have been written.'[19]

Nine thousand POWs of all nationalities died working on the Burma Railway. The 37,854 Far East Prisoners of War (FePOWs) who survived and returned home became 'as emblematic of the horrors of war as those of the Jewish victims of Hitler's "Final Solution". Systematically starved, beaten and worked to the brink of death by their captors, liberated FePOWs in the summer of 1945 were scarcely recognisable as human beings.'[20] The death rate amongst POWs in Europe was 5 per cent, five times lower than in the Far East. Those held in camps such as Changi had few, if any, of the comforts that POWs in Europe speak of in their memoirs. POWs in Germany had their food ration augmented by parcels from the Red Cross, the YMCA sent parcels with games and books, and letters from home were received. Stuart Mawson commented that 'We depended entirely on the Red Cross parcels to stay above starvation level' and that morale was aided by a padre who 'took in German newspapers and relayed BBC news bulletins from secret receivers in other camps'.[21] Yet, as Allport points out,

> that is not to say that the men returning from Germany were in good con-
> dition. Food and medical care were always unevenly distributed between
> one laager or campo and another, and became considerably worse as

Allied troops advanced on the territory of the Reich. By early 1945 tens of thousands of British Commonwealth and American POWs were being forced-marched hundreds of miles westwards from their former prison camps in Silesia, Poland and East Prussia to escape the advancing Red Army; an unknown number succumbed to disease, exhaustion and starvation.[22]

By spring 1945, 'around 40,000 British POWs had spent more than five years in captivity'.[23]

Allan Hanson joined the Territorial Army and 131st Field Ambulance RAMC in his hometown of Ashford, Kent, in 1939. 'As one of our friends put it, while not conscientious objectors we made the choice because we preferred to help put people together rather than blow them apart'.[24] On 2 April 1940, he and his unit crossed to Cherbourg 'and moved in easy stages to join the British Expeditionary Force (BEF) near the French/Belgian border.'[25] Ordered to move into Belgium from the west on 10 May 1940, when the German invasion of the country began, Hanson and his comrades set up an advanced dressing station and

> shared the duties of documenting the necessary details of the casualties while treatment was in progress ... all to go on forms in waterproof wallets attached to each patient en route for the CCS [casualty clearing station]. ... How long that went on and how much we achieved, I just don't remember. After that we seemed to spend most of our time stopping, unpacking, repacking, moving on, etc., etc. Our own casualties were mercifully few but directly and personally distressing.

Thus he finds the 'fortnight that followed ... impossible to describe. The scene everywhere was incomprehensible.' Civilians refugees flooded past and frequent strafing as well as 'terrifying spectacular dive-bombing by German aircraft' coincided with 'deafening artillery barrages'.[26] On 28 May 1940 he began his 'forced participation in the notorious march into Germany involving thousands of Allied prisoners ... But at least we were still alive! Most of the Ashford lads were together or in close touch as we joined an ever-growing column of captured men'.[27] He explains the position of medical personnel:

> Members of the RAMC were not officially regarded as prisoners of war even though in practicality we were always treated as such except for the type of work we did. Theoretically we could have been released immediately, but this was never known to have happened in practice and of course at least one of us would be needed to look after sick and wounded POWs.[28]

In an interview in 1977, Captain P. G. Seed, RAMC, recalled this so-called non-escape agreement: 'Of course from the medical officers point of view, our duty was not to escape. It was a duty not to escape. One is medical officer to fighting soldiers and one is medical officer to the same patients when they are prisoners of war.'[29] For Mawson, 'The question of escape for the doctors could only seriously be considered after the wounded had been evacuated to Germany.'[30] Philps, too, recalls being asked at times 'why we did not try to escape'. For him, as a medical officer, 'this was out of the question'. It was also 'impracticable … It was clear to everyone that there was only one way out of the camp and that was in a coffin.'[31] Death was the only release, but, as Philps also asserted, 'If we are going to die, we might as well die among friends.'[32] Moreover, Rosalind Hearder points out, for medics, 'As carers, for the sick, escape was an anathema to their professional and ethical code'.[33]

Allan Hanson describes his camp, Stalag VIIB at Lamsdorf in Upper Silesia, which was 'situated on a large flat stretch of land almost entirely surrounded by tall fir trees' and composed of four long single-storey buildings, each holding 350 men tightly packed in rows of three-tier wooden bunks, with an 'ablution room in the centre of each'.[34] Each building or hut had one latrine block for the 1,400 men in the four huts. Hunger and recurring dysentery were scourges. Letters and parcels from home, therefore, were a 'great tonic' for the POWs' states of mind.[35] Along with the Red Cross and YMCA parcels, 'the arrival of Army uniforms and underclothing also added immensely to our comfort, warmth and self-respect. All these aids helped us so much to face up to the things quite confidently again.'[36] Then, unexpectedly, he is moved to Ostrzeszów in Poland, where a former large school or college served as the camp. The hospital was increasingly staffed by British medics and also served the surrounding camps. From there he is sent to another Polish camp, Stalag XXID/13 at Krotoszyn, where medical orderlies went out with the working men each day 'because of the dangerous nature of the work'.[37]

Stuart Mawson described the camp hospital at Apeldoorn, as having 'three barrack blocks, each block a three-storey compact with a holding capacity of some three hundred and fifty wounded, provided some use was made of double bunks'. On the whole the facilities were very good, 'with central heating, good washrooms, bath-houses and showers, and modern sanitation', and the doctors were able to create 'a satisfactory working relations between ourselves and our captors'.[38] The Germans 'were co-operative and seemed anxious to do what they could to ease the shortages. More mattresses and blankets appeared to match the hospital's capacity and once saturation point was reached no more wounded were brought in. The situation became stabilised, all were comfortably berthed and hospital routine got into full swing.'[39]

Yet whilst POW medical personnel shared the hardships of their soldier-comrades, they were also in a unique position in having tasks to perform, decisions to make (who went on working parties; negotiating the wrath of camp commandants), ingenuity to employ (working with limited medical supplies within the confines of inadequate, insanitary conditions), and responsibility to save the lives of the men with whom they were imprisoned. Ken Adams, captured at Singapore in February 1942, remarks that in his situation, 'There wasn't much time for introspection. We were run off our feet with medical work. The routine kept us going: I think we were better off than blokes with time on their hands. Life for us was working and sleeping.'[40] On board a ship to Java, Philps felt he was

> in a fortunate position in that I had a job of work to do which forced me to keep going, though standing up was an effort. We really had no means whatsoever of treating the sick and dying on board, but at least it was possible to go round and talk to them. The determination necessary to perform even this simple action probably kept me alive at this time.[41]

Demonstrating resourcefulness and a sense of purpose, these doctors 'began to practise "POW medicine" rather than civilian or normal military medicine'.[42] In what MacCarthy described as 'My primitive medical work',[43] 'Doctors had to work creatively, and often at personal risk, to augment supplies'.[44] Beyond this, 'in an environment of great suffering, where much of the medical cupboard lay bare, basic psychology came to play an ever greater role in motivating less seriously ill patients and nudging them in the direction of recovery'.[45] As Hearder observes, doctors' 'sense of overriding purpose' was key to their psychological survival.[46]

Writing his memoir, *Stalag Doctor*, in 1956, where he noted how 'Our ideas on warfare were completely influenced by what we had read and heard of the battles on the Western Front in the First World War',[47] I. Schrire describes how 'The Red Cross and the YMCA provided us with a generous and varied quantity of books, and here, in the middle of Poland in 1942, I had re-read most of the classics at ease and with little interruption'.[48] Ion Ferguson similarly notes that 'When letters and Red Cross parcels began to arrive, we were about as well situated as prisoners could reasonably expect to be'.[49] Reading was also hugely important to R. B. C. Welsh, an RAMC doctor on the Burma Railway. His diary, which is sparse in its detail of conditions and his feelings, is littered with references to books. Records of the suffering, deaths and burials of comrades are punctuated with notations about his reading, everything from Dickens (*Nicholas Nickleby* is 'very enjoyable indeed'), Walter Scott ('quite pleasant but I am not an ardent enthusiast') and George Bernard Shaw, whose plays he labelled 'quite enjoyable', to the more popular Dornford Yates, whose *Adele and Co.* 'doesn't stand much re-reading', A. J. Cronin ('excellent'), and E. V. Lucas ('a book of pleasant, light essays, for odd moments'). He dubs J. B. Priestley's *Angel Pavement* 'a delicious book' while finding Beattie and Dickson's *General Pathology* 'quite a ray of light in this Pudu darkness'.

For Captain P. G. Seed and his comrades, books

> were terribly important to us. I remember when we were first captured as prisoners of war. We had enough to lug around with our kit and some colonel or other said 'Every man will also take a book' and I thought at the time 'What rot! Why lumber ourselves with literature in our predicament.' However, I again was quite wrong. We all took one book at least into the mining camp so there was a fair camp library and in retrospect those books were worth their weight in gold. There were all sorts of books: Novels, biographies, and I remember reading a geography book, a school geography book with great interest where I could really sit down and study the implications of this geography. Over all the rest of the books I think biographies were the most interesting. I still think so. I would say that the order to take the books into such conditions was almost the most important order we had. They were worth their weight in gold.[50]

The repetition of the phrase 'worth their weight in gold' reinforces the importance he attaches to these reminders of life outside captivity. And, as Aidan MacCarthy recalled, 'We played endless games of cards, and re-read our few books'.[51] Letters too were essential to maintaining any sense of morale. David Westlake, RAMC, also imprisoned by the Japanese, recounts that although the mail received 'from time to time … was always twelve to fifteen months old … it was great to have a letter or a postcard signed by our loved ones at home and, although they were so old, it did give us an added incentive to keep going'.[52] For Philps and his comrades, 'some special possession – something to take pride in' helped them to cope in 'these strange circumstances'. For some it was 'their aluminium eating-dish', which was polished with loving care 'until it shone', for others 'an old tin can', which with a piece of wire that 'fashioned a handle', 'made a mug'. Philps carved for himself from teak at Burabuya a 'little Kingfisher' and he was sure that 'the possession of these things had, in a strange way, a great survival value'.[53] Later on, a lute came into his possession at the hospital at Semarang: 'we derived great pleasure from it,' he notes.[54]

Trevor Gibbens's *Captivity* is a good example of how one's own writing and recording of daily incidents was a vehicle for keeping going. His memoir is also interesting for the ways in which what he recorded at the time in a diary while prisoner in Stalag 344 is contrasted with the recollections of his much older self which punctuate the diary entries in the typescript memoir. He describes how his diary 'was very largely notes of appointments with out-patients and lists of other patients, and it continued so throughout the time until the diary for the final March, but it included snippets of war news and events in the Stalag which I had forgotten or mistimed. It is very patchy and uninteresting, but nevertheless perhaps should be reproduced.'[55] Indeed, it is the 'very patchy' entries which themselves *are* interesting, for in their staccato snippets of detail we get a glimpse of the POW life, devoid of reflection, but telling in what Gibbens sees fit to record. Gibbens himself admits that the diary 'shows a lot of obsessional qualities … names and numbers of no significance' which to him were evidence of 'a sort of grim determination to hold on and persist in "doing one's duty", in spite of considerable inefficiency of mind'.

The diary begins on 25 April 1944. On 17 May, he notes how he spent the day: 'Two hours in block 5 including psychotherapy with Colonel Wilkinson. Played in goal later in hockey match between officers in lazarett revere officers 2 to 4.' 20 May is similar, though the war intrudes: 'Little work. Played hockey in goal for the Lazarett in match in the afternoon. Played records with Borrie, Lauste, and Hendy. *Italy Offensive.* Esperia and Pontecorvo. Papers full of it – is this the beginning of a Second Front?' 21 May: 'Wore my new suit for the first time. Fine day. Played hockey in goal again with RAF, 6 to 1. Duncan McCray a superb player. Started to write letters, but several sick patients, including Martin, etc., so did not have much inclination.' 24 May: 'Misery all day. Out-patients over here. Some censoring of material has come back, "Very final."' 26 May: 'Italy advance to Velletri and past Pontecorvo. Played Haydn's 99th Symphony – dullish except for last moments. Didn't sleep till 3.00 am, depressed and restless.' When Gibbens continues his post-war narrative reflection he echoes the use by other medical personnel considered in this book of the word 'strain': 'By 1944, most of us were beginning to be aware of *strain* … In 1943, when I started to feel the *strain*, and had many out-patients and in-patients to deal with who were showing manifestations, I realised I had some clinical material which might be expanded into an MD thesis' [our italics]. It is interesting how the POW is also clearly thinking as a medic, one keen to add to the literature of medicine on the diagnosis of some condition or syndrome. Hanson, too, describes how, in addition to physical infirmities brought on by poor diet and captivity, many prisoners increasingly began to show 'mental and emotional *strains*' [our italics] of restricted conditions and uncertain futures. He calls this being 'Stalag Happy', but it also known clinically as 'barbed-wire syndrome'.[56]

Barbed-wire syndrome, or 'barbed-wire disease', was coined by the Swiss physician, Adolf Lukas Vischer, in a seminal article in 1919, based on his observations of First World War POWs. Vischer argued that 'the prisoner comes to live in a grey, dreary shadowland … his emotions become blunted and give place to apathy'. This is the result of the loss of liberty, the crowding together and the uncertainty about the duration of captivity. Gibbens takes issue with Vischer's thesis that the decline into apathy is a continuous one from six months after being captured: some soldiers he knew had 'a strongly beneficial and constructive phase', but another POW, Ken Adams, notes that in his experience, 'Mental health problems started to emerge slowly and there was a handful of suicides about six months of captivity … several doctors warned us of a possible spike at the six-month mark … growing pessimism'.[57] Gibbens argues that after two years of captivity there is a crisis stage in which one either contemplates escape or develops a psychosomatic illness. Of himself, however, he wrote: 'I was, of course, extremely fortunate, like all the doctors, but more than most, in being required to make several changes of scene.' He was sent to various camps throughout his time as a POW, thus alleviating the stalemate of his position. He adds that 'All was not gloom and despondency, indeed a tendency to laugh perhaps too heartily was perhaps a [release] symptom.'

The idea that work was an antidote to apathy is reiterated by other POW medics. A. L. Cochrane, a captain in the RAMC, who was taken prisoner in Crete and sent to a camp in Germany, noted how

> Subjectively my own memory of the period is chiefly one of colossal inertia, which was thrown into relief by the fact that I had a lot to do. I was working at a small hospital, and as I was the only German-speaking MO had a fair amount to do in addition to the ordinary medical work. I remember waking each morning and being unable to get up. I was not tired – I was just apathetic; it was often an hour before the remnants of my Presbyterian conscience drove me down to start work. And during the whole of that

period every act, every decision, required an effort out of all proportion to the circumstances.[58]

This reflection is contained in what Gibbens called Cochrane's 'half-jocular' *British Medical Journal* article of 1946, 'Notes on the Psychology of Prisoners of War', in which Cochrane describes the psychology of imprisonment he terms 'Gefangenitis' ('chiefly because I like [the word]'). He claims that 'those who were best adapted to imprisonment found the greatest difficulty in readapting in England'.[59] Gefangenitis, 'antedates the surrender' in that for the 'very large numbers of prisoners' he spoke to 'practically none of them even considered the possibility of being taken prisoner'. Philps describes the experience of becoming captured 'thoroughly unreal'[60] and Adams

> felt a curious mixture of shame, embarrassment, anger and relief as we marched along. How could the British Army suffer such a humiliating defeat? ... The overnight transformation from being members of a beleaguered, but still powerful, army to becoming prisoners of war put an enormous strain on everyone. We were now totally isolated, at the beck and call of a ruthless enemy and had no idea what might happen next.[61]

Those POWs who succumbed to 'severe depression and lethargy', who remained 'apathetic ... became more and more horizontal, ceased washing, and ceased caring. They were difficult to treat; a few died of intercurrent infections.'[62] Dr Stanley Pavillard, who before his imprisonment, was appointed, age twenty-nine, Medical Director of the Bedong Group Hospital in Kedah, Malaysia, recalled that in the first two or three months of his captivity in Taiwan, 'I think we had about 30 deaths in 500 men and the killers were dysentery, and that usually passed on to diphtheria and it was linked with despair'. Similarly, according to P. G. Seed,

> it soon became obvious that people who fell into despair were signing their own death warrant. As a result they tended to recognize this and decided earlier in the course of their illness that they were going to get better. I do remember quite clearly that once even early in an illness a man yielded to despair, he was almost signing his own death warrant. In other words, it was an effective treatment of psychiatric illness by the Japanese in that a lot of people did not fall into depression who otherwise would have done. It's rather cruel to say this and very nasty to psychiatrists, but at the cost of a few deaths of despair, a lot of men did not despair.[63]

Those who survived were those, who like, Adams, 'reconciled ourselves to the facts that we were stuck, and it was going to be a long hard war. ...

Our growing resilience or perhaps acceptance of the status quo helped us to cope with some nasty shocks.'[64] Furthermore, 'we were young and optimistic we'd survive and eventually be freed'.[65] Philps, however, had a more fatalistic attitude: 'We did not, even in our most optimistic moments, really expect to survive. If we were not killed by starvation and squalor, we thought the Japanese would get rid of us just as soon as our usefulness to them had ceased', for they knew POWs were regarded only as cheap labour.[66] Stanley Pavillard asserts that 'Our thoughts became like dope to an addict',[67] and describes the adaptation to captivity as 'this mental camouflage of reality':

> We had to re-shape and re-direct our whole outlook: life became a game of make-believe and we acquired the knack of turning our attention entirely away from personal discomfort and deprivation. Together with a sense of humour this psychological technique saved morale as well as life. As a doctor I had many opportunities of studying the mental reactions of my fellow prisoners, and all too often I saw men failing to adapt themselves to this make-believe game, this mental camouflage of reality, and then in consequence becoming morose and gloomy and in the end inevitably dying.[68] .

For Philps, imprisoned on Haruku Island, 'we kept our spirits up – and tried to give hope to the sick – by imagining that one day, without warning, a fleet of Allied destroyers would sail into the harbour and rescue us'.[69] Yet, 'apart from this vague hope for the future', Philps and his comrades decided it was better 'not to look too far ahead'. They had experienced so much 'degradation and misery' that it was a case of taking one day at a time, not looking beyond the next evening, of dividing 'one's life into manageable lumps'.[70] Thus, as Allport observes, it was 'the steady attrition of their day-to-day captivity – their months and years of boredom, frustration and uncertainty, their almost total ignorance of what was going on in the outside world, and when or if they would ever get to see their homes and families again' that 'chipped away slowly but relentlessly at the inmates' mental health'.[71] Cochrane argued that 'one could say that the first year [of imprisonment] was spent in adaptation, the second year was the best year, the third year began to be a strain, and the fourth and following years left no one unscathed'.[72] Again, using the word 'strain', he falls in line with other memoirists in attempting to articulate the particular effect of wartime trauma in a term that underplays the severity of the reaction. For Westlake, 'strain' is also a key word: 'The morale and discipline of the troops throughout the whole period was very good although it was severely tested by a mental strain due to the lack of freedom, lack of definite news of the outside world and to the constant visits of the RAF although we had only two actual raids.'[73]

Cochrane's article stresses that 'In general, psychological medicine in imprisonment was very similar to that in peacetime. There were the same anxiety neurotics, hypochondriacs, compulsive neurotics, hysterics, and psychotics as in normal life. Whether they were more numerous than usual no one knows; no statistics or comparable group is available. One inevitable difference was the extent of the malingering.' This had particular relevance to POW army doctors, for it necessitated a 'change from the habitual severity with malingerers to an attitude of complacence if not actual encouragement. In many cases, the differential diagnosis between psychoneurosis and malingering was very difficult. Most prisoners felt it was their duty to malinger as much as possible to decrease the German war effort, and this idea strongly reinforced any hypochondriac tendency.'[74] For Stanley Pavillard, his decisions about the men working on the Burma Railway at Wampo, a twenty-seven-mile stretch of line, were more intense: 'It was a tough life and I did all I could to lighten the men's burden.'[75] He tried letting men 'go sick' to give them a day's rest, 'but it was a dangerous line to walk'.[76] The conditions at Kayu were 'horrible' because the railway was behind schedule and 'it was only with the greatest difficulty that we could get even the most seriously sick men excused from murderously hard work'.[77] 'The Japanese demanded a fixed quota of workers both for outside working parties and for inside factory work' which meant that MacCarthy and his fellow medics were often 'forced to pass unfit men'.[78] Adams recounts how the Japanese engineers had targets, pushing men ever harder, disregarding any claims of illness on the part of the prisoners. As an orderly, Adams did not have the authority of a doctor, but as a de facto medical officer for a working party at Phitsanulok in north central Thailand, he faced the bullying of the engineers and realised 'just how difficult it must have been for doctors earlier in our captivity to declare blokes unfit for work – and stick to those decisions – in the face of sustained and intense pressure to turn out full work quotas'.[79]

As excerpts from Adams's and others' memoirs demonstrate, POW medics from both theatres of war provide vivid descriptions of their conditions, peppering them with allusions and making historical connections with their current situation. For instance, Ion Ferguson recounts how 'In classical times, Corinth was the city of luxury to which visitors would come from all parts of the world to sample its sensuous pleasures. Now Corinth seemed to me to be the most blasted place on God's earth':

The conditions at Corinth were the worst I have ever experienced. The guards were selected for their brutality and took delight in breaking the spirits of the prisoners. The diet consisted of half a dry biscuit and a cup of watery rice each day, and a complement of a barrack-block built to accommodate two hundred and fifty was some three thousand men. The nights were like some horrible dream. We sat and lay about on the stone floors and tried to sleep, but our rest was broken by shouts and screams.[80]

Nightmarish scenes are commonplace, created not only by brutal guards but 'an appalling lack of drugs'. With 'most of the patients … suffering from incurable diseases such as pulmonary tuberculosis, anemias, cancer, kidney diseases and dysenteries', the many who died did so 'mostly slowly and painfully', so that, according to Aidan MacCarthy, 'the medical outlook was one of fatalism, and morale was at rock bottom … time passed very slowly'.[81]

David Westlake outlines how hygiene and sanitation in his camp in the Far East were 'difficult for two main reasons. The first one was that the water level was only a few feet below the surface and made the digging of latrines difficult especially in wet weather. The other reason was that the Japs kept a "Pig-sty" in the camp which was a first class breeding ground for flies.'[82] And while accommodation was 'very poor and inadequate' and the 'lack of medical supplies criminal', 'the fight the men put up against disease was simply marvellous' as the MOs 'did a wonderful job against terrific odds'. Westlake had to contend with 9,600 cases of malaria. The Japanese ignored all pleas from MOs that men were too sick with malaria, dysentery, beriberi, and other diseases to work on the railway.

As clerk to the hospital, Westlake's chief job was to keep track of the cases, and although the prisoners were not allowed to keep records, papers were secreted 'down the centre of bamboo shoots which support the sleeping platforms in the hospital'.[83] In addition to his huge number of cases of malaria, he recorded 1,380 cases of ulcers and other skin conditions; 900 cases of dysentery; 700 cases of deficiency diseases. Causes of death from disease were dysentery (amoebic and bacillary) (twenty-one dead) and deficiency (nineteen dead). Upon his release, Westlake handed the papers to the military authorities in Rangoon, hoping that 'someone in need of a pension will find help from these papers'.[84] Philps notes how, 'in our poor physical state, keeping records was extremely difficult or impossible and we had to rely on memory'. The keeping of records, though, meant that 'one was no dispassionate observer'. At the end of the voyage taking him to another camp, he 'concluded that 307 British had died', with the number of Dutch dead at sixty-three. There were 415 deaths on Haruku island, with 539 deaths due to the sinking of a ship taking the POWs from Haruku to Java. The total dead, he recalls, was '1325 among the 2075 who came on this ghastly expedition, leaving 750 survivors, a number of whom were too ill to go on much longer.'[85]

At Changi, Ken Adams, too, experienced 'a steady stream' of patients, in this instance with dysentery: 'The disease eventually overwhelmed us in the first three or four months of captivity. ... There were hundreds of patients – some desperately ill – who were so crowded together it was difficult to move between them, especially at night with the limited lighting. I never counted all the patients. It would have been too traumatic.'[86] Work was intense, with orderlies working twelve-hour shifts, and often helping out at other times: 'There was the never-ending drudgery of cleaning and washing ... critical for retaining morale and slowing the spread of disease. ... The pastoral side of nursing was in many ways the most rewarding. In my eight months or so at Changi, 200–300 blokes died from dysentery. This was roughly one half of the total deaths.'[87] And, as Adams poignantly notes, 'By the end of the year, the hospital camp's cemetery was populated well enough.'[88]

Although he declares that 'it is difficult to know how to describe the hospital conditions adequately', David Westlake paints a vivid account of an operating theatre in a Far East POW camp:

> Two wooden tressles [*sic*] are placed in the middle of the Ward with a sagging, dirty and half torn stretcher resting on them. This was the operating table. At the side were two wooden cases as instrument tables and two or three tressle forms on which were placed bowls of water for the surgeon's use. In comes the surgeon, rolls up his sleeves, washes his hands and the operation commences. This was the order of the day for all operations including appendectomies, amputations and all types of minor cases. Despite these primitive methods it should be stated that only one case proved fatal and that was due to a man being brought on a four-day journey from Up-country suffering from appendicitis with peritonitis.[89]

Pavillard describes performing an appendectomy at Wampo with 'no operating theatre' on a 'crude table out of bamboo', with rudimentary surgical equipment: 'three pairs of artery forceps, one rusty pair of scissors and some equally rusty surgical needles; also some gut and one large bottle of chloroform'. Borrowing a cut-throat razor from of one of the volunteer officers, Pavillard sterilises 'our few instruments by boiling them in a four-gallon kerosene tin, and we also boiled bits of towel and old shirts to act as dressings'.

Then we started. The cut-throat razor was extremely sharp and I had to be very careful not to go too deep: it would have been very easy to go straight into the peritoneal cavity and injure the bowel. There was very little fat between the skin and the muscles and I came down to the peritoneum almost at once. I grazed it with forceps and very carefully opened it with the razor, using the handles of two bent spoons as retractors. Gently moving the coils of intestines, I found an ugly gangrenous appendix, looking as if it might burst at any moment. This was carefully removed and we buried the stump with a purse-string suture in the caecum and then closed the peritoneum, sutured the muscles, and finally closed the wound with linen stitches.[90]

These POW medical memoirists do not shirk from graphic descriptions. Philps describes how ulcers, if allowed to spread, could prove fatal, but two forms of treatment proved successful: one using a combination of potassium permanagnate, iodoform powder and salt-water compresses, a second, for the worst ulcers, 'had to be quite horrible'. Surgery on ulcers had to be carried out without anaesthetics and the patient was subjected to scraping away of 'the diseased tissue' with a sharp spoon: 'the agony of this requires no description'. And for Philps and his assistant, 'the strain of doing this was such that, in one's undernourished state, it was difficult to not to pass out'.[91] MacCarthy's own 'primitive medical work' included the removal of rotten teeth with pliers without anaesthetic, which 'required courage, from both the doctor and patient'. More seriously, he had to operate on lung abscesses (empyema):

First I cut into the lung over the site of the abscess with a razor blade, taking care not to puncture the lung. Then I planted a drainage needle, which was inserted through a hollow tube (tracula), both home made ... These had been sterilized by immersion in potassium permanganate solution ... Using a home-made syringe the pus was sucked out. The protruding tube was left to bubble through water in a bottle. Every three days I removed the equipment, sterilized it and reinserted the tube.[92]

Dead toes, the result of dry gangrene, had to be treated like rotten teeth, 'with a quick snip of our pliers'.[93]

Adams recalls how the dental surgeon, Jimmy, would often assist in other operations. In the case of 'a badly ulcerated leg' that had to removed, 'Jimmy would be holding it and would place it reverently on the wooden floor. It was not just a cast-off piece of meat and bone. It had been part of a living man. It required respect.'[94] Thus, what the *Times*

Literary Supplement reviewer noted about Pavillard's memoir is true for the others under consideration here: such tales are 'not for the queasy'.[95]

Despite such physical pain and suffering, Pavillard marvels that 'so many men recovered after operations performed in such primitive conditions on patients in such very poor health',[96] and Adams is continually impressed by the 'stoicism of the badly wounded … they were either very brave or very traumatised, or both'.[97]

As Philps noted, these experiences clearly took an enormous mental toll on the doctors. Pavillard speaks movingly about how 'episodes' of such suffering and death 'left one completely washed out, and unable to control one's emotions, until in the long course of captivity, the repeated experience of such suffering ceased to affect one so violently, leaving only a vast tolerance of other people's shortcomings and a feeling of weariness and old age'.[98] In recalling being faced with 'the most appalling decisions',[99] whether of who to treat first with the medicine available or who to allow to go off sick from working parties, he asserts that 'In a sense our emotions were anaesthesized'.[100] Adams is not reluctant to admit his fear: 'With the Aussies we started treating a stream of wounded. Some were brought in on stretchers. Many blokes with bad wounds surprisingly walked in … first aid on a conveyor belt … I wondered how I would cope seeing dead men … I was scared.'[101] He was not alone, for after experiencing bombing and shelling,

> McDonald [Adams's colleague] and his team were treating several wounded soldiers and more were coming in. There was a good deal of work to do and three of his medical staff were traumatised. Two were corporals who walked around with paper and pencil in hand laboriously exacting names and unit details from incoming wounded, one even scribbling down the obscenities that sometimes greeted their enquiries.[102]

Having been captured by the Germans, E. Randolph, serving with the Australian Imperial Forces and the 2/7th Field Ambulance, noted how, with the 'staggering' number of wounded,

> By the end of the second day our morphia was all gone. From then on the nurses, who after all were mostly amateurs, found the shells of toughness they had gradually assumed cracking a bit. Pain was in the very air, with nothing to ease it but a squeeze on the shoulder or the casual offer of a drink of water. The most heart rending of all were the two cases of gunshot wounds in the abdomen. No possibility of operating – and for four or five days we had to watch these lads slowly die from agonising peritonitis. Nothing in our power could be done to ease them on their way.[103]

He gives 'praise of the highest order' to the stretcher-bearers of the unit and lauds the 'general duties chaps, nurses, doctors and cooks' who 'worked to exhaustion point' to care for the wounded, including '270 odd of our own boys, 290 odd Germans, and 40–50 Greeks'. His abiding memory is 'a sickly, sweet smell [that] drifted intermittently through the area gradually getting stronger until one could actually taste it in the mouth. The smell was of the *dead*' [original emphasis].[104] Pavillard describes his compound similarly as 'hellish in every way. The stench from the burial pit was everywhere. When one approached the pit to use it one saw bubbling millions of maggots'.[105]

Diseases such as cholera, dysentery, malaria, beriberi, dengue fever were the plagues of the Far East camps. Pavillard notes that 'One of the worst things' about cholera was 'the painfulness of the muscle cramps; we gave morphia when we could, but there was nearly enough to go round, and from the compound there arose continually, therefore, a faint desperate moaning which was terrible to hear, punctuated at intervals by appalling shrieks as some unfortunate's muscles snapped'.[106] Asian POWs had no doctors or orderlies to look after them in their camps, 'and the Japanese made no provision at all for them to have food or water. They were just dumped in our camp to lie on the ground in the open until they died or were taken by us into a tent. We did what we could to alleviate their sufferings'.[107] He makes a similar assertion elsewhere in the memoir, when he laments that 'We had no treatment for typhus: we had to stand by and watch, encouraging the patient as best we could'.[108] This single sentence is sandwiched between and set off by two longer paragraphs emphasising the ordeal.

Pavillard's assessment noted earlier that such episodes of suffering left one 'completely washed out' is relevant to MacCarthy who, at the death-bed of a young soldier, 'wept for his inexperience and his mistakes and for his lost youth'.[109] And, it would not be for the last time:

The days wore on – each filled with greater misery. One particularly grim memory I have is that of a dying airman in the dysentery hut. He was in the terminal stages of acute bacillary dysentery, and had not long to live. Because of severe abdominal cramps and pains it was a most painful way to die. His wasted body stiffened with each spasm and he had no control over his bowels and bladder. There was little or no medicine to be had and all that I could do for him was to pray and to hold his hand and whisper words of encouragement. As I tried to comfort him, I wondered if the dying man was able to find strength in the faith as I was. I remembered the devoutness of my own upbringing; I remembered our village priest, and myself as a child serving before the altar, and once again I thanked God for the faith that sustained me under these appalling conditions.[110]

Adams, too, 'couldn't stand to see blokes die alone', and spent much time 'holding their hands, and offering meagre reassurances that didn't changes outcomes in the vast majority of the cases. Those who died were best out of it.' Yet for those who did recover, he believed the 'pastoral care did change outcomes for blokes hovering on the borderlines of life and death'.[111] Much effort was put into easing 'the final days of patients':

> We decided to screen off blokes who were fading fast. The intention was good. Deaths in the ward produced a sombre mood. Everyone looked at the dead man. It was impossible not to, particularly if he'd died in the middle of the war. No one spoke as we orderlies pulled and shoved and hefted him onto a stretcher, and the sounds, and perhaps sights, were noticeable as we parcelled up the bloke, blocking up his passages to prevent drainage, tying up the jaw to prevent it flapping open, and wrapping him in sacking or whatever we had. Everyone wondered who'd be next. The sickest would look more fearful than ever, no thinking: I'm ill; I'm like the dead bloke was; am I next?
>
> We hoped that placing the sickest behind screens would remove some of the fear among the patients in the rest of the ward. We were badly wrong. Going through those red screens was seen as a death sentence.[112]

Adam's description elicits a profound sense of sadness, the red screen an apt metaphor for the descent into death, 'behind the veil'.[113]

P. G. Seed recounts how he and others tried to ease the dying on their way, with tenderness and intimacy:

> Up until that time [that Father Kennedy arrived] you might say men died in my arms metaphorically speaking. I was the last human being they would have contact with in this squalid death at the other end of the world from their homeland and that's a fact. As well as me, there would be medical orderlies and they were very tender. One or two of Queen Alexandra's Imperial Army Nursing Service experienced ward sisters would have been worth their weight in gold in a camp of thousands of men, rather like it must have been in the time of Florence Nightingale. Anyway, there were none, and of course, much less so in Taiwan, but in the absence of women – women's tenderness – one noticed developing remarkable tenderness in men and I note especially in the medical orderlies and the two RAMC orderlies – Donnelly and Thompson who joined about 1943. They almost seemed to develop a woman's tenderness in the nursing art, and this is very

astonishing when you consider the desperate and very rough surroundings in which they did their nursing – their medical care, but so it was.

In this passage, Seed is also quick to counter any suggestion that such tenderness and intimacy with other men might have encouraged homosexuality 'or the like': 'I don't think there was any.'[114] More importantly, however, he points to the kind of 'intense homosocial world' that Santanu Das has explored in the literature of the First World War, 'that amidst daily death and degradation, the body was primarily an object of pain rather than of desire ... Touch helps to open up our understanding of the ambiguous zone between diffuse homoeroticism and more conscious acts of homosexual intention. Touch is also aligned to emotions such as pity, vulnerability or maternity.'[115] In this light we may also see Pavillard's relationship with, and reaction to the death of, his good friend Captain T. E. Abrams, known to all as AB, who died of cholera. Pavillard notes simply how before AB took sick, 'I shared his blanket'. On his death:

> I had not the heart throw his body into the common pit, since we had lived together as brothers, sharing what little we had. So I took a shovel and dug a deep grave by a jungle tree, and his men in the lines afterward erected a rough wooden cross there with his name inscribed with a red-hot iron. ... His death was a blow to us ... I inherited his blanket, but missed his kicks and snores in the night.[116]

The physical intimacy continued after death, as doctors were responsible for preparing bodies for burial. When a body was not prepared properly on land, the results could be gruesome. Adams recalled the body of one soldier who had died of malaria:

> I wrapped him in sacks but didn't plug effectively all the outlets and tie up the chin to prevent the mouth from dropping down. Next day I was shocked to find froth on the sacking nearest his mouth. Air escaping from his body had produced it but it shook me. For a few moments I thought I'd trussed up an unconscious man and left him to die.[117]

Characteristically, the terse phrase 'it shook me' speaks volumes, while Philps's recollection of a burial at sea is equally horrific, if more matter-of-factly presented:

> because we had no means of weighting the bodies down, and after about twelve hours in the warm tropical sea, if the water was calm and we were near the shore, they would float up to the surface all around us. Sometimes, there would be as many as six, bloated, but unfortunately, often still recognisable.

Some of the stronger among us tried swimming to them and slitting them with a knife to make them go down. Fish finally finished the job.[118]

Amidst such horror and death, it is perhaps surprising to find passages in these memoirs that transcend the squalor. But the memoirists, however briefly, find themselves writing evocative descriptions of their surroundings. Ion Ferguson writes of his few months of captivity in Austria:

Autumn deepened into winter and, by the beginning of October, the beauty of the trees and mountains around us took on another splendour of its own. We lived in a scene reminiscent of the old-fashioned Christmas cards I used to see when I was a boy. The sight of snow was at first a great joy to some of the Australians and New Zealanders, who had never seen anything of the kind before.[119]

R. B. C. Welsh, an RAMC doctor on the Burma Railway in one of the longer perorations in his memoir from May/June 1942 notes:

Sun-rise and sun-set: here I go off into musing on nature, and only wish I could express myself on paper (or even verbally). Sun-rise is sometimes superlatively beautiful here – soft colours, beautiful cloud formations, a most pleasant temperature. … Sunset is usually more fierce and gaudy: fiery colours; large splashes of vivid orange and red gradually darkening through copper, then suddenly fading with the quick dusk, but the blues and purples are magnificent.[120]

And Philps, whose experiences in the Far East camps were truly horrendous, is able to see the beauty, which he also painted in watercolours, of

The island of Haruku … a coral island brought above sea level – indeed, turned into a small mountain – by volcanic action. It is beautiful, fertile and renowned throughout the world for its butterflies. The other islands in the Moluccas group are Ceram, Buru, Ambon and Saparua, all covered by lush vegetation and separated by narrow seas whose astonishingly clear blue colour has to be seen to be believed.[121]

Philps's imprisonment on the Spice Islands 'had a nightmare quality which makes some parts of it difficult to recall, indeed, up to this point in my life I have found the whole thing too painful to bring back to mind'.[122]

What, then, compelled ex-POWs, particularly medical personnel, to write of their experiences when '[M]emory seems to suffer a block when one tries to take from it incidents which are better forgotten'?[123] What role did this act of writing and publication play in these men's ability to endure and overcome the trauma of imprisonment and, as Adams called it, 'healing in hell'?

On one level it was an act of witnessing and of remembering those who did not survive. It is significant that a number of memoirs are dedicated to those left behind: Ion Ferguson dedicated *Doctor at War* (1955) to 'those who died in captivity' and Richard Philps provides a moving epigraph to his memoir published in 1996: 'To those of us who died so/ tragically and amid such squalor/but among friends.' As with all medical narratives discussed in this book, POW medical memoirs focus their acts of witnessing not so much on their own suffering, but on that of the countless men they treated, those who could not speak for themselves. Yet because they too were prisoners of war and shared in the misery of hunger or starvation, disease, squalor, confinement and the brutality of captors, doctors do reveal more of their own personal misery than medical personnel in other situations. These are not overemphasised, as the excerpts have shown, and they are often put in the context of hindering their role as healers rather than any claim for their own anguish. Yet, as Rosalind Hearder notes, and the memoirs discussed here attest, 'doctors were by no means immune to the psychological impact of captivity. While they may have blocked out or rationalised most of their experiences at the time, they too endured a painful legacy.'[124] Cochrane ends his *British Medical Journal* article with 'the plea that some attention should be paid to the psyche of repatriated prisoners. At my own medical board there was not one question which could in any way be construed as showing interest in my feelings, and they did not even measure my BP!'[125]

Prisoners of war returned to a post-war world that found it hard to accept the ravages wrought on the men who came home. MacCarthy describes a letter sent from 'some bright boy in the Ministry ... explaining that [POWs'] experiences had caused them to be slightly unbalanced. Not too much was to be expected of us and great patience had to be exercised. The letter did *not* help our rehabilitation and caused most of our relatives to view me with a kind of compassionate apprehension.'[126] As Allport suggests: 'Perhaps the POW experience was so alienating because it defied the national narrative of victory.'[127] Thus MacCarthy was right to use the plural pronoun when he declared, 'Now, with some reluctance, we faced life again.'[128] Adams described coming home as 'a reunion of strangers,'[129] and found himself 'changed fundamentally'. He lost his 'strong religious convictions', 'was aggressive' and found it immensely difficult to readjust to 'normal' society 'or to establish easy and comfortable relationships within the family. 'That side of me ... had been snap frozen.'[130] At times, memories would come to haunt them, unbidden. Pavillard, able, on the whole to contain his emotions in captivity, would sometimes find 'memory reasserting itself at night-time, and to wake up screaming from the black depths of nightmare: this still happens to me from time to time, and once again I see the jungle, the rain, and my friends turning liquid in a pit of flies and maggots.'[131] Adams 'can still hear those screams'[132] of men beaten to death, while, for MacCarthy, the body can prompt memories: 'nearly everyone developed pressure sores. I still have a spot on my left hip that becomes infected now and again, as though to remind me of past horrors.'[133] Hanson recalls, that 'In many small ways it took time to readjust – if ever we have! For a long time I had occasional nightmares in spite of persuading Eunice to thump me whenever I shouted in my sleep!'[134]

The family clearly had much to do with the readjustment or otherwise of these returned POWs. As Adams attests, it was not easy for wives and children to cope with men who had become virtual strangers and who carried what Hanson mildly calls 'some after-effects'.[135] Philps ascribes his ability to make 'the rest of my life happy' to three things: 'my marriage, my job [as a consultant pathologist at University College Hospital] and my liking for the company of wild creatures in quiet places – but by far the greatest of these is marriage.'[136]

It is usually at the prompting of these families that ex-servicemen and women write down their experiences, and POWs are no exception. J. B. Reid, in a 1994 letter which accompanied a copy of his memoir 'A Guest of the Fuehrer' explained that

> For the past few years my Grandchildren (now teenagers) have asked me to put it down on paper, as I know it is hard for people to understand what it was like. I have tried to stick to the humorous side as much as possible. I have asked a couple of people here [in Australia, where he was then living] what they thought of it and they said it is a 'Good Read'.[137]

The emphasis on trying to communicate the 'humorous side' is something that runs throughout other POW memoirs. According to Philps, this is why the 'human mind is strange', for, 'the best parts, the funny parts, are remembered with ease: the ghastly parts require great effort'.[138] Nevertheless, medical POWs are able to describe with great clarity the brutality of captors, squalid sanitary conditions, outbreaks of dysentery and other diseases, sparse medicines, poor food and vitamin deficiency, 'slogging work', starvation and needless, countless death. And for Philps, in particular, the truth is important: 'it was my responsibility to make it as accurate as a subjective statement can be.'[139] A journal he had been keeping for some time in captivity was confiscated by the Japanese and he regretted its loss, feeling 'somehow that I failed in an objective'.[140] He wrote about 'our experiences soon after the war' for his dissertation for a Diploma in Public Health in 1947, but 'after that, it remained on the shelf unread for 27 years simply because I was unable to face the stark truth of those days until I got older; my sixtieth year in fact'. He could not 'face re-living this time in any way' and 'also avoided discussing it as I have found that stories oft-repeated inevitably become exaggerated'. Thus, when he comes to publish his account, he is relying on a

> story, partly written soon after the time it occurred and then laid aside for the whole of the intervening period [that] does not suffer from this fault though I must confess that, had I read it for the first time now, many years after the events it describes, I should have some difficulty in believing it. I must ask the reader to understand I have attempted to tell the absolute truth.[141]

Had he been able to keep and bring home his journal, the raw evidence of his life in captivity, and turned it into a book, Philps believes he would have entered a world he did not want to be a part of:

> It would, in the climate of opinion at that time, have become almost inevitably a bestseller and I would have become known as the man who wrote that book about being a Japanese POW, perhaps, even, the man from whose book the film was made. I would then have become a professional ex-POW – and probably a crashing bore. Worse, I might have done nothing constructive with the rest of my life, always looking backwards, and worst of all, I would have lived on hate. The loss of that journal was therefore, for me, a highly significant event, possibly the most influential event in my later life. It enabled me to get on with living – to get on with being a doctor – and, I hope, perhaps to do a bit of good. It has also enabled me to put the events of those years into a broader perspective before setting them down – to see some sort of wood instead of a lot of trees.[142]

The comment about becoming a 'crashing bore' fits in with his inability

> to mix with the other men who came back, though we went through so much together. Until now I have shirked reviving these memories and have hardly discussed them (even Emmie did not know the details). This lack of discussion has had an advantage. Inevitably, a story often retold becomes distorted: the tale I have told is the truth as I saw it. My reluctance to enter into ex-POW activities has not been from any unsociable motive: it has been the result of my sadness at the loss of so many young men so unnecessarily. I trust that those who may be critical of me for not taking part in these reunions understand my point of view. I was kindly invited to a

Far-Eastern POW reunion a year or two ago. I went: they were charming to me, but I could not face it again.[143]

Philps's memoir charts the way that his older self is able to remember, and emphasises, like others, the ability to endure. Hanson argues that 'Though none of us would have chosen such experiences, nor claim to have done much to help win the war, we would probably all agree that we surprised ourselves by the extent to which it was possible for most of us, as ordinary human beings, to adapt to the changing conditions and keep going.'[144]

The emphasis on resilience is something that is clearly articulated in reviews of these published accounts. The *Times Literary Supplement* noted that although Stanley Pavillard's book 'reeks of filth, lice and sepsis … through it all shines the courage and resilience of the vast majority of those who went through hell on earth'.[145] It is 'a profound record of heroic endurance and of man's indomitable spirit.'[146] Similarly, despite his suffering the hardships of a POW in Colditz, Ion Ferguson 'lived to write it all down without bitterness or self-pity'.[147]

Yet, the memoirists are divided in their feelings for their captors, perhaps in an effort to further put the experiences behind them. MacCarthy claims that for all the suffering he witnessed and endured, he 'felt little bitterness for the Japanese'. Rather, he 'felt indifference. The totally different culture and religion of the nation made them so alien that I could hardly regard their actions as immoral. Everything my own world stood for had been turned on its head during my imprisonment.'[148] Philps considers the 'morality – or otherwise – of dropping the atomic bomb to finish the war':

> I must confess to a personal bias, so it is not for me to argue about the moral issue, but the practical results are undoubted. This action saved tens of thousands of prisoners from death … it saved native populations from the continuing miseries of war … and it undoubtedly saved the lives of countless troops of both sides as well … One tremendous advantage has resulted from the use of these devastating weapons: the effects were there for all to see and fear and so we have all been too frightened to use them again …. Only History can judge the rights and wrongs of the issue, but mankind has still a very bad conscience about it.[149]

Schrire is not so forgiving: 'I cannot forget these incidents [removal of Poles] when today the Germans are white-washing themselves and disclaiming all guilt for what we know they have done.'[150]

On the whole these ex-POW medical men use their memoirs less to castigate the enemy – perhaps an interesting omission – than to bear witness to suffering, and as we have shown, sometimes turning the lens from the suffering of others towards themselves. Writing was expiation, but also a testament to lives that were lived behind barbed wire, out of view, cut off from the regular interactions with the home front that sustained so many serving soldiers. Though those in European camps had more sense of the world outside and the progress of the war than those in the Far East, both sets of prisoners lived their lives in seclusion of the worst kind. They had to be witnesses to what went on behind the barbed wire, in the work camps and jails. That these medical men were not automatons, able to completely divorce their personal from their professional selves, is evident in the admissions however brief of their own mental strain and that oft-used term. MacCarthy noted how 'No one could go through such experiences without losing some of his sanity. There were some, of course, who never recovered it'[151] and these memoirs are also about remembering those who didn't survive.

As Hunt and McHale argue, the memories of aging war veterans 'have become molded and adapted over time according to individual narratives and the changing social discourses through which the veterans have lived'.[152] We argue that the memoirs discussed here evince the difference between traumatic memory and narrative memory that Hunt and McHale delineate. Traumatic memory is characterised by 'flashbacks or other ways of being unable to treat the past as history', and narrative memory is 'where the individual narrates the past as the past'.[153] These memoirists seem to able to narrate the past as the past, with traumatic memory returning in flashbacks, in dreams, or during the act of writing itself. The memoirists who published their accounts in the 1990s or 2000s use a very different language to describe their experiences from those who, like Ferguson and Pavillard, published in the 1950s and early 1960s. The word 'strain' is more often used by the latter, but 'traumatic' is frequently employed by Adams, in particular, perhaps the result of having his son as editor, one of a generation used to the terminology of PTSD that gives permission to admit its effects. Yet it is important to emphasise that this generation believed in stoicism, that what Hanson described as his pride in being able to endure such horrendous circumstances, was not about denying the anguish. And for Adams, who, 'being a medic I thought I couldn't grumble at the men who'd done the fighting', it was about being able to prove that medics were not 'gutless, robbing bastards'.[154] Thus, we must be wary of what Hunt and McHale observe as a contemporary prejudice 'where we expect people to break down after a traumatic event, and [find] there is something wrong if they do not'.[155]

Hearder's observation that '[c]aptivity for medical personnel could prove a consistently profound paradox: an experience encompassing optimism and sadness, influence and powerlessness, satisfaction and despair'[156] is equally applicable to their post-war lives in a world that Stanley Pavillard and his comrades found difficult to understand. Although 'the hunger, the blood and the cruelty had vanished with so many of our friends into the past; we wore new uniforms, and a new life lay before us. But we had not been issued with new unmarked memories to match, and the scars inflicted on us during those terrible days are there for life.'[157]

Notes

1 Nigel Hunt and Sue McHale, 'Memory and Meaning: Individual and Social Aspects of Memory Narratives', *Journal of Loss and Trauma* 13: 1 (2008): 42–58; p. 52.

2 Alan Allport, *Demobbed: Coming Home after the Second World War* (New Haven, Conn., and London: Yale University Press, 2009), p. 208.

3 Allport, *Demobbed*, p. 194.

4 Allport, *Demobbed*, p. 196.

5 Allport, *Demobbed*, p. 196.

6 Robert A. Zeiss and Harold R. Dickman, 'PTSD 40 Years Later: Incidence and Person-Situation Correlation in Former POWs', *Journal of Clinical Psychology* 45: 1 (Jan 1989): 80–7; p. 80.

7 Zeiss and Dickman, 'PTSD 40 Years Later', p. 81.

8 Allan Hanson, 'The Story of POW 12415. 1940–1945' (revised 1995), Army Medical Services Archive (RAMC/PE/1/607/HANS M70), pp. 7–8.

9 Richard Philps, *Prisoner Doctor: An Account of the Experiences of a Royal Air Force Medical Officer during the Japanese Occupation of Indonesia, 1942–1945* (Hove: The Book Guild, 1996), p. 66.

10 Aidan MacCarthy, *A Doctor's War* (London: Robson Books, 1985), p. 120.

11 MacCarthy, *A Doctor's War*, p. 56.

12 MacCarthy, *A Doctor's War*, p. 57.

13 MacCarthy, *A Doctor's War*, p. 15.

14 MacCarthy, *A Doctor's War*, p. 56.

15 Philps, *Prisoner Doctor*, p. 9.

16 MacCarthy, *A Doctor's War*, p. 58.

17 MacCarthy, *A Doctor's War*, p. 60.

18 MacCarthy, *A Doctor's War*, p. 63.

19 Philps, *Prisoner Doctor*, p. 33.

20 Allport, *Demobbed*, p. 197.

21 Stuart Mawson, *Doctor after Arnhem: Winter to the Fall of the Third Reich* (Stroud: Spellmount, 2006), p. 46.

22 Allport, *Demobbed*, p. 200.

23 Allport, *Demobbed*, p. 201.

24 Hanson, 'The Story of POW 12415', p. 1.

25 Hanson, 'The Story of POW 12415', p. 5.

26 Hanson, 'The Story of POW 12415', p. 6.

27 Hanson, 'The Story of POW 12415', p. 8.

28 Hanson, 'The Story of POW 12415', p. 10.

29 P. G. Seed, The Second World War Papers of Captain P. G. Seed, Imperial War Museum, London (91/35/1), p. 12.

30 Mawson, *Doctor After Arnhem*, p. 9.

31 Philps, *Prisoner Doctor*, p. 55.

32 Philps, *Prisoner Doctor*, p. 105.

33 Rosalind Hearder, *Keep the Men Alive: Australian POW Doctors in Japanese Captivity* (Sydney: Allen & Unwin, 2009), p. 15.

34 Hanson, 'The Story of POW 12415', pp. 10–11.

35 Hanson, 'The Story of POW 12415', p. 13.

36 Hanson, 'The Story of POW 12415', p. 16.

37 Hanson, 'The Story of POW 12415', p. 19.

38 Mawson, *Doctor after Arnhem*, pp. 6–8.

39 Mawson, *Doctor after Arnhem*, p. 8.

40 Ken Adams, *Healing in Hell: The Memories of a Far Eastern POW Medic* (Barnsley: Pen & Sword Books, Ltd., 2011), p. 45.

41 Philps, *Prisoner Doctor*, p. 99.

42 Hearder, *Keep the Men Alive*, p. 27.

43 MacCarthy, *A Doctor's War*, p. 119.

44 Adams, *Healing in Hell*, p. 64.

45 Adams, *Healing in Hell*, p. 65.

46 Hearder, *Keep the Men Alive*, p. 172.

47 I. Schrire, *Stalag Doctor* (London: Allan Wingate, 1956), p. 15.

48 Schrire, *Stalag Doctor*, p. 115.

49 Ion Ferguson, *Doctor at War* (London: Christopher Joseph, 1955), p. 110.

50 Seed, Second World War papers, p. 34.

51 MacCarthy, *A Doctor's War*, p. 70.

52 David Westlake, RAMC, 'An Account of Life as a POW', typescript, Army Medical Services Archive, p. 11.

53 Philps, *Prisoner Doctor*, p. 63.

54 Philps, *Prisoner Doctor*, p. 104.

55 Trevor Gibbens, 'Captivity: Trevor Gibbens' Experiences as Prisoner of War in Germany, 1940–1945', Army Medical Services Archive, p. 85.

56 Hanson, 'The Story of POW 12415', pp. 32–3.

57 Adams, *Healing in Hell*, p. 45.

58 A. L. Cochrane, Capt. RAMC. 'Notes on the Psychology of Prisoners of War', *British Medical Journal* (23 February 1946): 282–4; p. 282.

59 Cochrane, 'Notes on the Psychology of Prisoners of War', p. 282.
60 Philps, *Prisoner Doctor*, p. 7.
61 Adams, *Healing in Hell*, pp. 31, 35.
62 Cochrane, 'Notes on the Psychology of Prisoners of War', p. 282.
63 Seed, Second World War papers, p. 14.
64 Adams, *Healing in Hell*, p. 45.
65 Adams, *Healing in Hell*, p. 47.
66 Philps, *Prisoner Doctor*, pp. 62–3.
67 Stanley S. Pavillard, *Bamboo Doctor* (London: Macmillan & Co., Ltd., 1960), p. 78.
68 Pavillard, *Bamboo Doctor*, p. 52.
69 Philps, *Prisoner Doctor*, p. 67.
70 Philps, *Prisoner Doctor*, p. 67.
71 Allport, *Demobbed*, pp. 201–2.
72 Cochrane, 'Notes on the Psychology of Prisoners of War', p. 283.
73 Westlake, 'An Account of Life as a POW', p. 11.
74 Cochrane, 'Notes on the Psychology of Prisoners of War', p. 283.
75 Pavillard, *Bamboo Doctor*, p. 96.
76 Pavillard, *Bamboo Doctor*, p. 96.
77 Pavillard, *Bamboo Doctor*, p. 148.
78 MacCarthy, *A Doctor's War*, p. 76.
79 Adams, *Healing in Hell*, p. 106.
80 Ferguson, *Doctor at War*, p. 60.
81 MacCarthy, *A Doctor's War*, p. 70.
82 Westlake, 'An Account of Life as a POW', p. 9.
83 Westlake, 'An Account of Life as a POW', p. 9.
84 Westlake, 'An Account of Life as a POW', p. 10.
85 Philps, *Prisoner Doctor*, p. 103.
86 Adams, *Healing in Hell*, p. 39.
87 Adams, *Healing in Hell*, pp. 39–40.
88 Adams, *Healing in Hell*, p. 60.
89 Westlake, 'An Account of Life as a POW', p. 9.
90 Pavillard, *Bamboo Doctor*, pp. 97–8.
91 Philps, *Prisoner Doctor*, pp. 87–8.
92 MacCarthy, *A Doctor's War*, p. 119.
93 MacCarthy, *A Doctor's War*, p. 120.
94 Adams, *Healing in Hell*, p. 73.
95 *Times Literary Supplement* (10 June 1960), p. 374.
96 Pavillard, *Bamboo Doctor*, p. 105.
97 Adams, *Healing in Hell*, p. 25.
98 Pavillard, *Bamboo Doctor*, p. 107.
99 Pavillard, *Bamboo Doctor*, p. 106.
100 Pavillard, *Bamboo Doctor*, p. 137.

101 Adams, *Healing in Hell*, pp. 18–19.
102 Adams, *Healing in Hell*, p. 25.
103 E. Randolph, *An Unexpected Odyssey: The Chronicle of a Field Ambulance Private, 1940–1945* (1981), IWM Documents 3504, p. 26.
104 Randolph, *An Unexpected Odyssey*, pp. 27, 30.
105 Pavillard, *Bamboo Doctor*, p. 136.
106 Pavillard, *Bamboo Doctor*, p. 136.
107 Pavillard, *Bamboo Doctor*, p. 137.
108 Pavillard, *Bamboo Doctor*, p. 164.
109 MacCarthy, *A Doctor's War*, p. 36.
110 MacCarthy, *A Doctor's War*, p. 68.
111 Adams, *Healing in Hell*, p. 41.
112 Adams, *Healing in Hell*, p. 41.
113 Alfred Lord Tennyson, *In Memoriam*:

O life as futile, then, as frail!
O for thy voice to soothe and bless!
What hope of answer, or redress?
Behind the veil, behind the veil.

114 Seed, Second World War papers, p. 25.
115 Das, *Touch and Intimacy*, pp. 25–6.
116 Pavillard, *Bamboo Doctor*, p. 140.
117 Adams, *Healing in Hell*, p. 101.
118 Philps, *Prisoner Doctor*, p. 99.
119 Ferguson, *Doctor at War*, p. 116.
120 R. B. C. Welsh, 'POW Diary of Captain R. B. C. Welsh: A RAMC Doctor on the Burma/Siam Railway 26 January 1942–24 October 1945', Army Medical Services Archive, p. 39.
121 Philps, *Prisoner Doctor*, pp. 51–2.
122 Philps, *Prisoner Doctor*, p. 32.
123 Philps, *Prisoner Doctor*, p. 32.
124 Hearder, *Keep the Men Alive*, p. 200.
125 Cochrane, 'Notes on the Psychology of Prisoners of War', p. 284.
126 MacCarthy, *A Doctor's War*, p. 156.
127 Allport, *Demobbed*, p. 205.
128 MacCarthy, *A Doctor's War*, p. 159.
129 Adams, *Healing in Hell*, p. 133.
130 Adams, *Healing in Hell*, pp. 140, 142, 143.
131 Pavillard, *Bamboo Doctor*, p. 137–8.
132 Adams, *Healing in Hell*, p. 95.
133 MacCarthy, *A Doctor's War*, p. 102.
134 Hanson, 'The Story of POW 12415', p. 44.
135 Hanson, 'The Story of POW 12415', p. 45.

136 Philps, *Prisoner Doctor*, p. 125.
137 J. B. Reid, letter to G. W. King, dated 10 October 1994, 'A Guest of the Fuehrer (POW)', typescript, Army Medical Services Archive (RAMC/PE/1.611/REID M 70).
138 Philps, *Prisoner Doctor*, p. 32.
139 Philps, *Prisoner Doctor*, p. 33.
140 Philps, *Prisoner Doctor*, p. 102.
141 Philps, *Prisoner Doctor*, p. 33.
142 Philps, *Prisoner Doctor*, p. 130.
143 Philps, *Prisoner Doctor*, p. 129.
144 Hanson, 'The Story of POW 12415', p. 45.
145 *Times Literary Supplement* (10 June 1960), p. 374.
146 *Times Literary Supplement* (29 April 1960), p. 268.
147 *Times Literary Supplement* (15 July 1955), p. 402.
148 MacCarthy, *A Doctor's War*, p. 156.
149 Philps, *Prisoner Doctor*, pp. 130–1.
150 Schrire, *Stalag Doctor*, p. 64.
151 MacCarthy, *A Doctor's War*, p. 101.
152 Hunt and McHale, 'Memory and Meaning', p. 42.
153 Hunt and McHale, 'Memory and Meaning', p. 43.
154 Adams, *Healing in Hell*, p. 31.
155 Hunt and McHale, 'Memory and Meaning', p. 50.
156 Hearder, *Keep the Men Alive*, 36.
157 Pavillard, *Bamboo Doctor*, p. 206.

5

Claiming trauma: women in
the Vietnam War

The Vietnam Women's Memorial in Washington, DC is an isolated island of suffering (Figure 5.1). Placed at a distance from the Vietnam Veterans Memorial – the Wall– and the 'Three Soldiers' statue, it exists outside these more traditionally masculine commemorative narratives of war: the warrior and the dead (see Figures 5.2 and 5.3). Instead, it depicts the women's war story, particularly that of the nurse. She is locked forever in the moment of holding the dying soldier – a pietà in which there is no redemption, only the circular monument reflecting an ongoing circle of pain which refuses to direct the viewer beyond it. Its exclusion from the dominant motifs of warriors and Wall which work interdependently – the warriors gazing at their own or their comrades' names on the Wall[1] – is a reminder not only of the historical exclusion of Vietnam women veterans from the history of the war, but of the exclusion of their community, the wounded and sick and their healers, as represented in the nurse and the dying soldier.[2] This community is central to the accounts by nurses from the Vietnam War, since it is through that community that they claim their legitimacy as war veterans, and by extension the trauma that they suffered in caring for the wounded and sick.

But their writing does not focus only on the physical and emotional suffering engendered by war. It extends the narrative to include the politics of the war and its legacy: both nurse and combatant are depicted as victims of a meaningless war and of the malign American policies that sent them there, and as victims of the anti-war response that greeted them on their return home. Further, the politics of their involvement goes beyond the relationship between nurse and wounded soldier depicted in the monument. Sculptor Glenna Goodacre's original concept had included a nurse holding a Vietnamese child. This model was rejected on the grounds of being too political.[3] The nurse accounts under

Figure 5.1 The Vietnam Women's Memorial, Washington, DC

Figure 5.2 'The Three Soldiers'

Figure 5.3 The Vietnam Veterans Memorial – the Wall

discussion, as well as their poetry, reclaim the wounded civilian as essential to the narrative. In particular, Patricia Walsh's *River City*, an account of her work as a civilian nurse caring for wounded and sick Vietnamese civilians, reminds us that, while the combatant injury narrative may have been relegated to the peripheries, the story of Vietnamese civilians and those who cared for them is nowhere represented in the public remembrance of the war in the United States.[4]

The writings examined in this chapter take us from the representation of women at the periphery to their central claim of a traumatic legacy that places them in war. These women's accounts are thus more overtly political than nurses' accounts from the Second World War. In addition, they move beyond the kind of political statement we find, for example, in Mary Borden's writing which rejects war in the context of combatant suffering and death, to claim the legitimacy of *their* experience as traumatic, placing themselves in the political debate surrounding the treatment of Vietnam veterans post-war. At the same time, these accounts continue to represent care-giver and care-receiver as indissolubly linked; bearing witness to her own trauma, the nurse inevitably holds up the damaged bodies she nurses to public view as the source of her psychic wounding.

Yet even as she does so, the relegation of this act in the Vietnam Women's Memorial to the periphery of remembrance is also, as one nurse explains in her response to the Wall, a removal of the unpalatable facts of injury from American consciousness to a place where they cannot intrude on the management of mourning:

> It was seeing the names so carefully carved out. So much neater and cleaner than any of them died. … It was almost too neat, almost too precise, almost too lined up. It somehow can't reflect the horror of holding a young man while he dies. It was terrible watching your children die, it was awful. Mr and Mrs America, Mr and Mrs Congresspersons, all of the people who declared the wars, it was terrible watching your children die. You have no idea what that looks like. If you did you wouldn't have another war.[5]

The narratives of this community of suffering thus have as their mandate the revealing of death and injury, of showing what it is like to treat the wounds and watch not only soldiers but civilians, especially children, die. Even as these women claim their own trauma, like their predecessors they still take on the burden of bearing witness to war as it is represented through the wounded and dying. Moreover, in spite of the inclusion of civilian deaths, the American combatant remains at the forefront of these narratives. In this sense the Women's Memorial is paradoxically both radical and conservative. While it claims a cultural and political space in the commemoration of the war (even as it is placed on the periphery and did not receive state funding), something women had not done previously, as in the First World War it represents the nurse through an image that reinforces her role as healing and grieving mother, defined by the wounded soldier she supports. Yet, as we have shown in our discussion of both world wars, this role is the source of much of the psychological suffering these women endured. The emotional stress involved in taking on this role not just commemoratively but actively is outlined by Norman:

> After the neurosurgeon and chaplain had left the 'expectant' patients [patients who were expected to die], it was the nurse's job to monitor the patients' vital signs until their hearts stopped beating. … All a nurse could do was touch and speak to these men. While listening for a heart-beat, a nurse would hold a man's hands and whisper in his ear. In Vietnam, and in other wars, women learned that nursing was more than healing. The women learned to measure death and soothe the way.
>
> These expectant soldiers were strangers. … For the nurses, it was crucial that these anonymous soldiers not die alone or unattended. … 'I would just stand near them. I felt that his mother would feel better knowing that

someone was standing with her son when he died.' This timeless scene is one of sadness and loneliness. The soldier was every young man who went off to fight a war and never returned. The nurse was every woman who mourned the wartime loss of a husband or son or brother.[6]

As in earlier wars, many of them remark that as nurses they had to be mother, sister or girlfriend to the wounded, so in writing and telling these stories they still carry this burden. This role is brought home in Lynda Van Devanter's Vietnam War memoir, *Home before Morning*, where a crucial image is represented in the dream she records on the ending of the war in 1973: '*Thousands of American mothers were walking in the streets of Saigon, carrying the bloody bodies of their dead sons. Above the wailing, screaming, and gnashing of teeth, one word was constantly repeated: Why?*'[7] [original italics]. The image of collective suffering not only positions the nurse as mother, putting on public display 'the bloody bodies' in a performance that demands an answer, but also uses her to make a political statement. The burden these women carry is both the psychic burden of caring for thousands of wounded and dying, and the question that constantly hovers about the war itself: 'Why?' This question disrupts the iconic pietà even as it exploits it. In doing so, these writers represent war through the emotional rawness and graphic depictions of injury and death. War memoirs by Van Devanter, Winnie Smith, Patricia Walsh and others, and Sharon Grant Wildwind's diary of her time in Vietnam, take us beyond the writing of nurses from the First and Second World Wars to an explicit interrogation of the evil and absurdity not just of this war but of all war.

The anger and sorrow pervading Van Devanter's image of the mothers with their sons' bodies is the anger and sorrow that is the legacy of that war. The politics of meaningless death and the community of young men and women who carried the burden of that meaninglessness and the Vietnamese civilian deaths are central to their texts. That death in war is meaningless was certainly not a new concept in Vietnam; we see nurses in the First World War, such as Mary Borden cited in Chapters 1 and 2, confronting its absurdity, but with the political divisions at home and the social inequity of the draft system it became increasingly difficult to impose any form of meaning on the death and maiming. Van Devanter's mothers' public display of mourning is thus simultaneously a funeral procession and a protest march. As the absurdity and sorrow of war are foregrounded in this image, so is the demand for an answer. The challenge to the state implied here and throughout *Home before Morning* marks an important change in nurses' responses to their war service.

The racial equality and second-wave feminist protests of the late 1960s and early 1970s clearly influence this demand for a public voice, and in doing so present a generation of nurses who claimed their war service as the impetus behind their demand to be heard. Notably, they would also become the first nurse veterans, in fact the first medical personnel, to make public the psychological damage wrought on them by their war service.

Exchanging nurses for mothers points to Van Devanter's own internalisation of the role of nurse-mother. Her memoir enacts the role of the mothers in her dream. The wounded soldiers are not just on external display for political purposes, they return home inhabiting the psyches of the women who cared for them. This community of suffering is not left behind in Vietnam – Saigon comes to America, carried back in traumatic images that haunt the nurse. Norman writes of the nurses in her study that:

> PTSD was the psychological fallout of their service in Vietnam. Two central features characterized their disorder. On the one hand, the women with PTSD reexeperienced the war in painful recollections, and recurrent dreams and nightmares. On the other, they also felt numb and experienced a loss of emotional reaction to the world around them.[8]

This haunting in the form of nightmares is represented in *Home before Morning* in the image of a young 'bleeder', Gene, whom Van Devanter tries unsuccessfully to save. Although the horrific nature of his injuries haunts Van Devanter, her inability to forget him arises because she inadvertently discovers him as a person, not just another wounded soldier.

> Leading to the operating table was the largest trail of blood I had ever seen. I tried to walk quickly through it but slipped. … Three intravenous lines ran from bags of blood to his body. … The lower portion of his jaw, teeth exposed, dangled from what was left of his face. It dragged along the canvas litter and then swung in the air as he was moved from gurney to table. His tongue hung hideously to the side with the rest of the bloody meat and exposed bone.[9]

As she keeps pumping blood and changing IV tubing she notes 'It was all just another simple job where I could turn off my mind and try to forget we were working on a person'.[10] But at that point she sees a photograph that has fallen out of his pocket:

> the picture was of a young couple – him and his girlfriend, I guessed. … Straight, blonde and tall. … But the thing that made the picture special was

how they were looking at each other ... I could see, in their faces, the love he felt for her and she for him. ... On the back of the picture was writing, the ink partly blurred from sweat: 'Gene and Katie, May 1968.'

I had to fight the tears as I looked from the picture to the helpless boy on the table now a mass of blood vessels and skin so macerated that nothing could hold them together. *Gene and Katie, May 1968.*[11]

No longer able to ignore his identity as a human being 'who can love and think and plan and dream' Van Devanter herself is unable to maintain the necessary wall nurses report building to protect themselves from the intrusion of emotions that would lead to breakdown. As she records it, this experience with Gene causes a breakdown similar to that Mary Borden describes in *The Forbidden Zone*, discussed in Chapter 1. The point where the anonymous wounded becomes a person rather than an injury is the point where the emotional detachment is breached. That moment forces a confrontation with the larger meaning of war contained in the injury and refuses to allow the nurse to return to her role as detached automaton. Where Borden becomes aware of 'the wounded packed round us, hemming us in'[12] and feels herself 'to be breaking to pieces',[13] Van Devanter begins 'seeing all of them – the double and triple amputees, boys with brain injuries, belly wounds, and missing genitals. ... Then all the images came crashing back on me. I lost control and became hysterical.'[14] On returning home Gene inhabits her mind as a representative of all the young men who died or were mutilated. As she falls asleep on the plane, 'I saw an image that startled me awake. It was the bloody, blown away face of the young bleeder into whom I had pumped blood six months earlier. Gene and Katie, May 1968. He was wearing his tux and dancing with Katie, but his face was all exposed meat and bone. ... Her face, too, was blown away.'[15] The discrepancy between these images and the way the war was advertised to potential nurses in recruiting material is explored by Kara Vuic in her discussion of recruitment advertising. An advertisement 'showed an army nurse tending a wounded soldier' telling the nurse audience 'that a nurse can "bandage a war ... a wound at a time. A person at a time. With your skills as a nurse. With all the cheerfulness in your heart. You do it because you want to do it. You do it because you are an Army nurse." '[16] As we show in the Introduction, towards the conclusion of *Home before Morning*, Van Devanter reminds us that the disconnect between the idealisation and the reality of war nursing has been a part of the experience in all wars and war nursing must be recognised for what it really means to those who undertake it: 'even to talk about Vietnam is not the whole story. During World War II, hundreds of women were killed. ... In all of our wars, women have been killed, maimed, disabled, and psychologically injured.'[17]

The conflict played out in Vietnam nurse accounts is, arguably, the same as we have shown in the two world wars only more overt; that is, the immediate need to repress emotion in the interests of patient care and professionalism exists simultaneously with an emotional strain that for many medical personnel can be uncontainable and uncontrollable. The Vietnam nurses' willingness to unleash graphic depictions of the wounded, dying and dead in their memoirs goes beyond that of earlier writers so that such images not only bear witness to the suffering endured by combatants as a form of protest, as mentioned earlier, but also become essential to the woman's claiming of her post-war trauma. The political climate surrounding the war paradoxically works both for and against such a claim. One the one hand, the negative response to those who had served on their return home initially silenced their war experience and possibly contributed to the PTSD experienced by some women. On the other hand, the representation of the war as unethical and damaging to its participants allowed for a cultural context within which graphic depictions of violence to the human body and mind could be represented. This is in contrast to the kind of silencing we have discussed in relation to the Second World War, and certainly influenced the differences in accounts from these two wars. Thus, while initially Van Devanter was rejected by an editor who told her of her proposed work on women's experience of Vietnam that 'nobody wants to read that kind of book',[18] subsequently *Home before Morning* was acclaimed as a crucially important contribution to the understanding of the war and of the war nursing experience more generally.[19]

The investigations by psychiatrists such as Charles Figley, Chaim Shatan and Robert Jay Lifton into post-war traumatic response which resulted in the inclusion of PTSD in the *Diagnostic and Statistical Manual of Mental Disorders* (DSM-III) in 1980 legitimised the relationship between wartime exposure to violence and later psychological repercussions. However, as we stress in the Introduction, PTSD was still seen as a combatant 'disorder', predicated upon being in an environment of killing and dying. It was not until women such as Van Devanter discovered the relationship between their own post-war symptoms and those defined as symptoms of PTSD years after their return from the war that they recognised their own experience as traumatic. Van Devanter writes:

It sounded like I was reading my own psychological profile. The psychologists had not thought to include women in their studies, but I began thinking that if I had the same problems as the men, there must be plenty of women in similar circumstances. There could be thousands of women vets experiencing PTSD who thought they were alone.[20]

Yet women, as non-combatants, remained excluded from the diagnoses. The efforts by Van Devanter and others to have their own post-war trauma legitimised, and to be accepted as veterans, became a hugely important furthering of the nursing experience (and by extension that of all medical personnel) as traumatic.[21]

Remarque's observation that 'the real war' takes place in the hospitals is more immediately relevant when we consider it in relation to these women's fight for recognition.[22] The relegation of the hospital to an experience 'behind the lines', outside combat and thus officially excluded from the psychological strain of war not only placed nurses, especially women, outside the war, but also allowed the damage of war, made visible in the wounded, sick and dying soldiers and civilians, to be concealed. In fact, as Van Devanter finds, nurses literally didn't count: 'neither the VA [Veterans Association] nor the Defense Department could give an accurate total of women who served in Vietnam, let alone who they were, where they lived, and what their physical and mental health might be.'[23] Even during the war, Sharon Grant Wildwind asks herself in her diary 'Are women, are nurses real veterans? Sometimes it doesn't seem as if we should be. We live in hooches, eat in a mess, work under conditions that are at least comfortable.'[24] At the same time she is annoyed to be called an REMF (rear echelon motherfucker). In a comment added after the war she returns to this issue and claims the validity of her war experience:

> For those of us working in hospitals being called REMF hurt. We joked about it with the patients, allowing them to call us that. What did we know of fire fights, hot landing zones, snipers, napalm, trees defoliated by Agent Orange, mud, rice paddies filled with leeches, ambushes and cho-com grenades?
>
> I had stood ankle-deep in purple potassium permanganate solution, pouring gallons of it on white phosphorous burns, trying to keep the W[hite] P[hosphorous] from burning to the bone.
>
> I had gone to tag 'em and bag 'em in the body shed, pulled the tags from a man with no face, read the name, and realized we'd had coffee together the day before.
>
> I had spent long nights sitting beside beds while guys smoked and talked in the dark about all those things REMFs didn't know about.

I had nursed two men through minor injuries and sent them back to the field only to hear two weeks later they were on the orthopaedic ward with their legs blown off.

There was no bad guy in the field killing and good girls in the hospital saving lives. I was a soldier; I supported soldiers.[25]

In claiming she is 'a soldier' Wildwind is claiming the legitimacy of her experience. Those who would categorise her as REMF are, in fact, colluding in Scarry's concept of the 'disowning of injury', since to designate the hospital as 'rear echelon' is to refuse to acknowledge those who inhabit it as having been damaged by war. In this context it is crucial to see Van Devanter's representation of 'Gene and Katie' and of her mothers carrying their wounded sons as important public acts of defiance against this disowning. The concept of a community of suffering and victimisation is central to such representation. While nurses like Van Devanter are arguably the first medical personnel to claim their own psychological stress in this very public way, like their predecessors they cannot decouple that suffering from its source: the physical and psychological pain of those they cared for and their own intimate relationship with suffering. As Das has argued of First World War nurses, touch marked the point of intimacy that brought nurses into an often unbearably close relationship with the injured. Wildwind explores her feelings about this kind of intimacy in her diary:

The soaks, dressings and other procedures take most of the evening. Our work is close and intimate. ... What I do involves touching: changing dressings, turning helpless patients, back rubs, sometimes just a hand on an arm or holding a man's hand. There aren't any pictures of me doing this. Sometimes I am embarrassed to have others ever see me do it. I want to be private about caring. This is the hard part of nursing. ... There's something terribly personal about the intimacy of some of the care I give.

...

Ward work is exhausting. It isn't just the new medicines and the treatment routines, but what is more tiring is the intensity of these contacts.[26]

Such intimacy thus contributes to emotional as well as physical exhaustion. Moreover, a particular response to this intimacy is the need for patient advocacy. Nurses' accounts therefore often become a form of advocacy for the combatants and in some instances the Vietnamese civilians as well as for themselves.[27]

The paradox inherent to these accounts is thus one we have encountered before: to represent their experience medical personnel must also represent that of the injured or sick combatants and civilians they care for. Representing their own pain is impossible without representing, and foregrounding, the pain of others – particularly a suffering that seems so much greater than their own. The impetus behind this need to foreground the patients' suffering is, as we have noted, a characteristic of medical personnel accounts across time. In the Vietnam War context it is reinforced as part of the war nursing narrative established in recruitment advertising. Kara Vuic points out that:

> Recruitment materials routinely suggested that army nurses worked on the front lines in Vietnam, sometimes showing nurses working in field hospitals, but more often by showing wounded soldiers. … The ANC [Army Nurse Corps] minimized the real danger many nurses would face by suggesting 'Your greatest and most rewarding challenges will be in the care of wounded soldiers. Many Army Nurses find their finest hours in the combat zone.'[28]

Moreover, she notes, 'recruitment literature challenged nurses to "[M]atch your skill and dedication to your patients' courage and sacrifice".'[29] When such representation is compounded with nurse probationary training, the ideal version of their wartime role is reinforced. Elizabeth Norman asserts that '[t]he concern for preserving life begins where self-preservation ends. Dock and Stewart, in a classic history of the nursing profession, refer to this behaviour as the "mother nurse" characteristic, where tenderness and devotion to the sick and helpless came before all personal needs.'[30] Former Vietnam nurse Joan Furey describes the relationship between that training and the inadmissibility of psychological repercussions.

> I think that a big part of it was that the majority of women were nurses. Nurses in the sense we were from a very traditional kind of nursing educa tion background. Most of us were graduates of three-year hospital schools of nursing. People don't always appreciate what this means. We were indoctrinated with professionalism, the tradition of nursing, the honor, the self-sacrifice – all this stuff was part and parcel of what was engrained into us during those three years in hospital student nursing. One of the things that I think most of us believed was that if we were having any difficulty, it made us less of a nurse – somehow we weren't good enough, or that we somehow hadn't learned all that we should have. We couldn't own the very human emotions of being exposed to high levels of trauma. We couldn't get comfortable with feelings. They were very frightening to us, very confusing. We had expected we would have a degree of detachment and in no way were prepared for the experience of being a nurse in a war. It's not gall bladders

and heart attacks. It's young men – your own age or younger – and, again, I would like to point out: we're talking about young women, I was 22 years old, and I wasn't the exception. Most of us were 21, 22, 23. We didn't have a lot of experience, and, all of a sudden, we were dealing with our peer group of young men who had devastating injuries – had been blown to bits! We were doing things we never thought we would have to do, seeing things we never thought we would have to see. In some ways the experience was incredibly empowering, in others, so incredibly destructive.[31]

Such training – to consider patients' needs first – thus informs the way these nurses construct their narratives both during and after the war, especially in relation to the emotional toll of their nursing. As we note in our discussion of American nurses in the First World War, their position as members of the Army Nurse Corps involved further stress as their role existed in tension with the concept of the nurse as healer. Lynn Hampton interrogates the motto of the Army Medical Corps, 'To Conserve the Fighting Strength', and her role in its function, using it as the title of her memoir. In her chapter with that title she writes:

I had never really liked the motto, 'To Conserve the Fighting Strength' which we saw on banners and signs in hospitals in Vietnam. I understood it, but it seemed too 'utilitarian' or something ... somehow it seemed to fall short of humanity, and it always gave me a mental image of someone recycling dented tanks through a garage. I often wondered how it would make someone feel who had been wounded too seriously to have their 'fighting strength conserved' to see that motto over the door of the hospital.[32] [original ellipsis]

Her questioning of the motto and image of recycling reflect Mary Borden's fragment 'Conspiracy', in *The Forbidden Zone*, where she employs the domestic image of patching and mending and eventually discarding clothes to represent the 'conspiracy' of wounding and restoring and eventual dying in which she participates. Sharon Grant Wildwind comes even closer than Lynn Hampton to reflecting Borden's representation of war. Aware that each time she sends men back to fight they may return more severely wounded or dead she remarks in her diary:

I feel like I'm part of this 'conspiracy' for lack of a better word: this conspiracy to get men crippled or killed. Sometimes I think I should say 'no', make some kind of protest like refusing to send someone back to the field. I know I'd last about thirty seconds if I tried that. Whatever I do has to be sneaky and subversive, like coaching the patients on how to answer the doctor's questions or learning which doctors are more likely to send someone home.

I feel it's us, the patients and the hospital staff, against them, the Army.[33] (16 December 1970)

The understanding of the practicality here is important. All the nurse can do is work subversively to try and mitigate the conspiracy. Within the environment she has no political power; she can only try to undermine it in an ad hoc fashion. Yet her guilt at her role in the war clearly weighs on her. The idea of the healer and the advocate for the patient, so deeply instilled in nurse training, is at odds with the concept of army medicine which asks practitioners only to 'conserve the fighting strength', the motto itself a representation of the 'conspiracy' of which the healers are a part.

The image of the nurse portrayed in the advertising described by Vuic above does not allow for this conflict inherent in wartime nursing that both Hampton and Wildwind confront. Rather, it works together with the professional training outlined by Norman and Furey to reflect idealisations of the female nurse role that have dogged the war nurse for over a hundred years. Such rhetoric encourages self-effacement even as it implies that the war offers an exciting and rewarding experience. As we have seen in the two world wars, such idealisation disallows the nurse's own feelings. She must be entirely subservient to her work and her patients. Feelings that undermine or contradict the ideal, or her role in the war, may thus become very difficult for the nurse to acknowledge or express, and the cultural milieu of nursing (as well as of the military) may make it impossible to speak. The guilt Wildwind indicates thus becomes a further burden the nurse has to carry and, as Van Devanter tells us and as we have seen in accounts from the First and Second World Wars, emotional survival in the immediate term demanded repression: 'I must be tough', she records repeating to herself both during and in the aftermath of the war. Since voicing one's own needs runs counter to the culture of nursing, Vietnam nurses' accounts represent what Kali Tal defines as the 'aggressive' nature of bearing witness that we present in the Introduction: 'Bearing witness is an aggressive act. It is born out of a refusal to bow to outside pressure to revise or repress experience, a decision to embrace conflict rather than conformity, to endure a lifetime of anger and pain rather than submit to the seductive pull of revision and repression.'[34]

Tal's valorisation of such witness carries problems even as it identifies the need to employ trauma for political purposes, however. The survivor's burden carried by Kate Finzi that we have seen in her First World War account discussed in Chapter 1, 'I alone am left to tell the tale', arises out of a compulsion to keep the shattered combatant body on public view as well as to bear witness to one's own pain and to the pain of medical personnel as a community. Yet taking on this role can become problematic if it stands in the way of resolving the very real lived experience of post-traumatic stress. As we note in the Introduction, Dominick LaCapra posits that '[t]hose traumatised by extreme events … may resist working through them because of what might also be termed a fidelity to trauma' and that in 'reengag[ing] in life, one is betraying those who were overwhelmed and consumed by the traumatic past'.[35]

Similarly, Hunt finds that some suppression may contribute to resilience. Although we find little evidence of effective repression in most of the Vietnam nursing narratives we discuss here, they do indicate Hunt's further assertion that where suppression is impossible, narrative processing, such as writing the kind of memoirs and diaries we are highlighting, plays an important role in resilience. As will be seen below, we further find that, for some women, the experience was highly rewarding in spite of the stress. Emphasising that her memoir was a 'form of therapy', Van Devanter also moves beyond her individual experience to the community of which she is a part and which the act of writing the memoir creates: '[m]y story is only my own, but many other women and men shared similar experiences both during and after the war. I hope to let them know that they are not alone.'[36] Van Devanter's words suggest a balancing of the problem defined earlier. While she retains the feelings as a personal and political motivator against war, it 'no longer owns her'. Bearing witness here thus becomes part of the 'processing' which contributes to resilience.

Another Vietnam nurse veteran, Winnie Smith, turned her response to Van Devanter's account into an equally compelling memoir: *Daughter Gone to War*. Smith's initial reaction to reading *Home before Morning*, is first a denial of any emotional legacy and then a reliving of the trauma she had repressed. Initially sceptical of Van Devanter's blaming of the war for her sleepless nights, the image of wounded soldiers triggers an immediate emotional and physical impact:

> A vise grips my chest. … Still, I read: 'With his eyes closed, he might have been just another tired soldier resting. However, the bloody mess that was once his body told a different story.'
>
> I can smell the blood now, the stench of Vietnam in its humid tropical air. I see the dazed stare in the haggard face of a young soldier. I hear the choppers, the sound of more wounded on their way;
>
> …

For the next week these ghosts of my past are my constant companions, and the past is more real than the present. Somehow my mind has crystal-lized them, brought their tortured faces and tormented voices back to life.
...

> When they come, they bring everything with them: the sights, the smells, the sounds, the tastes, the very essence of that time and place. ...
>
> These are flashbacks, though I do not yet know the word. I am reliving, not just remembering, the past.[37]

Like Van Devanter, she finds that narrative, as Hunt represents it, becomes the means by which she can process the experience:

> I discover writing helps me regain control of my mind. The reels won't stop, but I can slow them enough to record portions, and once they've been put to paper, they fade into the past, change from experience to memory. Only there are too many of these scenes, no end of new ones to replace those that writing puts to rest.[38]

The range of writings by woman veterans reflects the differences in pro-cessing their seemingly 'traumatic' experiences. The complexity of the war experience means that there is not necessarily a common pattern of response. While both Van Devanter and Smith record the extreme emo-tional pain that attended their Vietnam experience and followed them home when they left, they also relate more positive experiences, especially those which became crucial for their survival at the time, such as close friendships and love relationships even though these were also charged with pain as individuals left or were killed or disappeared. Moreover, as we have seen in accounts from earlier wars, and as Furey states in the interview cited above, many nurses report the paradoxical experience of their work as being simultaneously 'destructive' and 'empowering'. Thus for Maureen Nerli, 'Vietnam was for me, then and now, a powerful growth experience, I'm glad I served.'[39] Likewise, Charlotte Miller responded that 'Vietnam is one of the most positive experiences of my life ... it was so good and yet it was so awful.'[40] Cheryl Nicol further articulates the paradox inherent to war nursing: 'It was the best year or worst year of your life. But I knew what I could do ... I felt like I was really doing some good.'[41] At the same time she voices the need to suppress emotion during her time in Vietnam for her own survival, echoing the war experience of generations of war nurses before her:

> You had to completely turn off. ... No matter how bad the stuff was that you had seen, you didn't think about it. You just didn't allow yourself. Because you'd never have been able to come and work on the next chopper load that

came in. I think a lot of problems that I had later were caused by dragging it all up to where I came home.[42]

In an interview with Olga Gruhzit-Hoyt, nurse Diane Corcoran also represents her time in Vietnam as one of learning:

> I learned a lot about living and dying, friends, work, skills, and how very clear you must be on values, goals, and how short life can be. There were many sad times. Some really fun times, and some intense times, but all of them I believe I integrated in a way to make me a better, wiser me. I was very lucky; I believed in my ability to help. I did not believe in the politics of the war. I was able to separate the two things.[43]

Given the emphasis on Vietnam nursing as a traumatic experience, we need also to pay attention to these more oblique responses, especially as they bear out Hunt's call for a more nuanced examination of the war experience. Nicol's statement is important in suggesting that repression and avoidance can be appropriate coping skills, and that revisiting the experience had negative repercussions. This is a useful reminder that the kind of forgetting that Gask, for example, writes of in the First World War could be advantageous in avoiding the emotionally overwhelming experience and its memory.

For writers like Van Devanter and Smith, however, the trauma needs to be translated into a narrative to be contained and controlled. For both women this means revisiting the experience. As Van Devanter writes in her foreword, 'there is so much of that year in Vietnam ... that I cannot remember. I needed to forget during those early years, and now that I want it back I have to struggle to regain it. But it is coming back, and I'm learning to live with it.'[44] For Winnie Smith the processing takes place not only in her book but in a support group for women veterans. Describing it, Smith articulates the psychological responses that attend the war experience. Where Brenda McBryde in the Second World War and Vera Brittain in the First both write of the 'shutters' that aid forgetting, Smith describes 'layers of forgetfulness [that] have welded into steel bars that lock out emotions.'[45] The nurse's training that insists she be strong, a term Van Devanter also uses constantly, plays an important part in creating those bars: 'We're here [therapy group] to dismantle the cages, to free our emotions. ... It's a scary process, worsened by an underlying sentiment among us the we have to be strong and the fear that we'll be considered weak.'[46] Such confrontation must dredge up the psychic wounds that lie behind that experience: 'We learned to accept death there, and it erased our sense of immortality. We met our human frailties, the dark side of ourselves, face-to-face.'[47] Elsewhere she describes the connection between her responses and those of the combatants; like the other women veterans, her account emphasises the community of suffering that brings together medical personnel and combatants:

> We all survived the same way, by numbing ourselves to what was asked of us. They [the combatants] swallowed their fear in order to face the enemy. I buried compassion to face the wounded. Back in the world with hearts desensitized and minds numb we shut out the horrors of the war zone and turmoil on the home front, and our self-administered anesthesia has been wearing off in variable times.[48]

Once the anaesthetic no longer works, the memories must be confronted. Telling the story as a memoir is both a process of unlocking emotions and a reflection on that process.

These women's responses show how understanding the trauma of war is much less simple than imposing the label of PTSD on someone who is suffering severe psychological pain from their war service. They reinforce Hunt's argument that we need to have 'a diagnostic category of war trauma distinct from PTSD, as PTSD covers only a proportion of the symptoms experienced by people suffering from war trauma. ... [W]e may help victims of war more effectively using a narrative approach that takes into account the breadth of their experience.'[49] The memoir, and in the immediate term the diary, thus become the ideal site through which individuals can create a narrative of the experience that goes beyond trauma or symptoms of PTSD, and as political as well as personal documents offer the reader a way of understanding the nuances and contradictions inherent to the experience. This complexity is what individuals such as Van Devanter, Smith and Walsh, as well as the diverse range of nurse veteran responses outlined in the interviews above, offer us. Wildwind summarises it: 'The ambivalence never leaves. There are days I wouldn't go to war again for anything. There are days, like when I see casualties being carried from a bombed building in Beirut, I would give anything to go again. There is no final word, no complete epilogue on Viet Nam.'[50]

Accounts from earlier wars include such contradictions and represent physical wounds directly, as we have seen; what often sets the Vietnam accounts apart from these is the unflinchingly graphic focus on injury. Perhaps because the war itself was much less mediated or censored than previous wars, writers felt permission to describe what they saw in an equally uncensored way. Both Van Devanter and Smith report being silenced by their mothers on their return home and having families turn away from their photographs and stories, making the later breaking of that silence so much more emphatic and arising out of a very particular need to speak. As already noted, the political agenda that runs through-out all these accounts also sets them apart from earlier narratives: they politicise women's experience in relation to the trauma suffered, and at the same time demand that their audience be made to observe the injury they witnessed on a daily basis. Needing to speak on behalf of their patients, and creating a community of suffering – an evocation of the 'world of hurt' in which they all exist and which they carry home – they also go much further that most previous writers in extending the damage of war and its repercussions beyond the warzone. Smith and Van Devanter, for example, relate their war experience in the context of their return home and the years of psychological suffering that ensued. The aftermath narrative is as important to their accounts as the war service experience. It also extends the war suffering more generally, reminding us of the effect on all those whose lives are damaged by the war. Thus when Van Devanter tells the story of Gene and Katie, she doesn't end at the hospital. She returns the reader to Gene's home and the announce-ment of his death to his family and Katie. The nurse's experience is only a part of the larger picture of grief. The community of suffering extends far beyond the front to the grieving family, who as yet don't know that Gene is dead: 'and Katie? She would probably hear over the phone.'[51]

As already noted, this event and all those leading up to it precipitate a breakdown. Van Devanter thus sets up the related tensions that recur throughout these women's writings: emotional survival and effective nursing in the warzone demand suppression of feeling; survival on their return home means leaving the emotions that attend war experience in Vietnam. When the image of Gene and Katie continues to intrude into her nightmares after she returns, the distinction between the arenas of war and the home front is blurred. For all those affected by war home is not a separate space. There is no return. As she had realised at the time of the Gene and Katie episode, 'The Lynda I had known before the war was gone forever.'[52]

Winnie Smith's title, *Daughter Gone to War*, reflects a similar sense of loss: having 'gone to war' she can no longer return as the daugh-ter who left. Loss is central to her narrative, both her own losses and those of others, especially combatants. While Van Devanter employs the photograph of Gene to reveal what has been lost and mutilated, Smith's account is permeated with an underlying tension between pres-ence and absence which she subsequently carries home. Soon after her arrival in Vietnam she attends an expectant – a young soldier who has been wheeled behind curtains to die. Her narrative begins by affirming his presence so the viewer/reader shares her gaze: 'The soldier's face is deeply tanned, not discoloured like so many in death. The dirt of battle gives him the air of an athlete at rest after a workout. Sweat streaks outline helmet straps along his jaw.'[53] Smith manipulates her representation of the image, so that the initial impression is of a warrior – the physical details of her description evoking an almost tangible physical presence. Yet as she moves us beyond the immediate impression, she sets this presence against an absence that completely destroys the initial illusion: 'He could be a high school football player after a scrimmage in the mud – except for the misshapen form under the sheet, flat where there should be arms and legs.'[54] The impact of this story is held in the tension that accompanies the pause: 'He could be … except for …' The absence is indicated rather than described, 'flat where there should be …'; the war has taken what was present – vibrant, young, physically strong – and reduced him to an absence. The image of the 'high school football player' returns us home, to what was. But in this wartime present, the absence of limbs becomes a synecdoche for the absence of self. The future is further defined by absence as his death becomes the extreme form of absence in the home that will receive the news.

When 'Pops', the close comrade and sergeant of Smith's lover, Larry, is brought to her ward with a head injury that has rendered him vegetative, Smith takes this concept of absence even further. She remembers his vivid presence 'In my mind's eye he flashes a grin at Larry on a Saigon street. … Pops' turn comes. It's not Pops turbaned and decerebrate I see but the expressionless face of a head injury, just another casualty of war. … Goodbye old friend, your Freedom Bird is waiting for you.'[55] The real individual has gone, his 'expressionless face' reducing him from the vibrant human being she had known to an anonymous 'decerebrate' defined only by his injury. For Smith, the need to survive the emotions of seeing a friend so severely injured means retreating to her professional nurse's dissociation. When Larry visits him she recognises a similar form of retreat. Touching Larry on the back as he sits by Pops's bed:

> He whirls on me, instinctively reaching for his weapon. His eyes are wild. The reflex lasts only an instant. When the instant has flown, Larry has the 'thousand-yard-stare'.
>
> Suddenly I understand that look. It's a retreat from too much pain. It puts a safe distance between the pain and the soldier.[56]

In bridging the experience of nurse and combatant, each of them retreating from the pain of witnessing a friend reduced to the nothingness of a vegetative state by the war, Smith explores how, for both, an instinctive avoidance or retreat from pain is crucial for survival in the immediate instance. It also, as Smith discovers on her return home, results in a numbing of all emotion. Equally, it reveals how the community of suffering is not just that of injury or witnessing injury. In a warzone both medical personnel and combatants are constantly confronted by the pain of loss. Shutting down pain is also a shutting off of grief which, as Shatan asserts, causes 'unexpiated' grief which can be central to post-war forms of traumatic stress.[57]

Smith's memoir explores this experience and accompanying avoidance further when later she is confronted by Larry's absence and presumed death. Shortly after he gives her his Combat Infantry Badge and asks her to marry him,

> I see Larry's jeep parked alongside our hooch. A corporal is leaning against it with his arms crossed, waiting. Could he have a message from Larry? No, Larry would have come himself. It must be about Larry.
> Before he sees me, I slip around the officers' club and sneak through the back door of our hooch. Whatever he has to say I don't want to hear it. If Larry's dead, I don't want to know. If he's messed up for life, lying in some hospital bed without arms or legs, I don't want to see him. I want to remember him with a light in his eye and the catlike grace of a warrior.[58]

Here, Smith's avoidance is a refusal to face and thus be forced to accept that absence. As Larry's own response to seeing his friend in a vegetative state is to retreat, so Smith's defence mechanism means 'putting a safe distance between [her] pain' and the soldier who would force her to confront it.

What this narrative does is draw attention to such communal bonds: nurse and warrior perceive themselves to be equally victims of this world of hurt. Like the Vietnam combat memoirs, the nurse memoir sets her community of medical personnel and those they care for apart from those who have never been in the war. Once the individual returns home, however, that community is lost, and a profound isolation, defined by its absence, takes its place. The isolation and absence are particularly felt in relation to the family, especially the mother, who should offer support, but who refuses to hear the war story. Both Smith and Van Devanter explore the way their respective family's unwillingness to listen to their war experience becomes representative of the larger silencing imposed by the country. When Van Devanter begins to show slides of her wounded patients her mother suggests

'I don't think you really want to show those slides. ... Maybe it would be wise to put them away.' ... I stored [the slides] in the back of a closet. ... Vietnam would never be socially acceptable. Not here, not anywhere in the world. ... I felt a deep emptiness inside, a longing for someone who might understand. I didn't belong in this place.[59]

Thus the rejection of her experience is directly linked here to her sense of not belonging. As Vietnam is not 'socially acceptable' in America, neither is she. Smith similarly finds that when she describes the patients in her neurosurgical ward her mother responds, 'Nobody wants to hear that stuff ... [s]ome things are better left unsaid'.[60] Smith points to the incongruity of the world she now finds herself in which refuses to listen to her representations of the war, but watches it on television. The world of the hospital with its vegetative soldier patients must not be made visible, but the representation of the war as combat is still present during family mealtimes, beamed into the living room from the television. He father tells Smith she must 'forget about it and go on with [her life]'. 'How can I forget?' she asks and he replies, 'Just don't think about it.' 'Then shut off the damn TV, I think miserably. Stop the nightly news footage of all those warrior faces, of choppers with Red Crosses, of wounded with bloodied field bandages and glazed eyes staring out of the screen while we eat steak and potatoes and fresh salads and drink real milk.'[61]

The silencing extends into the public realm. Prior to being interviewed on a local radio station about her Vietnam experience, Smith is confronted with the censorship of the images she had chosen: a picture of a Vietnamese boy shot in the head by America troops is rejected as too political, as is a 'nurse holding a child all bandaged up,' burnt by American napalm.

On the air he asks me what kinds of wounds I saw there, and a sharp vision of a ward full of maimed and dying soldiers fills my head. I blink down the image, shut down the part of me that wants to cry how awful it was ... no one wants to hear that stuff.

I say gunshot wounds, burn wounds, head wounds, blast wounds. I don't say bellies full of pus, or crispy critters, or blown-off arms and legs, or fixed and dilated pupils left to die alone.[62]

Language plays a role in obscuring the real story here. It brings us back to poet Siegfried Sassoon's words during the First World War about a public who prefer to censor certain unpalatable aspects of war, acknowledging only those wounded in 'a mentionable place'.[63] Externally imposed censorship becomes self-censorship that prevents Smith from articulating publicly the memory of war that she carries. The enforced silencing is here internalised so that the memories are driven deeper into the psyche and the sense of alienation increases. While the larger world participates in the disowning of injury, Smith, Van Devanter and others find themselves carrying the burden of what they witnessed home with them and for years afterwards. For both women, the mutilated bodies they cared for return insistently in their dreams so that their war experience increasingly defines them in its aftermath. Their alienation derives from their position: physically they are removed from the warzone but mentally they are unable to leave it. Moreover, for both women the rejection of their experience is seen as a rejection of self, precipitating a downward spiralling into depression and self-destructive behaviour. As noted earlier, for Van Devanter it is not until 1979 when she is asked to form the VVA [Vietnam Veterans Association] Women Veterans project that she becomes 'familiar with a syndrome called post-traumatic stress disorder'[64] and begins to explore this condition in women veterans.

Later she enters therapy specifically designed for Vietnam veterans, a process that allows her to reconceptualise her experience: 'It was as if I were exorcising a ghost that had haunted me for a decade.'[65] Central to this is a reconstruction of the narrative that has for so long been defined by the image of Gene, the soldier she could not save. She is given permission to 'hurt' and to 'ask for help' with a therapist who reinforces the value of the nurses' role: 'Our job was overwhelming, he said, but we nurses triumphed. And most importantly, we saved the lives of people who might otherwise have died.'[66] Ultimately her written account is, as she notes, a form of therapy that takes her from naive trainee nurse, through the experience of the war and the post-traumatic stress that followed in its aftermath. In writing and publishing the book she defies (like Smith, Hampton, Walsh and others) the larger culture of the United States that didn't want to 'hear that stuff'.

Particularly important, her telling, along with her work for VVA women, constructed a community that enfranchised the Vietnam War nursing experience for the many women to whom that legitimacy had been denied. For some nurses, as for some combatants, the isolation both from the community at war and from the meaning it offered them was so profound that they returned to duty in spite of the working conditions and the danger to their own lives. Of extending her tour in Vietnam Pat Johnson says 'I was happy to go back to Vietnam because that was where

I felt secure. I went back there feeling that I didn't know what I was going to do with myself when I came home. I didn't know where I was going to fit in.'[67] Nurses record feeling a sense of purpose in their work that could not be equalled at home and there was guilt associated with leaving their patients and friends:

> I would have loved to have gone back. I remember when the plane took off from Cam Ranh Bay, most of us were crying … I was thinking how guilty I felt that I was leaving. There was still so much to do. And I was leaving the best friends that I'd ever had in my life there. Then, when I got home and saw the stuff on the news and read the papers – that was so Godawful, I just couldn't believe it. I wanted to go back right away. It's like they say, 'The best year or the worst year of your life.' But I knew what I could do as a nurse and as a person. I knew I could stand up to whatever they had to throw at me, and I felt like I was really doing some good.[68]

As noted earlier, Hunt's approach to war experience that affirms the validity of the heightened intensity, the sense of purpose and of feeling needed, must be set alongside the trauma and the post-trauma response if we are to understand the multi-faceted experience of medical personnel in a warzone. These women's accounts, and particularly the paradoxical sense of the Vietnam experience as simultaneously their best and worst experience, thus become crucially important in understanding not just the relationships between trauma and resilience at the psychological/emotional level, but how individuals articulate this paradox and use their narratives to negotiate it.

Memoirs like those of Van Devanter and Smith created a community of medical personnel in their writing, and furthered that community after the war as women responded to these accounts. Although the perspective in these narratives is specific to the individual narrator, at the same time, these memoirs, and the interview with Nicol earlier, emphasise the community and comradeship that were a salient feature of wartime service. Mary Reynolds Powell's *World of Hurt: Between Innocence and Ignorance in Vietnam*, returns to those friendships in a collective account that unites her experience with the voices of those who worked with her in Vietnam into a single story. In telling this collective story she brings together those who fought and those who cared for them with the object of holding to account those responsible for the war:

> Eighteen and nineteen year old kids carried the burden of the war we asked them to fight. They carried it in the jungle, they carried it when they were spat upon, they carried it when they could not get jobs. They carry it today

in their destroyed bodies, in their nightmares, and in their genes altered by Agent Orange. They did what we asked them to do and we turned from them.

As a nation it is time for us to take the burden from the kids who fought our war. All of us were part of the lie that wasted an American generation and devastated an ancient culture half a world away. Until we acknowledge the wrong that we did in arrogance, we will not have learned. And if we have not learned, we will do it again.[69]

Powell's book was published in 2000 and this final comment resonates ironically in the aftermath of the invasion of Iraq in 2003. Powell's use of the term 'lie' takes us back to First World War poet Wilfred Owen's famous repudiation of the 'old lie', *dulce et decorum est pro patria mori* (it is sweet and fitting to die for one's country), as one told to children by their elders to encourage them to fight.

While Smith and Van Devanter focus primarily on their own post-war suffering as representative of those who served, Powell integrates the experience of other nurses, doctors, corpsmen, dustoff crew, soldiers and a Vietnamese medical orderly into her story, alternating her account with theirs to build a sense throughout her narrative of a community forged from individual experiences in the larger wartime and post-war context. Van Devanter's work was crucial in giving other women veterans permission not only to speak and write but to legitimise their experience as important as well as massively traumatic. Powell's work, coming twenty years later, in many ways extends that legitimacy, drawing out stories from those who might otherwise have remained silent. In doing so, she offers a range of voices that extend the community of carers beyond their Vietnam service to the legacy of the war in the 1990s.

One nurse in particular, Stephanie Grenthon, who worked with Powell at the 24th Evacuation Hospital, speaks to the contradictory responses that attend war nursing: 'It was always somebody's son or boyfriend', she said, 'They were so nice, so young, and so scared, it made it twice as hard to see them die.'[70] 'Sometimes', Powell adds, 'it was harder for the staff to care for soldiers who did not die immediately – the GIs who were still under attack in their nightmares or those who died after days of misery.'[71] The inability to confront the politics of the war in the immediate term is voiced by Stephanie, a crucial point in Powell's narrative, since it is through Stephanie's voice especially that Powell questions the war so many years later:

Beneath the goodnatured teasing [between nurses, medics and doctors] lay a sadness that could not be expiated and an anger that had to be concealed. No one spoke about the war. 'The patients needed to believe in what they were doing,' explained Stephanie, 'It was the glue that held them together. If they lost that, it would be all over. We were just taking care of sick people. They were out there fighting. How could we be critical of the war? They needed to believe that what they did was worthwhile.'[72]

At the same time Powell notes that after nine months Stephanie requested a transfer to the intensive care unit, afraid she would verbalise what could not be said. The paradox of war nursing is embodied in Stephanie's story. Telling Powell that '[t]here was just so much I could allow in … or it would have ruined me', Powell narrates the following account by a friend and fellow nurse:

> *Finding her [Stephanie] sobbing I went in. She was working on what looked like a long tape of paper. Through her tears, she was scribbling the full names of every kid who had died in the last couple of days. The list was enormous. She had been doing it all along. I told her to stop. She had to let them go to survive herself. I remember she turned to me solemnly and said through her tears, 'But someone has to. Someone has to remember their names.'*[73] [original italics]

In the same way that Stephanie names the dead, these accounts are all concerned with a kind of naming – individuals like Gene and Pops become representative of the thousands whose names the nurses would never know.

While Van Devanter, Smith and to a large degree Powell and others focus on the army nurse experience and explore the extent to which their trauma arises out of the interdependent nature of their relationship with the wounded combatant, the narrative that has been particularly silenced is that of the civilian American nurse caring for wounded and sick Vietnamese civilians. Patricia Walsh's account of her time nursing in a civilian hospital ostensibly under the auspices of USAID was originally published as fiction under the title *Forever Sad the Hearts* (1982) Rewritten as a memoir, *River City: A Nurse's Year in Vietnam*, it was published in 2009. The images of the naked Vietnamese boy shot through the head and the baby burnt with napalm that are censored from Winnie Smith's television interview are given representation in Walsh's account.

River City confronts us with the murky nature of American involvement in the war through USAID which, while purporting to use medical aid to reach 'hearts and minds', in reality had little or no concern for the Vietnamese population. It refused to listen to reports from Walsh's hospital of the terrible conditions caused by lack of supplies, or to acknowledge the numbers of casualties that were brought to the hospital because of American military action. An early scene in Walsh's memoir presents the absurd context in which she works. While military nurses tell their war story primarily through wounded combatants, the confusion of war where civilians are caught in crossfire points to even greater ethical questions:

> [T]wo military field ambulances sped through the gates. A Navy corpsman unloaded victims, who had lain for hours in a rice paddy after being caught in the middle of a firefight. In some cases sufficient mud had oozed into their wounds to stop the hemorrhage, but others had not been so lucky. One canvas stretcher was piled with small children; limp corpses mingled with the wounded, who whimpered pitifully as we eased them from the tangled mess. Mothers clutched dead children to their breasts and wailed unconsolably as they swayed back and forth in their squatting position. Children screamed in terror as they tried to arouse dead parents in a room that now looked and smelled like a slaughterhouse.
>
> When all of the patients had been carried inside, one of the corpsmen approached Shelly and me in the screened corridor where we worked. 'Sorry we can't stay and help,' he said. 'We have to get back to the field.'
>
> 'That's all right,' Shelly said kindly. 'Thanks for bringing them in.'
>
> 'Please don't thank us.' The corpsman nervously adjusted his blood splattered helmet. 'We're sorry about the kids.' He turned abruptly and joined the other corpsman waiting for him down the corridor.
>
> 'It's hardest on the medics and corpsmen,' Shelly told me when they were gone. 'They aren't part of the killing, but they have to witness it and try to patch up the injured.'
>
> 'But why are American military called to pick up injured civilians?'
>
> 'They don't have to be called, Pat. The Marines you saw carrying in the patients were the other half of the firefight they were caught in.' ...
>
> I went back to work, but I was having difficulty assimilating what Shelly had said. American military were shooting people, who they later picked up and brought to a hospital staffed by American government workers to be cared for with supplies cumshawed from the military.[74]

Nursing injured Americans only occasionally confronts American nurses with the issues Walsh presents. Her situation is even more conflicted, however, by the need to develop relationships with the American military in order to keep the hospital supplied. This in turn leads to a romantic involvement and engagement to an American Marine who is killed just before Walsh is due to return home. Walsh's work is with Vietnamese civilians and her book presents the effects, mental and physical and social, on these men, women and children, but she makes us aware of the complexity of emotions in wartime. While most of her memoir is concerned with describing her experience in treating civilians and with representing them as victims of the American war machine, she acknowledges that her more intense emotional response is to the wounded Americans. Visiting an American military hospital to beg supplies, she sits with a severely wounded Marine and comforts him as he dies: 'I had seen injuries like this – and worse – in our own triage, but my feelings were different. The frustration I felt caring for Vietnamese in an ill-equipped, civilian hospital was worlds apart from the revulsion that filled me as I looked down at the Marine's sunken blue eyes in a pallid face.'[75] Her reported conversation with her companion articulates her apparent discomfort at her response: ' "I care about our patients," I said, "But they're all strangers to me in a strange country. Coming out here where they look like my kid brother makes it my war too." '[76] ' "The military medical teams have a tougher psychological burden," Leo said, "We have it a little harder physically." '[77] Walsh thus suggests that maintaining detachment is easier in an environment where there is little emotional connection with the individuals under her care. The 'psychological burden' is arguably heavier when the patient is familiar, a 'kid brother', rather than 'other'.

All of the works discussed here focus on physical and psychological trauma, the impossibility of containing that trauma at the level of physical treatment of the wounded and dying and the psychological repercussions of that failure for medical personnel. As in accounts from earlier wars, the lasting images are those of fragmented bodies and the psychological fragmentation that afflicts the psyches of those who witness such damage. At the same time, the imposing of order through writing, whether in a memoir or the more immediate diary, offers a form of control over the experience, but also claims its essentially uncontrollable nature. In addition, the psychological stress that comes out of the conflict involved in the actual experience, whereby the medical personnel must confront the ethics of the war made visible in the individuals they treat, both soldier and civilian, makes for a particularly difficult aftermath response. That this is especially problematic for medical personnel in the Vietnam War is shown in the doctors' and medics' memoirs discussed in the next chapter. In these, the relationship between the personal response and the politics of a war where both civilian and combatant come to represent dual aspects of the same ethical quagmire is made even more central.

Notes

1 This was not Maya Lin's intention when she designed the Vietnam Veterans Memorial (the Wall). It was intended to be self-sufficient.

However, the subsequent placing of Hart's 'Three Soldiers' created a connection between the two. For further discussion on this controversy see Elizabeth Wolfson, 'The "Black Gash of Shame": Revisiting the Vietnam Veterans Memorial Controversy', at www.art21.org/texts/the-culture-wars-redux/essay-the-black-gash-of-shame-revisiting-the-vietnam-veterans-memorial- (accessed 9 October 2014).

2 Although this representation of the nurse and wounded soldier as a commemoration of war is unusual in the English-speaking world, especially the United States and Britain, First World War commemoration in France does include similar representations. Alison Fell writes that '[c]ertain evocations of the nurse in the interwar years effectively combine the roles of nurse and grieving woman, with the nurse depicted as a Pietà with a dead or wounded soldier presented as a Christ figure. This is particularly the case in France. ... The war memorial in Charlieu (Loire) is of this type. ... [I]t features a nurse wearing a First World War uniform and cradling a dead French soldier, his helmet by his side. This rare appearance of a realist sculpture of a uniformed nurse on a French memorial is perhaps explained by the fact that the mayor of Charlieu was Dr Jean-Louis Vitaud, who had worked as a doctor in the French army during the war' ('Afterword: Remembering the First World War Nurse in Britain and France', in Alison Fell and Christine Hallett (eds), *First World War Nursing: New Perspectives* (New York and London: Routledge, 2013), p. 174).

3 See 'Vietnam Veterans Memorial' history at www.saylor.org/site/wp-content/uploads/2011/06/Vietnam-Veterans-Memorial.pdf (accessed 9 October 2014) for an outline of the history of the three memorials and controversies. On the baby missing from the original prototype see the report from the *Los Angeles Times*, 8 August 1993, which reported that 'The Vietnamese baby has disappeared from the bronzed arms of the American Army nurse. No political statements are allowed at the Vietnam Veterans Memorial on the Mall in Washington. "I had thought of the baby as part of the casualties of war", says sculptor Glenna Goodacre, touching the tiny model of the infant that was eliminated from her original design for the Vietnam women's statue' (http://articles.latimes.com/1993-08-08/news/mn-21736_1_vietnam-memorial).

4 In 1982 Patricia Walsh published a fictional account of her time in Vietnam, *Forever Sad the Hearts* (New York: Avon Books, 1982). *River City: A Nurse's Year in Vietnam*, was published as a memoir in 2009 (Boulder, Colo.: TOA Press), but there is little difference between the two accounts.

5 Judy Hartline Elbring in Ron Steinman, *Women in Vietnam: The Oral History* (New York: TV Books, 2000), pp. 153–4.

6 Elizabeth Norman, *Women at War: The Story of Fifty Military Nurses Who Served in Vietnam* (Philadelphia: University of Pennsylvania Press, 1990), pp. 38–9.

7 Van Devanter, *Home before Morning*, p. 361.
8 Norman, *Women at War*, pp. 144–5. For a fuller overview see pp. 141–54.
9 Van Devanter, *Home before Morning*, p. 194.
10 Van Devanter, *Home before Morning*, p. 197.
11 Van Devanter, *Home before Morning*, p. 197.
12 Borden, *Forbidden Zone*, p. 158.
13 Borden, *Forbidden Zone*, p. 159.
14 Van Devanter, *Home before Morning*, p. 201.
15 Van Devanter, *Home before Morning*, pp. 250–1.
16 Kara Dixon Vuic, *Officer, Nurse, Woman: The Army Nurse Corps in the Vietnam War* (Baltimore: Johns Hopkins University Press, 2010), p. 30.
17 Van Devanter, *Home before Morning*, p. 358.
18 Van Devanter, *Home before Morning*, p. 344.
19 For a discussion of the reception of *Home before Morning*, including some nurses' rejection of it as representative see Vuic, *Officer, Nurse, Woman*, pp. 163–9; see also Joan A. Furey, Interview with Donald Anderson, 'Visions of War, Dreams of Peace: A Conversation with Joan A. Furey', *War, Literature, and the Arts* (Fall/Winter 1999): 118–33.
20 Van Devanter, *Home before Morning*, p. 343.
21 For a comprehensive overview of post-traumatic stress and guidelines for treatment of women nurses from the Vietnam War see D. H. Price and J. Knox, 'Women Vietnam Veterans and Post Traumatic Stress Disorder: Implications for Practice', *Affilia* 11: 1 (Spring 1996): 61–75. See also J. Wolfe, P. J. Brown, J. Furey and K. B. Levin, 'Development of Wartime Stressor Scale for Women', *Psychological Assessment* 5: 3 (1993): 330–5.
22 Remarque, *All Quiet on the Western Front*, p. 173.
23 Van Devanter, *Home before Morning*, p. 343.
24 Sharon Grant Wildwind, *Dreams that Blister Sleep: A Nurse in Vietnam* (Edmonton, Alberta: River Books, 1999), p. 104.
25 Wildwind, *Dreams*, p. 196.
26 Wildwind, *Dreams*, p. 134. Wildwind is well aware of the connections between her caring here and that performed by First World War nurses. In her post-war comment after this entry she quotes from Vera Brittain's *Testament of Youth*: 'Short of going to bed with them there was hardly an intimate service that I did not perform for one or another in the course of four years.' Wildwind ends: 'That hadn't changed. It was as much a reality in the Viet Nam war as it was in World War I' (p. 136).
27 For further discussion of nursing and advocacy see Barbara Jo Foley, Ptlene Minick and Carolyn Kee, 'Nursing Advocacy during a Military Operation', *Western Journal of Nursing Research* 22: 4 (2000): 492–507.
28 Vuic, *Officer, Nurse, Woman*, p. 32.
29 Vuic, *Officer, Nurse, Woman*, pp. 32–3.
30 Norman, *Women at War*, p. 146.

31 Furey, Interview with Donald Anderson. Vietnam nurse Ann Cunningham draws a connection between her youth, the youth of her patients and the emotional toll of the work: 'I thought I was doing really good for 15 years. 'Course I never talked about Vietnam or anything, and um, and especially when the Iraq War started, and then I took part in a, in a study up in New Hampshire at the VA center for women in combat and I don't know what that did, but it kind of just really stirred up a lot of stuff. And I was telling him [a friend] that I was looking at the *Army Times* ... and it has a casualty list every week for Iraq, and I said that, I said, "You know it seems to me that soldiers are older than they were in Vietnam" ... There wasn't anyone under 20 ... And in Vietnam, they had a lot of 18 and 19 year olds. Um, they were just kids you know. I mean we were, shoot we were kids too, and they were younger than we were. And they have said, that the studies that they have done, that they sent the youngest group of nurses to Vietnam than they'd ever sent to any conflict, any war, ever before' (Ann Catherine Cunningham Collection (AFC/2001/001/48446), Veterans History Project, American Folklife Center, Library of Congress, Washington, DC).
32 Lynn Hampton, *The Fighting Strength: Memoirs of a Combat Nurse in Vietnam* (New York: Warner Books, 1990), p. 38.
33 Wildwind, *Dreams*, p. 130.
34 Tal, *Worlds of Hurt*, p. 7.
35 LaCapra, *Writing Memory*, pp. 22–3.
36 Van Devanter, *Home before Morning*, p. ix.
37 Winnie Smith, *Daughter Gone to War: The True Story of a Young Nurse in Vietnam* (New York: Warner Books, 1992), pp. 296–7.
38 Smith, *Daughter Gone to War*, p. 299.
39 Nerli in Keith Walker, *A Piece of My Heart: The Story of Twenty-Six American Women Who served in Vietnam* (New York: Ballantine Books, 1985), p. 179.
40 Miller in Walker, *Piece of My Heart*, p. 327.
41 Nicol in Walker, *Piece of My Heart*, p. 368.
42 Nicol in Walker, *Piece of My Heart*, pp. 359–60.
43 Corcoran in Olga Gruhzit-Hoyt, *A Time Remembered: American Women in the Vietnam War* (Novato, Calif.: Presidio, 1999), p. 47.
44 Van Devanter, *Home before Morning*, p. x.
45 Smith, *Daughter Gone to War*, p. 308.
46 Smith, *Daughter Gone to War*, p. 308.
47 Smith, *Daughter Gone to War*, p. 308.
48 Smith, *Daughter Gone to War*, p. 322.
49 Hunt, *Memory*, p. 59.
50 Wildwind, *Dreams*, p. 197.
51 Van Devanter, *Home before Morning*, p. 199.
52 Van Devanter, *Home before Morning*, p. 199.

53 Smith, *Daughter Gone to War*, p. 121.

54 Smith, *Daughter Gone to War*, p. 121.

55 Smith, *Daughter Gone to War*, p. 207.

56 Smith, *Daughter Gone to War*, p. 213.

57 Chaim F. Shatan, 'Stress Disorders among Vietnam Veterans: The Emotional Content of Combat Continues', in Charles Figley (ed.), *Trauma and Its Wake*, Vol II (New York: Brunner/Mazel, 1978).

58 Smith, *Daughter Gone to War*, pp. 236–7. Wildwind gives us the opposite reaction as she hears of the disappearance of a close friend: 'Even burned, wounded, disfigured, I want him alive' (*Dreams*, p. 36).

59 Van Devanter, *Home before Morning*, p. 259.

60 Smith, *Daughter Gone to War*, p. 251.

61 Smith, *Daughter Gone to War*, p. 251.

62 Smith, *Daughter Gone to War*, p. 265.

63 Siegfried Sassoon, 'The Glory of Women', in *The War Poems*, ed. Rupert Hart-Davis (London: Faber, 1983), p. 100.

64 Van Devanter, *Home before Morning*, p. 343.

65 Van Devanter, *Home before Morning*, p. 350.

66 Van Devanter, *Home before Morning*, p. 351.

67 Johnson in Walker, *Piece of My Heart*, p. 59.

68 Nicol in Walker, *Piece of My Heart*, p. 368.

69 Mary Reynolds Powell, *A World of Hurt: Between Innocence and Ignorance in Vietnam* (Cleveland, OH: Greenleaf, 2000), pp. 160–1.

70 Grenthon in Powell, *World of Hurt*, p. 37.

71 Powell, *World of Hurt*, p. 37.

72 Powell, *World of Hurt*, p. 37.

73 Powell, *World of Hurt*, p. 41.

74 Walsh, *River City*, p. 24.

75 Walsh, *River City*, p. 69.

76 Walsh, *River City*, p. 71.

77 Walsh, *River City*, p. 71.

6

Crying silently: doctors and medics in the Vietnam War

In his Second World War memoir, *The Other Side of Time*, American battalion surgeon Brendan Phibbs writes: 'We were lucky in 1942. We didn't have to shrink from pictures of screaming Vietnamese about to be raped and murdered by American soldiers at My Lai. There were no dead students scattered across the grass at Kent State. Where we stood in 1942 the air was charged, clean, dangerous, honest.'[1] While our discussion of the Second World War, and Phibbs's own book, shows that the air was not as 'clean' and 'honest' as he saw it in 1942, his comment does point to the burden carried by his medical successors who came to articulate their war experience in Vietnam. Even as Phibbs represents the insanity and absurdity of killing and dying in his war and his Vietnam counterparts do the same, the latter must also struggle with coming to understand their experience in the political context of 'a filthy and unfathomable war'[2] both as it was being fought and in its aftermath.

Central to the politics of remembering this war and the trauma of that remembering is the bringing together of civilian and combatant injury and death; its legacy persists in iconic images: Haeberle's photographs from My Lai, Kim Phuc running naked and burning, American soldiers with the 'thousand-yard stare'. Two representations of injury from Vietnam War surgeon Allan Hassan's 2006 memoir *Failure to Atone* show, at the most extreme level, a doctor's compulsion to bring to public view atrocities visited on the Vietnamese civilian population and, at the same time, the apparently flagrant disregard for the lives of young Americans. In spite of the images that came home from the war, Hassan presents the stories embedded in his narrative as hidden from the American public. As in Van Devanter's image of mothers carrying their dead sons, where memory and nightmare merge as the images bring together personal anguish with the politics of the war, so Hassan's memoir opens with an episode that initially appears to be a nightmare representing the psychic burden he and other doctors carry:

I have a recurring dream of the past, or perhaps it is a nightmare. It is late May 1968, and I am a doctor in the jungles of South Vietnam …

Suddenly, three uniformed helicopter pilots hurry into the foyer of the hospital, carrying stretchers heaped with young children …

…

Spread out before me are the writhing, dying forms of approximately 40 very young Vietnamese children. Many are infants, the oldest perhaps five years of age. The children all wear plastic medical armbands. They are struggling to stay alive. … They have all been shot through the head. I quickly realize that these young children were probably lined up and shot, execution style.

… I desperately stuff Gelfoam into the bullet holes in the children's heads, trying desperately to save them.

I remember the moment of cold despair, a moment every doctor feels after fighting to save a patient only to see them slip away. I am losing forty patients at one time, and I cannot save even one. I am not only a doctor, I am a former Marine. I take a look at one of the arm bands on the children. The arm bands say 'Interrogated USMC'.

… As the last innocent child dies, I wonder if it will ever be possible to atone for such an inhuman slaughter, one of the many continuing atrocities of war.[3]

Later in the memoir we find that this 'nightmare' is an actual event. Moreover, when Hassan tries to investigate the apparent execution of the children by the Marine Corps, he is visited by two men whom he suspects are CIA agents, warning him to take his inquiries no further. Shortly after this event he is invited to visit a hospital with severely injured Marines at Dong Ha, a few dangerous miles from his hospital.

Most of the wounded men had neither arms nor legs, and were quadruple amputees … Well-muscled young bodies had been reduced to trunks and heads. I walked past row after row of horrible quadruple amputees. Tubes linked to their heads, chests, and abdomens drained into a maze of tubes and bottles hanging around and below the severely wounded Marines. … The main thing that struck me was that the faces and eyes of these men were hopeless and shattered.

…

'We can do some good for twenty or thirty percent of these guys if we send them home *quick*,' I said, feeling a medical urgency in the horrible spectacle I was witnessing.

…

'We can't send these guys home, Doc,' a young medic explained ... unless they go home in a body bag.'

'What? Why?'

'They're too grotesque,' a medic explained.

'They'd stop this war the second they saw the horrors up this close. As soon as that Medevac plane landed back in the world, and everybody saw those guys, they'd riot, and the war would be history.'

...

'At the very least,' I said again, 'these young soldiers should go home to die.'

...

'You must be joking, Doc ... We can't send these guys home ... Don't you get it? They can't handle the truth back in the world.'[4]

For Hassan, setting these events alongside each other is a way of bringing the unpalatable 'truth' they carry back to 'the world'. It is a knowledge he must live with privately, but at the same time it demands that the reader witness not only the physical horror that confronts medical personnel during their time in Vietnam and in the later remembering and telling of that experience, but also to understand that the damage visited upon Vietnamese civilians and the killing and maiming of young Americans are part of the same politics, as we have seen in Walsh's *River City* in Chapter 5. As in other wars, the 'disowning of injury' that Hassan is concerned to counter through these descriptions was part of the larger representation of the war to those at home. In spite of this being dubbed 'the television war', and the wide distribution of the iconic images noted earlier, real rather than celluloid injury came home to America in tin boxes. When the dead were returned, corpses were marked 'viewable' or 'non-viewable' to prevent families receiving the bodies from witnessing injury that was considered too shocking. In commenting on the 'non-viewable' designation, Robert Jay Lifton asserts that 'the larger symbolism of these instructions lies in the general collusion – asked for by the military and acceded to by civilian society – in turning away from the actualities of war, in keeping the corpses "non-viewable"'.[5] He quotes a veteran as saying, ' "[t]he only way Americans could begin to understand what this war is would be for them to have to see a few corpses right in front of them"'.[6]

Medical personnel like Hassan thus feel compelled to challenge the civilian and military collusion by making public the injury that is being 'disowned'. They must also confront their own feelings of guilt that arise from their participation in the war, even as healers. As John Parrish explains in *Autopsy of War*: 'I wanted to accept responsibility for every-thing I saw, yet wanted to hide from it at the same time'.[7] The impetus behind Hassan's memoir is both public – the 'failure to atone' speaks to the legacy of the war in political terms – and private, as it speaks to the legacy of personal guilt carried by those who participated, even those whose job was to heal rather than hurt. Writing about combatant sur-vivors of the war, Lifton stresses guilt as 'the fundamental psychological legacy of this particular war'.[8] Even though most doctors did not par-ticipate in killing, guilt arises out of witnessing deaths, surviving where comrades did not and being present in the warzone and thus complicit. Medic Charles Kinney writes in *Borrowed Time: A Medic's View of the Vietnam War*, 'I can't help thinking that there should have been chap-lains ... before we departed [for home] ... to give us their blessing and absolution for all we had to do and endure in the name of War'.[9] Lifton asserts that

> [i]mages and feelings of guilt are generally associated with transgression – with having crossed boundaries that should not be crossed. ... Here the transgression has to do with two kinds of death; that which they witnessed and 'survived' and that which they inflicted on Vietnamese. Though the two involve different experiences, they merge in the absurdity and evil of the entire project.[10]

While Hassan was not in the position of battalion doctors in the field who at times had to participate in fighting and killing, his setting of the Vietnamese children's deaths alongside the mutilated soldiers reveals just how much his sense of guilt at the 'failure to atone' arises out of this 'mer-ging' to which Lifton refers. In the search for atonement and absolution, the compulsion to speak publicly cannot be disengaged from the psycho-logical need to recount the experience as a form of private therapy. And, as with the Vietnam War nurse memoirs, these accounts are particularly important for their writers' willingness to acknowledge and often to fur-ther examine their own psychological damage, unlike those from other wars under discussion which seem reticent to expose psychological stress because of the stigma attached to breakdown.

In *Autopsy of War*, John Parrish's second work to examine his own leg-acy of the war in the larger context of American politics, he claims that he must keep 'writing and rewriting [his] war story' in an attempt to 'get it right'.[11] The compulsion to return to the experience in an attempt to articulate it to the writer himself as well as to a public audience is char-acteristic of all of the works discussed here. Titles like Hassan's *Failure to Atone* and Lunati's *Time Never Heals*[12] speak to a similar need to confront a lasting psychological legacy that is common across the memoirs of American doctors and medics who served during the Vietnam War.[13] Published over a broad timespan, from 1971 to 2012, all explore the relationship between the politics of the war, the literal immersion in wounds and death and the psychological burden of that experience, what Hassan calls the 'torment [that] clings to your soul'.[14] They range from the immediate experience of combat (although all of them were officially non-combatants and one, Ben Sherman, was a conscientious objector) described by medics Ben Sherman, Charles Kinney and Daniel Evans and battalion surgeon Byron Holley, through accounts by doctors who treated both American combatants and Vietnamese civilians in less dangerous areas, to Ronald Glasser's narratives of the patients he treated as a surgeon outside the warzone, receiving casualties at Camp Zanna in Japan, as well as John Parrish's *Autopsy of War*, an exploration of his post-war struggle with PTSD.

In spite of representing injury visited upon Vietnamese civilians by the American military, the memoirs tend towards a privileging of the American combatant. It is unsurprising that their emotional allegiance is to their own troops, but the focus on the American soldier would also seem to arise out of the need to retrieve his image from the narrative of murder and rape employed by Phibbs, and to offer a more nuanced representation. It also points to the emotions behind the impetus for writing these accounts. The psychological trauma that accompanies doctors and medics home often comes out of their caring for individuals who may be comrades. This is particularly the case for the medics and for Dr Byron Holley. The memoirs, or in Holley's case, letters, are written as an outlet for emotion, to explain their experience to themselves as well as to others, and as a confession for which they desire absolution; as they do so they position the American combatant as voiceless, one for whom they must speak. Doctors like Hassan also manage to direct our attention to the voiceless Vietnamese civilians. Others such as Carl Bartecchi, in *A Doctor's Vietnam Journal*,[15] try to retrieve something positive from the horrific nature of the war by looking for an affirmation in their bringing medical care to the Vietnamese.

Hassan's opening nightmare points to the problem of communication. The problem is inherent to all war experience, but for Vietnam veterans is claimed as particular to that war for reasons pointed out by Glasser in *365 Days*: 'There is no novel in Nam, there is not enough for a plot, nor is there really any character development. If you survive 365 days without getting killed or wounded you simply go home and take up again where you left off.'[16] He concludes: 'my wish is not that I had never been in the Army, but that that book could never have been written.'[17] What Glasser suggests here is what Mary Borden, writing in the First World War, identifies as the fragmentary and ultimately untellable nature of the experience of the wartime hospital. There is always that which 'can never be written'. Conventional narrative cannot capture it and those who carry the burden of witness would prefer never to have had the experience they must try and articulate. Like Borden, Glasser calls the segments of experience that make up his memoir 'sketches', and confronts the dilemma inherent in writing about this war:

'Why write anything?' Peterson said. 'Who wants to be reminded?'
    There are no veteran's clubs for this war. ... For those who haven't been there or are too old to go it's as if it doesn't count. ... Only the eighteen-, nineteen-, and twenty year olds have to worry, and since no one listens to them it doesn't matter.
        ...
    Perhaps Peterson's right. And if he is, then everything is a bit closer to what Herbert said when he woke up in the recovery room and found they'd taken off his leg. 'Fuck you – fuck you one and all.'[18]

The individuals who fight war are politically powerless; their stories do not count as part of the larger American narrative, and for those uninvolved the war is diminished to the images on a television screen. The problem of articulation exists as much at the level of language as structure or narrative. The collapse of a language that can convey what the war means to those who suffered it is summarised in Herbert's comment. Can anything more be said but 'fuck you one and all'? As we note in the Introduction, Kali Tal asserts that it is not the lack of language to describe the experience that is behind the inability to articulate it, but the breakdown in meaning between signifier and what is signified: 'Traumatic experience catalyzes a transformation of meaning in the signs individuals use to represent their experiences. Words such as *blood, terror, agony* and *madness* gain new meaning, within the context of the trauma, and survivors emerge from the traumatic environment with a new set of definitions.'[19]

If, given this breakdown in meaning that Tal defines, the only retelling by the soldier can be 'fuck you', then Glasser, who listens to the war stories, must try to reconstruct them both for themselves and to bring their voices to the larger public. To tell his Vietnam story then, is to tell the stories of the men and one woman, a nurse, who are his patients, noting that initially there was no thought of putting these sketches on paper, for that is what they are – sketches, not finished stories. I did not start writing for months, and even then it was only to tell what I was seeing and being told, maybe to give something to these kids that was all theirs without doctrine or polemics, something they could use to explain what they might not be able to explain themselves.[20]

Taking it on himself to tell these stories is arguably Glasser's making himself accountable as the impersonal 'they' who have removed Herbert's leg.

Like medical personnel and combatants before him, Glasser thus takes on the burden of speaking for the troops; his experience is integrated into theirs to the point where he is almost entirely absent from the narrative or there only as an impersonal medical force. It is only in his sketches of the patients that we see his experience reflected back. His words at the end of his comment above strikingly resemble those by the First World War poet Wilfred Owen. Writing to his mother on his return to France in October 1918 he says: 'I came out in order to help these boys – directly by leading them as well as an officer can; indirectly, by watching their sufferings that I may speak of them as well as a pleader can.'[21] Speaking the 'suffering' is central to these doctors' and medics' accounts and informs the struggle to communicate. It is, as for Owen, less the desire to tell one's own story than to plead on behalf of others.[22]

Glasser's introduction points to the narrative problems inherent in communicating the 'suffering' in a war that seems impossible to represent. For Parrish, as already noted, a single telling of the war was not enough: 'Despite numerous attempts, for more than forty years, I have not been able to stop writing and rewriting my war story. I don't know why. Primarily I persist because I can't get it right.'[23] The problem is common to war experience more generally: how to communicate to those outside war an experience they can never fully understand. In *12, 20 & 5*, Parrish goes outside straight reportage using an unbidden dream-state that comes during his tour of Vietnam to reach towards the overwhelming sense of helplessness at the absurdity of war where the only response can be 'why?':

Each young man wore a dark, three-piece suit, a dark tie, white gloves, and black shoes. They did not notice my approach. Their pupils were widely dilated. … Some had missing arms or legs. One had a missing head.

…

'Excuse me, son,' I said to the young man closest to me. … 'Your leg is missing.'

'Why?' he said.

…

I encountered another group of boys in white dinner jackets. Their bodies had great holes in them, and their black pants were torn. Each boy had
blood on his chest and shoulders.

'You boys are all badly hurt!' I blurted out.

They looked at me as if I had told them some surprising news.

'Why?' they said.

I turned to run back, but the path had become an eight-lane superhigh-
way. It was filled with elderly women – thousands of them. Each lovingly
cradled a small bundle covered with a flowered baby blanket. Filing past
me, each carefully exposed her burden – an arm, a leg, a foot, a hand, or a
head. Some carried torn Vietnamese babies.

They showed me their precious packages with smiles of pride. They were
surprised and hurt if I showed any disgust and shock. Each pointed to her
beloved object and said 'Why?'[24]

Parrish ends his dream-hallucination with the image of a bored couple in
America switching off their television: 'And with a loud snap the whole
world became black and quiet. "Somebody will have to tell them," I said.
"Someone has to tell them what this war is all about." '[25] Parrish's dream
brings together his sense of responsibility for the wounds of these 'boys',
with the helpless witnessing of massive damage to the human body that
is beyond his control. The repeated question 'Why?', as in Van Devanter's
post-war dreams, emphasises the lack of purpose behind the war, the ability of those at home literally to switch off and, in the face of such indifference, his own urgent responsibility: 'Someone will have to tell them.'

The urgency behind this telling means, in addition to representing
injury, representing the soldiers as 'boys'. Their extreme youth – they
are often portrayed as little more than children – becomes a mechanism
by which Parrish and other memoirists represent them as victims of the
military-political system that exploits their voicelessness by sending them
to war and treating them as expendable. As already noted, Glasser begins
his reflection on the absence of a war narrative by considering the lack of
both voice and audience for those eighteen- and nineteen-year-olds who
fight the war. To address an absence which is complicit in the continuing
'injuring', he creates a narrative with them at the centre, asserting of the
young men he treated in Camp Zanna in Japan:

Growing up in a hypocritical adult world and placed in the middle of a
war that even the dullest of them find difficult to believe in, much less die
for, very young and vulnerable, they are suddenly tapped not for their

selfishness or greed but for their grace and wisdom, not for their brutality, but for their love and concern.[26]

And later, in a sentence that could as easily be used to describe the tone of much First World War writing, he presents a world of suffering and death 'where the young are suddenly left alone to take care of the young'.[27]

The youth of the patients is a dominant trope in the narrative of injury as it is represented in these accounts. As already noted, if, like the medical personnel in other wars, bearing witness means the 'owning' of injury, then Glasser's description of what that means is echoed by many other doctors: 'the stark reality of it – not just a sick patient, but a dying healthy kid who's just been blown apart'.[28] As a paediatrician, Glasser confronts the damage done to the 'child's' body:

> to save one child is to save the whole thing.
>
> But to save him only to see him blown apart or blinded, to help him grow properly only to have his spinal cord transected, or to have him burned to death, puts all effort in doubt; the vaccines, the pediatric research, the new techniques and the endless concern – suddenly it all seemed so foolish, so hopeless. To lose a child at any time along his life, is really to lose the whole thing ...
>
> Literally thousands of boys were saved. But the effort had its price; after a while it began to seem so natural, even the blind seventeen-year-olds stumbling down the hallway, or the shattered high school football player being wheeled to physical therapy.[29]

The emphasis on the youth of dead and wounded Americans that positions the soldier as a pawn in the larger political morass of the war is a constant preoccupation in these accounts, one that identifies it as a major contribution to the doctors' emotional stress. After a mass casualty Peter Caldwell records signing the graves registration: 'There were 18 – all young, all very much alive this morning, and now suddenly gone.'[30] Parrish opens his description of his arrival in Vietnam with the image of damaged youth: 'On the first stretcher lay a boy whom earlier in the day any coach would have wanted as a tackle or defensive end.'[31] His work becomes defined by these wounded 'boys': 'Everyday – all day – we saw wounded American boys who had been intact and healthy earlier in the day and who now were mangled, bleeding, torn, and dying – the cost in bodies, the debt in minds.'[32] Lunati likewise draws attention to 'the majority of these soldiers [who] were young, very, very young – kids'.[33] Parrish writes that on his return home he responded to questions about his war experience by telling people, 'I started each day examining recently dead teenagers'.[34]

The overall sense of futility inherent in this war is compounded by the witnessing of these young deaths. Even where individuals try to impose meaning at the immediate level of treating injury and illness, it becomes increasingly difficult to maintain. As Glasser writes, '[w]ar's maximum efficiency is the reduction of twenty years and one hundred sixty pounds into a telegram and a statistic.'[35] Medic Ben Sherman sums up his first Vietnam duties in the morgue: 'Repeatedly before me, on a cold stainless steel table, lay the one common denominator of escalated conflict: dead bodies. No matter what provokes nations to war upon each other – land, oil, trade, religion – this bagging of boys is as fundamental to war as a haiku is to poetry. / *High speeding metal / Slamming through muscle and bone / How war begins, ends.*'[36] [original italics] These writers struggle with their position as carers whose very presence makes them complicit in this destruction of youth. 'If I allowed myself to think beyond the immediate task the sense of waste was overwhelming – nineteen-year old bodies with firm muscles and years of learning.'[37] Parrish might have heeded the warning by Mary Borden from over sixty years earlier: 'It didn't do to think.' And, like Borden, the thinking that might arouse emotion plays no role in the immediate instance: 'I barely had time to experience any of my emotions, much less express them.'[38]

Such an emphasis on youth reflects the concerns we have found in the Vietnam nurses' accounts where the soldiers are seen as kid brothers and high-school football players. The travesty of the war from the American side at least, is the killing of boys. Van Devanter's symbolic dream of the American mothers carrying the bodies of their sons through the streets is reflected in the actual experience represented by these doctors and medics. Their emphasis, as we have seen in Glasser's representation of the young left alone to care for the young, suggests their abandonment by state and family to the horror of war. As the nurse takes on the burden of surrogate mother, so the doctor must take on the responsibility of bearing witness on their behalf that comes with the role of surrogate father.

Parrish's nightmarish scenes quoted earlier imply that 'telling' includes not just the story of those who are injured, but the psychological effect on those who participate in their care. As we have seen in earlier discussion, acknowledging one's own psychological wounding is especially problematic for those in a profession which stresses the need for control and detachment. Glasser, who in exploring the difficulty in creating a narrative structure out of the Vietnam War uses a collection of 'sketches' that are the voices of his patients rather than himself, points to this difficulty. Hassan and Parrish foreground the damage war visits on soldiers and civilians; as they acknowledge their own pain they at the same time recognise the professional pressure to keep it silent. Treating wounded civilians at Quang Tri, Hassan admits '[a]fter work, the thought of all the dying and wounded left me profoundly shaken, crying silently to myself in the early morning hours'.[39] He speaks of '[weeping] with agony and exhaustion' while at the same time stressing that 'I was a surgeon and I could not let these things affect me'.[40] Later he asserts what others imply but do not often state directly: 'A torment sticks in your soul when you have witnessed the wholesale destruction of human beings.'[41] This image of a private hidden emotion says much about the relationship between the culture of stoicism and the professional detachment needed to cope on a daily basis as a doctor in war that we have also seen in doctors' writing from the two world wars. While such detachment is necessary to save lives, the unwillingness to show emotion or to engage in forms of debriefing outside the actual practice, meant that there was no direct professional context in which individuals could deal with the stress of work. As in earlier wars, doctors needed to find sources of resilience within themselves; however, these doctors admit us into situations which threaten to overwhelm their coping ability in the immediate term and persist as the lasting legacy of their work. As noted in the Introduction, Charles Figley's outlining of the stresses carried by a medic with PTSD with whom he worked can equally be applied to the wartime surgeon: 'by the pain and suffering he experienced from treating those in harm's way; by the guilt he felt each time one of his patients died; by being obsessed with reacting quickly enough to save lives'.[42] The tension between the need to sustain an emotional detachment and the point at which the 'torment' becomes so intense that it breaks through the detachment in an expression of the extreme anguish which we have seen expressed by Mary Borden and Lynda Van Devanter, is represented in Lunati's *Time Never Heals*. Initially, he writes, 'I kept my feelings to myself, not letting on to others and not wanting my frame of mind to trouble them'.[43] Yet one particular death pushes Lunati past his ability to remain stoically silent. Confronted by the friendly fire death of 'another young American',

> I could feel strong emotions, rage, sadness, confusion welling up within me. I had never felt such rage before and … it consumed me. … My hands clenched into fists … I raised my fists to the heavens and screamed at God …

Words and spittle flew from my mouth as I screamed and vented into
the jungle ...
'Listen to me! You're supposed to be the God of love. I demand that you
stop all this killing; this foolish nonsense, this senseless waste. Stop this
now ... Stop it! Stop it all.'
... I fell on my knees from both frustration and fatigue. Anguish and despair devastated me. ... The events of the last few months and especially this
day and night tore at my heart and tortured me.[44]

The accounts discussed here are all attempts to exert control over this
frustration, anger and helplessness at the deaths and injuries of soldiers
and civilians the medical personnel treat, to convey the uncontrollable
nature of the experience, and to bear witness to what they see.

Lunati's rage is momentary; he must return to a calm, professional
detachment if he is to care for the wounded, but Parrish, in *Autopsy of
War*, takes us into the aftermath of the war experience and the ongoing
psychological damage wrought by that experience. In looking back at
his war and post-war experience from a distance, he succinctly summarises how the doctor's immediate dilemma in a mass casualty situation
reflects the larger tensions between professional control and the underlying emotional narrative: 'Rapid, scientific and professional appraisal
of the torn bodies replaced responses to the emotional tug of an out-
stretched hand or a trembling cry. All the doctors knew that the greatest compassion was expressed by efficiency.'[45] This need for professional
detachment necessarily extended outside the actual work. Avoidance
becomes the primary means of coping. Parrish writes that 'off time
involved discussion of injuries and procedures or even jokes [which]
replaced any serious debriefings or discussions of an individual doctor's
fear or response to horror.'[46] Acknowledging their own and others' psychological fragility many years later allows Parrish and the other writers
discussed here a 'debriefing' that addresses that avoidance by confronting the emotions it represented.[47]

While some medical personnel appear to have maintained the necessary avoidance and distance during their tour, only to suffer from the
trauma post-war, others reveal how the constant treating of casualties,
whether American or civilian Vietnamese, especially in the context of
physical danger, wears down the psychological defences needed on a
day-to-day basis, so that resilience becomes more and more difficult to
maintain. Such a pattern is apparent in Byron Holley's letters to his wife,
published as *Vietnam 1968–1969: A Battalion Surgeon's Journal*.[48] Not
only does Holley's role as battalion surgeon mean he comes to know the

men he cares for as comrades and hence is much closer to them emotionally than a doctor working in an evacuation hospital would have
been, but in 'humping the boonies [going on patrol]' with them he is, as
he writes 'fifty-percent doctor and anywhere from fifty to one hundred
percent soldier depending on circumstance'.[49] Holley's letters give a vivid
account of the stress and danger that were a part of his role. In particular, his relationship with the soldiers means that he is unable to maintain
the detachment that would protect him emotionally. Arriving in Vietnam
on 17 October 1968, a few days later Holley is assigned as surgeon to
the 4/39th Infantry Battalion at a forward aid station near Dong Tram.
Writing to his wife on 19 December 1968 he describes the wounds and
deaths of these 'kids' and his attendant feelings:

> I had a bad day today. I had to dust-off six seriously wounded boys with
> a variety of booby-trap injuries. One, a real nice kid from Alabama, had
> a fragment of steel pierce his skull, and a large piece of gray matter was
> protruding. God, how do you fix that out in the boonies, or even in the
> OR? ... One poor kid had a fractured tibia and was shot right through the
> genitals. Baby, most people have no idea of the hell these young kids are
> going through over here while those SOBs in Paris argue about the shape
> of the damn conference table.
>   Darling, I still feel like I am the same Byron, but I can't help getting
> bitter towards the Viet Cong when I see so many of America's young
> men being blown up, killed, and maimed. I would get immense pleas-
> ure from killing a VC [Viet Cong]. It's something you have to live with
> to fully understand. Seeing the last breath of life leave a young GI, I just
> stand there, feeling so damned empty, and helpless ... and sad. [original
> ellipses][50]

In January 1969 that emotional connection comes so much closer when
he must try and save the life of his friend, Corporal Rollins. Holley
describes in detail the three-and-a-half-hour surgery to try and repair
Rollins's injuries. Here, he loses the detachment normally crucial for a
surgeon in his position:

> I looked over at the window of the OR door and was surprised to see eight
> of our good buddies looking over each other's shoulders, crowded around
> the small porthole of a window. I just shook my head and looked down
> as I felt the tears well up in my eyes. They dripped down into my friend's
> chest cavity as I struggled to maintain my composure. ... Not Corporal
> Rollins, our own John Wayne ... One of America's finest, dead at nineteen.
> He would have been a star on anybody's football team. ... My heart aches
> for his mom and dad who are probably at this very moment preparing for

his homecoming. [He had less than a week to go.] Oh God, how senseless it all is! When will it ever end?'[51]

On 29 January he again reiterates the emotional stress of knowing 'so many of them. To see them all blown up, it's so pitiful.'[52] Preparing to meet his wife on leave in Hawaii in March he tells her, 'Baby, I'm still a little concerned about how I will seem to you. I know I've changed some. … I've had so many casualties brought in to my little aid station at Giao Duc. I know most of them well, and I can tell you it's getting through to me. It's breaking my heart. A little bit of you dies each time you see one of your friends mangled, killed or mutilated.'[53]

In his later memoir, *Vietnam: A Battalion Surgeon Returns*, Holley notes that at a certain point he stopped referring to individuals by name in his letters as unconscious avoidance: 'By the time Rick [Hudson – one of his medics] was wounded I was so burned out I didn't mention anybody's name in my letters to Sondra which shows just how powerful the mind is when it decides to bury unpleasant memories.'[54] This is the detachment we see throughout medical personnel accounts that allows an individual to function in the immediate term, and it is clear in reading Holley's letters that he is able to maintain the detachment until the danger is past and he can let down his guard. At the same time he is aware that he will not be able to maintain it indefinitely. On his arrival back from leave with the prospect of his transfer to an evacuation hospital he tells his wife, 'I don't feel like I can take another six months of seeing so many good friends killed and mutilated. At least at the evac hospital the casualties will be unknown to me. It hurts so much more when they are boys you have lived with, laughed with, and cried with, day and night for months on end.'[55] In April, waiting for his transfer, he confesses, 'I do worry about the effect all this killing and dying and sorrow has had on me. I may come home without any visible scars, but I can assure you there are many scars way down deep inside me that may never heal.'[56] Notably, once he is transferred to a safer, less stressful environment, his psychological fragility becomes increasingly apparent. He tells her that he feels 'like I am held together by Scotch Tape and would fall apart if somebody shook me real hard. … I feel like I am going to burst out crying over nothing.'[57] Yet at the same time he admits trying 'to put on a facade of happiness.'[58] While Holley is never wounded in spite of spending six months in a dangerous combat environment, he writes to Sondra towards the end of his tour that he 'may not have a Purple Heart … but I am coming home with a bruised and broken heart'.[59] The comparison with Wilfred Owen's 'foreheads of men have bled where no wounds were' is inevitable here. Holley's private acknowledgement to his wife, so astutely captured in his image of feeling 'held together by Scotch Tape', reveals the wounds that are hidden by his outer 'facade'. Those hidden psychological wounds compel his return to Vietnam years later. As he writes in his opening dedication to the memoir of his return, '[o]f those who survived the war to return home physically, very few were able to come back emotionally. This book is written to and for those people, who like myself, tried to hide their Vietnam experience in a closet.'[60] Holley's very direct reflections on his state of mind illustrate the difficulty in defining resilience: holding oneself together enough to perform adequately may not equate to resilience; rather, it may be a form of psychological survival that is revealed to be temporary: once the individual leaves the stressful environment the traumatic response becomes increasingly evident.

In combat the job of medical personnel at all levels is 'to preserve the fighting strength', yet, as we have seen throughout this book, the cold detachment this phrase implies does not reflect the emotional demands of what it means in practice. Doctors treating patients they do not know work to maintain an emotional distance, but this becomes virtually impossible for surgeons like Byron Holley or medics who serve together with combatants in a particular unit. Medics Daniel Evans (who served with Byron Holley) and Charles Kinney, who treat wounded comrades in the field, very much reflect Holley's description of the emotional toll exacted by his closeness to the wounded and dead. Yet the struggle between such detachment and the underlying reality of an emotional connection with friends that we have seen in Holley's letters is perhaps even more central to the experience of medics. The bravery of medics is constantly reiterated in the doctors' memoirs. In his foreword to Evans's account, Colonel David Hackworth, commander of his unit, writes: 'There is no job in the insanity of close combat that requires more bravery, steadfastness and coolness under fire than that of combat medic. Medics go into the very center of the hell-storm of battle – where grunt has fallen and where the enemy waits to strike again – and perform major and minor miracles.'[61] The professional demands in the immediate instance are thus ones that require emotional detachment. Ben Sherman, faced with his first casualty in the field, remembers the words of his instructor at Fort Sam Houston: ' "You *will* do that *well!* I be-*lieve* you. And you *will* do everything you learned here – [...] you will do *everything* abso-*lute*-ly perfect." [...] "And you will do *all* of these things with tears in your eyes ... and your stomach in your throat" '[62] [original italics; our ellipses in square brackets]. Evans tells us, 'making friends on the line carried a high price'.[63]

Yet in spite of allowing us to see his own emotion underlying the professional care, that emotion is bound up with Evans's concern for his comrades rather than for himself. His detailed narrative of one particular incident shows what this means emotionally, and also demands that we reflect back on Glasser's comment about medics where 'the young are left alone to take care of the young': 'They are suddenly tapped not for their selfishness and greed but for their grace and wisdom, not for their brutality but for their care and concern.'[64]

> I was the medic. The Doc. My men needed me. I couldn't let them suffer while I watched, booby traps or not.
>
> An initial medical assessment told me Dale's condition was much worse than Gauerke's. Shrapnel from the mine had shredded both lower legs. Blood and greenish bowel material oozed from deep lacerations in his abdominal cavity; his intestinal tract had been punctured. There was a ragged hole the size of my finger through his neck and esophagus. As if this wasn't enough, the center of his left hand had been blown out, leaving shards of bone and dangling tendons and nerves exposed. The fingers twitched spasmodically.
>
> I crooned reassurances as I worked over him. I pretended this was some stranger, a soldier from another outfit. I didn't want to see the farm boy lying there suffering and perhaps dying. It couldn't be Dale. Not my Dale who always took out photographs of his prize porkers to show to the cherries, not the farm boy with whom I had eaten and slept and shared Vietnam experiences so personal that only those of us who lived them would ever understand them. A Doc had to rise above his emotions. A Doc must never let his tears show.[65]

Evans's narrative begins with a detached medical assessment. In spite of the graphic representations of injury, emotion only begins to emerge as he describes treating Dale. 'I crooned reassurances' evokes the relationship between the two – the image is maternal, caring. He is not just treating wounds, but offering moral support. As the narrative progresses he reveals an increasing closeness. The very attempt to detach himself from the emotions of treating a friend reveals the impossibility of doing so, 'It couldn't be Dale. Not my Dale', using a first name rather than a last name or more commonly amongst troops, a nickname. The tone moves from maternal to big brother, and then to the deep emotional ties that define the intense intimate relationship born of shared combat experience: 'experiences so personal that only those who lived them would ever understand them.'[66] He ends the paragraph with the emotional demands: 'A Doc had to rise above his emotions. A Doc must never let his tears show.' The statement itself, of course, communicates the mental effort involved in hiding, as opposed to not feeling, emotion. A few days after the episode with Dale Gass, again with his platoon under fire, Evans goes to treat a wounded man 'lying directly in front of an enemy bunker'.[67] 'I recalled what Doc Holley had told me that time when I walked point, about how most Medals of Honor were awarded posthumously. He had also said no one would think less of me if I didn't try to reach the wounded under fire. *But that was my man out there, hurt. A medic had no choice*'[68] [our italics].

For the medic, ownership of his role is everything – it demands self-sacrifice. As Evans's introduction notes, over 1,300 medics were killed during the war.[69] The ownership extends to those of his platoon who have been killed or wounded: 'Doc Whitmore had warned me … not to become personal friends with the troops, but he knew I wouldn't follow his advice. And I hadn't. Grunts who were no longer with the platoon were now lined up wearing their bloody bandages as they marched through my mind. I saw their faces.'[70] Evans lists their names and then muses on the burden of witness he must carry as a medic: 'What was it I had thought to prove when I volunteered for this … How to watch your friends die in the sun?'[71]

Medic Charles Kinney offers advice to medics in the preface to his memoir that defines the combat-medic persona: 'To survive you must save the sorrow and tears for later … gathering and tucking these memories away', while acknowledging that 'the memories become the baggage you will carry with you for the rest of your life'.[72] For Ben Sherman the emotional weight of his first casualty cannot be tucked away. In a situation that echoes *Catch-22*, he treats an entry wound before realising that the soldier is losing most of his blood through a large exit wound. Sherman is unable to save him. His narrative details the sorrow and guilt that pursue him afterwards:

> Walking in the rear, I shuddered and sobbed and tried to mute my choking, until darkness and a ten degree drop in temperature eased my lament. Drying my eyes and biting the inside of my cheek, with each step I fought the urge to collapse in tears.
>
> The look and feel of my hand full of sticky blood returned. It was like Lady Macbeth's 'damned spot' and the bucketload of blood that haunted her into madness … I felt the caked blood on my pants, against my thigh, sticking and releasing with every step.[73]

Even as Kinney advises on how to survive psychologically, his account explores the cost of that immediate term survival: 'it would be 36 years before I would be able to completely give voice to all that I experienced and felt during my time in Vietnam.'[74] The actual process of returning to his memories and writing about them, rather than being therapeutic, has catalysed a traumatic response:

> For many years now, I have skated on the edge of losing my sanity. ... In writing this book ... I've had to peel back my protective cover and let all these memories of war flow back into my consciousness. It has been the most emotionally painful experience of my life. Now I fear that I may not be able to tuck away the memories and nightmares again.[75]

His emotional pain arises directly out of the loss of his friends from Vietnam: 'there are so many souls "on the other side" whom I still love, treasure, and desire to see again, that some days my loneliness for them is almost unbearable.'[76] As we note in Chapter 5, Chaim Shatan identifies such grief as inherent to the war experience, but notes that it is often 'unconsummated' and thus 'impacted', contributing to PTSD: 'The "post-Vietnam syndrome" confronts us with the unconsummated grief of soldiers – "impacted grief" in which an unending, encapsulated past robs the present of meaning. Their sorrow is unspent, the grief of their wounds is untold, their guilt is unexpiated.'[77] Sherman's description of his visit to the Wall in 1985 at the end of his memoir, where he looks for the name of his first casualty, enacts this grief, although there is little to suggest that the visit does more than allow him to express his emotion.

> I returned to the wall to find the panel and line, and I found his name about face high ... On the pavement, leaning my forehead against the ebony wall, I sobbed as I remembered my palm soaked with blood from his exit wound, the same palm now clutching a rubbing of his name ... I just yearned so deeply that it hadn't happened. I wanted more than anything to get that day back. I didn't know him, we had never spoken, but he mattered to me.[78]

Holley, Evans, Kinney and Sherman all articulate multiple and complex psychological responses to the war experience, especially the profound sadness at the loss of intimate comrades. Doing so means uncovering what, even long after the events, may still be raw emotional wounds. These losses are particularly painful when they are the result of a futile and absurd war rather than one that could be constructed in terms of a greater good. The euphemism 'wasted' which was used by the troops to describe death in Vietnam also, of course, included the attitude towards their deaths in the war itself, especially in the last two or three years. Moreover, the grunts coping phrase, 'it don't mean nothin' likewise says much about how the war was experienced at the level of the individual soldier on the line.

It is arguable that the psychological aftermath is more severe when a war loses the veneer of just cause, but it is also in this context that we find individuals more willing to reveal their psychic damage. It is striking that the war which has always been touted as 'good', the Second World War, is the most silent on its psychological pain. The complete loss of moral certainty that informs writing from the Vietnam War can find no meaning in death. It thus more often finds connection with the disillusionment represented by many writers in the aftermath of the First World War.[79] It is not surprising then, but coincidentally noteworthy, that Parrish, at the Marine Headquarters in Da Nang, recounts how

> one day in a desk drawer I found a handwritten statement
> > Finished With the War
> > A Soldier's Declaration
> I am making this statement as an act of wilful defiance of military authority, because I believe the war is being deliberately prolonged by those who have the power to end it. ... On behalf of those who are suffering now I make this protest ... I believe that I may help to destroy the callous complacency with which the majority of those at home regard the continuance of agonies which they do not share.[80]

Not recognising poet and writer Siegfried Sassoon's famous open letter to *The Times* from the First World War, Parrish's 'first thought was that this declaration had been written by the doctor I was replacing or found by him on the body of a Marine'.[81] But the date and author, 'S. Sassoon, 1917', are written at the bottom. Parrish copies it into his notebook but only later learns who Sassoon was. The immediate relevance of Sassoon's statement to Parrish's own feelings about the war again draws attention to the connection between these two wars that Lifton points to in *Home from the War*, and that becomes increasingly apparent as we read these accounts side-by-side in this discussion. Noting that First World War recollections come closest to those from the Vietnam War, Lifton asks that 'we keep constantly in mind a dialectic between the specificity of the Vietnam War and its relationship to all war. As always, the particular is the only path to the general, but cannot itself be comprehended outside of the general.'[82]

Soldiers, doctors, nurses, medics, all confronting the seeming pointlessness of the war, whether the First World War or the Vietnam War, thus reflect each other as we have seen earlier in the chapter. Struggling with ways to survive the emotional burden that comes with witnessing these deaths and injuries for no cause, Glasser's *365 Days* confronts the reality of the combatant lot in a war of attrition that has much in common with the war Sassoon condemned as he wrote his famous protest. Glasser concludes his collection of sketches with the narrative of a patient dying of burns:

> That's the great thing I learned .... His death is expected. It is expected since there are 80 percent burns, and it is expected that 80 percent will become septic. The whole thing is expected. You're supposed to get burned in Nam; you're supposed to get your legs blown off; you're supposed to get your chopper shot down; you're supposed to get killed. It's just not something that happens. It's expected.[83]

The medical diagnosis and treatment and the military operation that results in injury and death are made part of the same ideology here. While Glasser does not state it directly, this section and the larger 'sketch' 'I don't want to go home alone' of which it is a part, explore the way the doctor becomes complicit in further injuring and causing pain to a dying patient by refusing to give up his increasingly pointless intervention. The patient goes from being the pawn of the military to the pawn of the doctor because neither can see him as a suffering human being. While there is no evidence that Glasser read Borden, the exploration of the doctor's complicity in furthering the injury caused by war and similarly violating the human body is strikingly similar to her writing – the war inflicts pain and injury; the doctors inflict further pain and injury.[84]

The accounts discussed so far are by doctors and medics who primarily treated American troops. Doctors played various roles. Some cared for American troops and also volunteered to treat civilians in what were known as MEDCAP visits to outlying villages. Other doctors such as Peter Caldwell, Allan Hassan and Carl Bartecchi treated both soldiers and civilians in American facilities, but developed particularly close emotional ties with the civilians they cared for. When these individuals' accounts are set beside the intimate relationship with the troops that we find in writings by medics such as Evans and Kinney or surgeon Byron Holley and the weight of sorrow and grief at the death of close comrades they carry, the experiences may appear to be radically different, yet, as we have already seen in Hassan's memoir, the narratives are interdependent. Bartecchi begins his memoir by noting how, within the 'turmoil and chaos of the war [p]ositive existed … though insufficient to balance the negatives'.[85] Although he acknowledges the corruption that characterised USAID, something Patricia Walsh writes about at length in *River City*, he also felt that his aid to civilians exerted some positives in an otherwise negative situation. Peter Caldwell, in *Bac-Si: A Doctor Remembers Vietnam*, records that the sense of achievement in treating civilians (including repairing a hare-lip on a small child) helped balance the sorrow and stress of treating mass battle casualties.[86] The emphasis on relationships with civilian Vietnamese, especially children, is borne out by the many photographs of children in his book and, of course, by the title itself, Bac-Si being the form of Vietnamese address that honours the doctor. Of his MEDCAP ventures Caldwell writes:

> Any session of triage after a couple of chopper loads of DMZ area casualties arrived left us drained, depressed and filled with sadness at having to do such a job. Working with the civilians, we were sometimes able to balance the mental efforts of such devastating destruction by participating in some healing and constructive treatment which was good therapy for us as well as our patients.[87]

Yet overall Caldwell's memoir struggles to place the positive to the fore. Resilience becomes, for him as for others, a conscious detachment: 'Even after eleven months of it, there was no getting hardened to the devastating sights. You just had to put yourself on a kind of numb automatic pilot and do the best that you could under the circumstances.'[88] Like Caldwell, Bartecchi looks to find a way of constructing his time in Vietnam as positive through his accounts of aid to the Vietnamese civilian population. In particular he gives time and expertise to an orphanage at Soc Trang. Even though the MEDCAP missions were of dubious design politically, created out of a desire to 'win hearts and minds', doctors like Bartecchi felt that they were making a difference at a micro level. In contrast, Parrish, much more cynically, represents his own scepticism in *12, 20 & 5*. After a MEDCAP visit he records an exchange with a fellow doctor, where Parrish begins by saying, 'We may as well try to help though. As long as we are over here', but is interrupted by his counterpart, 'We can help them the most by not being here in the first place'.[89]

In spite of the attempts to offer some positive representations of medical help, all of the medical personnel discussed here carry the burden of a war where the casualties they care for, American and Vietnamese, are representations of its pointlessness. Writers such as Parrish, who confesses to a need to write and rewrite compulsively, or Byron Holley who must return to Vietnam and write a further memoir in order to gain some control over his past, show the lasting effect the war had on those who cared for the injured. At the same time, however, as Hunt notes, war experience is paradoxical: it can be defined by futility and post-traumatic stress, while at the same time being the most fulfilling and most import-ant experience of an individual's life. These doctors' and medics' accounts demonstrate the extent to which those conflicting responses make up that experience. Thus Daniel Evans can write of the sense of futility he felt watching 'his friends die in the sun' while at the same time acknowledging the intensity that came out of the paradoxical nature of the experience. In the concluding chapter of his memoir, Evans quotes one former medic:

> The Vietnam experience was so intense, so nerve-wracking, and so prob-ing, it dissected your brain and really made you aware of who you were as a person. It exposed all of your strengths and weaknesses. ... For all of the good and bad (mostly bad) I experienced in Vietnam, I never knew any other feelings equal to the ones I felt when I was able to save someone's life.[90]

Evans's response to his own experience is contradictory:

> My tour of duty as a combat medic was by far the most rewarding part of my life. I never had nightmares about Vietnam, but for many years I couldn't go to sleep at night until I relived every second of March 25, 1969. I was convinced that because I didn't die that day I didn't do enough, and the only logical explanation for that would come under the category of cowardice.[91]

For Evans the guilt of not doing enough in one particular action out-weighs the lives he has saved. His need to remember more generally is reinforced in the conclusion of his memoir which ends with a list of 'KIAs: 4/39th Infantry Unit'. It is his private memorial to his dead made public in the act of telling. Yet he does not seem willing or able to con-front the complexity of the issue he raises: the paradox whereby the war can give the medic's life intense meaning and, at the same time, an anx-iety and guilt that refuse to leave him. Similar elements of this contra-diction are voiced by Caldwell in remembering the day he left Vietnam:

> The long-awaited moment turned out to be quite a let down for me – even a strange kind of sadness ... I seemed to know that part of it was the know-ledge that the excitement and intensity of living fairly close to the edge would be gone. In addition, I was surprised to find strong feelings of some-how running out on a job where I was really needed. ... Now it was even more clear why the degree of emotional involvement in some individuals led as far as extension of tours of duty in spite of all the hazards.[92]

Guilt at not doing enough in a specific situation translates into guilt at leaving at the end of a tour. As we have seen in the previous chapter these feelings, compounded by a sense of alienation on the return home, lay behind the decision of some individuals to sign on for a second tour of duty. In addition, the sense of unfinished business compounds the psychological legacy of a war that itself had no conclusion. While telling us in his memoir that, although his first tour was only two months 'it felt like a lifetime',[93] Hassan recognises that returning to America on 4 July 1968 does not feel like a return home: 'Without quite realizing it I had developed a crop of personal demons, horrible memories of Vietnam and the atrocities I had seen. In some ways, at that time, Vietnam already seemed like my real home.'[94] Hassan returns to Vietnam to evaluate and treat injured Vietnamese children under the Committee of Responsibility in January 1969. Yet ultimately he cannot avoid confronting the legacy of his time there. The later part of his memoir explores his final return home, drawing attention not only to his own psychological damage but that of other medical personnel.

> Soldiers called the return from Vietnam to America 'back to the world'. Many doctors who went to Vietnam also experienced a profound culture shock when they returned to the United States, and some were haunted by memories of Vietnam. Dr Ralf Young, a paediatrician who helped train me when I arrived in Hue, committed suicide sometime after he returned … I was changed in a way I could not immediately understand.[95]

A qualified psychiatrist as well as a surgeon, Hassan treats Vietnam veterans with PTSD. As we have seen, his memoir brings deeply political concerns to his own knowledge of war and the psychological as well as physical damage it causes. He writes: 'If you have never been to war, any war, and seen action, you may not understand what I am saying. A torment clings to your soul.'[96] And when Hassan, like Van Devanter, voices the political need never to forget, he foregrounds not the American combatant, but the Vietnamese child:

> As a doctor, I never want to forget what I saw. It wasn't because I relished the spectacle of death and dismemberment, or had some sense of accomplishment in witnessing atrocities, or even because I felt good that I had survived it all. I want to remember the disturbing feeling of the warm blood of a child whose arm has been blown off … I want to remember surgery to open up the bellies of children looking for shrapnel and bullets, trying to save their lives, remembering the horrible moment I notice that a child's spinal cord has been severed. … Because after I experienced all this, the feeling I had

when I got back to civil society was: don't try to put one over on me. Don't try to tell me how heroic war is. ... Don't talk blandly about 'collateral damage'. Those who have experienced war have seen suffering and sorrow and death and destruction. Advocates of more and more war have not seen the dead children, or the buckets of arms and legs as you amputate feverishly, trying to save lives. A torment sticks in your soul when you have witnessed the wholesale destruction of human beings.[97]

Hassan's own trauma of treating and bearing witness to injury that he brings home thus carries important political weight. In making public his memory long after the actual events and in the context of another American war, he reinforces the importance of speaking the traumatic legacy. The insistence on replacing the euphemism of collateral damage with graphic images of injury that would disown it is also significant in Parrish's second account of his Vietnam experience, *Autopsy of War*, which deals primarily with the aftermath. In his prologue he juxtaposes intrusive flashbacks of the injuries he confronted in Vietnam with the casual discourse of collateral damage at a meeting of the Defense Science Board of which he is a new member.

[M]embers start to speak, and soon the discussion centers on how best to defeat or coerce the enemy while causing the least 'collateral damage' ...

...

Foreign civilian casualties are weighed against American civilian intolerance of their own dead and wounded soldiers. Tables and charts of costs, hearts and minds, kill zones, quantification of civilian casualties, ratios of dead women and children to total dead civilians, soldier morbidity and mortality, combat casualty care and medical evacuation time are used to compare present wars with the American War in Vietnam and other US military actions.

...

A steady stream of women and children blown apart and badly burned flows though the door as the conference room becomes a makeshift hospital. A dead baby charred black, is still warm to the touch. ... Mourning mothers cling to dead children and terrified children cling to dead mothers. ... The conference room is further transformed to a forward triage center. The smell of burned flesh causes my eyes to water ...

I cannot keep up. I have no control over the flow of casualties ...

...

Slowly the carnage retreats. Once again I begin to absorb the calm male voices around me talking about ways to wage war.[98]

Both Hassan and Parrish use their own 'torment', the images of the dead and wounded that will never leave them, to make a political point, as nurse Judy Hartline Elbring, quoted in Chapter 5, implores to 'all of the people who declared the wars, it was terrible watching your children die. You have no idea what that looks like. If you did you wouldn't have another war.'[99] While Elbring focuses on American 'children', Hassan and Parrish use images of civilian women and children to take the point further. The politics of war are not only about deaths of Americans but deaths of those designated 'other'.

As we noted in Chapter 5, post-war accounts struggle with the tension between the need to remember and bear witness as a political act – to remember is constantly to bear witness to the injury that warring states would prefer to disown – and the extent to which such remembering can be psychically destructive to the one who carries the burden of the memory. In Parrish's prologue to *Autopsy* quoted above, for example, his intrusive flashbacks are essential to his message: they need to be juxtaposed with the cold, impersonal number games and euphemism to reveal the so glibly disguised ('disowned') horror. Flashbacks and intrusive memories represent the unforgettable nature of such witnessing and the breakdown and potential breakdown that are the consequence: Lunati's screaming to God; Holley's feeling of being held together by Scotch Tape; Kinney's post-Vietnam acknowledgement that 'for many years now, I have skated on the edge of losing my sanity'.[100] They would seem to be the price paid for bearing witness to the unbearable. At the same time, all of the writers discussed here have managed to organise and control their experiences through their writing, itself an act of resilience. Yet even as the writing, the making public of their accounts, may be therapeutic, it is also psychologically dangerous. If, as Kinney tells us, 'peeling back the protective cover … has been the most emotionally painful experience of my life',[101] the re-experiencing involved in remembering puts his sanity at risk as much as the original experience. Resilience is thus not an opposing state to breakdown but held in tension with it.

The growing awareness of war trauma and the definition of PTSD in *DSM*-III in 1980 offered writers composing their accounts after that date a definition through which to view their experiences. In particular the permission, not offered to psychological casualties from other wars, to see their experience as a complex psychobiological response meant that they could confront it in themselves. Although, in these early years, PTSD was defined as a combatant issue, Hassan recognises himself in Robert Jay Lifton's now renowned work on trauma and Vietnam, *Home from the War* (1973), which predates the *DSM* definition of PTSD. For Hassan, reading Lifton 'triggered memories of my Vietnam experience, which hit me like a scream in the dark. "The witnessing of children's and old people's deaths wrote an indelible script into my psyche. Shot in the head, why?" I wrote in the margins as I was reading the book. "I can never let this be forgotten."'[102]

Hassan's response surely resonates with Glasser's assertion that

> the ethical issues facing physicians in the military have not changed since medicine came to the battlefield. It is basically the result of that conflict between the Hippocratic Oath to heal the sick and relieve suffering, and General Patton's universal and timeless speech to troops that they were not there to die for their country but to make sure that the enemy died for theirs.[103]

But Glasser does not take into account the innocent civilians that are so central to Hassan's memoir. Lifton's discussion of psychiatric (and one could construe that this applies to all medical personnel) collusion with the destruction of war takes Glasser's point further:

> For when he [the psychiatrist] serves with the military he becomes integrated with, and to a significant degree the advocate of, a group 'the aim of which' according to Bloch, is 'admittedly a very pragmatic one … to conserve the fighting strength'. Yet the psychiatrist's long-standing personal integrity is likely to be dependent upon a very different form of advocacy: that of individual well-being and larger humane principles having to do with justice and realized lives, as opposed to killing, premature dying, and especially widespread atrocity. During World War II psychiatrists experienced this integrity-integration conflict … but they could, in that war, achieve a measure of reconciliation between group integration and personal integrity through the realization that their collusion in killing and dying was in the service of combating a force that promised killing and dying on an infinitely larger and more grotesque scale.[104]

Parrish ends *12, 20 & 5* with a single death certificate. In this he gives us the pared-down medical story of an individual death which carries in it the waste of life and sorrow that it represents: one life here stands for the many that he treated and the death certificates he signed. The brevity of the factual details urges the reader to fill in the missing story. 'Date of birth: 1/19/49' and further down the list 'Date of death: 6 Jul 68'; 'Death or condition directly leading to death: Penetrating missile wounds of chest, abdomen, neck.'[105] Entering the details of a war death on what might also be a stateside death certificate presents the disjuncture between home and warzone, reinforcing the wrongness of the death of a healthy nineteen-year-old in this war. Placing it at the end of the book, Parrish offers us a comment on his own burden as the doctor who writes the certificate, caught between professional detachment and personal emotion. In his later *Autopsy of War*, Parrish tells us that he cannot stop writing his war story, but it is not until the publication of this second memoir in 2012 that he publicly confronts the psychological legacy of the war, noting of the definition 'PTSD' that 'my story begins before the term existed'.[106]

As with some of the other doctors (and the nurses' experiences discussed in Chapter 5), Parrish finds an unwilling home audience for the knowledge he brings. While he tells them that 'I started each day examining recently dead teenagers', like the home audience that silences Smith and Van Devanter, 'they didn't want the truth in detail'.[107] Parrish finds that the process of writing allows him to articulate what the home audience does not want to hear: 'writing did help. Now that I had a place where I allowed expression of my feelings, they were no longer so intrusive.'[108] Of his first draft of the work that would become *12, 20 & 5*, he notes that although 'it led me to episodes of painful grief, the structure was helpful'.[109] At the same time he struggles with the emotions that are essential to remembering and attempting to impose control over the experience. He asks: '[was it] more helpful to remain stuck in re-experiencing specific painful episodes or to work through the traumas by providing history, context, venue and outcome and the moving on. Should I pull the most painful, horrible and soul-damaging scenes and events into a story?'[110] Continually trapped in the writing and rewriting in an attempt to get the story right – 'if only I could find my voice I could explain the sadness and waste and horror that surrounded the death of each soldier'[111] – he becomes a prisoner of his own traumatic remembering. Writing thus may not be a therapeutic means of finding resilience, but a kind of entrapment in remembering. If, as Tal points out, traumatic knowledge cannot really be shared because of the collapse of meaning carried in language between those who have participated in war and those who have not, these accounts ask us to consider the dilemma inherent to traumatic remembering: is it possible to move beyond Parrish's writing and rewriting or the image of Hassan 'crying silently into the early morning hours'?[112]

Notes

1 Phibbs, *The Other Side of Time*, p. 27.
2 Robert Jay Lifton, *Home from the War: Vietnam Veterans: Neither Victims nor Executioners* (New York: Simon and Schuster, 1973), p. 100.

3 Allan Hassan, *Failure to Atone: The True Story of a Jungle Surgeon in Vietnam* (Sacramento, Calif.: Failure to Atone Press, 2006), pp. 13–14. Later in his book Hassan writes that the image of the babies persisted in his dreams, to become the focus of his post-Vietnam trauma: 'After thirty years, I realized, I still dream of lifting up the limp arm of a baby killed by a single shot to the head … I could not shake the memory of the blood-spattered hospital foyer, the horror, and the shock of all I had seen' (p. 188).

4 Hassan, *Failure to Atone*, pp. 145–6.

5 Lifton, *Home from the War*, p. 368.

6 Lifton, *Home from the War*, p. 368.

7 John Parrish, *Autopsy of War: A Personal History* (New York: Thomas Dunne Books, 2012), p. 109.

8 Lifton, *Home from the War*, p. 101.

9 Charles M. Kinney, *Borrowed Time: A Medic's View of the Vietnam War* (Victoria, BC: Trafford Publishing, 2003; 2005), p. viii.

10 Lifton, *Home from the War*, p. 100.

11 Parrish, *Autopsy*, p. xi.

12 Frank Lunati (as told to Gene Ligotti), *Time Never Heals: The Memoirs of Capt. Frank Lunati, Battalion Surgeon 2/5 1st Cavalry Division (Air Mobile) 1965–1966* (Bloomington, Ind.: Xlibris 2003).

13 Vietnam context Army medics are soldiers trained to give emergency medical treatment in the field.

14 Hassan, *Failure to Atone*, p. 182.

15 Carl E. Bartecchi, *A Doctor's Vietnam Journal* (Bennington, Vt.: Merriam Press, 2006).

16 Ronald J. Glasser, *365 Days* (New York: George Braziller, 1971), p. xii.

17 Glasser, *365 Days*, p. xii. In *Home from the War*, Lifton writes 'We may say that there was no genuine "script" or "scenario" of war that could provide meaning or even sequence or progression' (p. 38). He goes on to note that 'veterans have always come to terms with their war experience through some formulation of their survival that permits them to overcome much of their death anxiety and death guilt, diffuse suspiciousness and numbing. Crucial even to this partial resolution of survivor conflict is the veteran's capacity to believe that his war had purpose and significance beyond the immediate horrors he witnessed. He can then connect his own actions with ultimately humane principles, and can come to feel that he had performed a dirty but necessary job. … But the central fact of the Vietnam War is that no one really believes in it' (pp. 39–40).

18 Glasser, *365 Days*, p. 5.

19 Tal, *Worlds of Hurt*, p. 16.

20 Glasser, *365 Days*, p. xi.

21 Wilfred Owen, *Selected Letters*, ed. John Bell (Oxford: Oxford University Press, 1985), p. 351.

22 Lifton points out one important issue that such pleading leads to in Glasser's work. Commenting on how Glasser uses the term 'gook' as his own observation, apart from describing the soldier narrative, Lifton calls Glasser's book 'profound and honest' but also notes that [p]aradoxically, his very compassion and empathy for suffering Americans assigned to his care at an evacuation hospital in Japan propelled him toward the gook syndrome – at least in terminology and in certain moments. The extraordinary sensitivity of the book ... makes one realize that such was the pervasiveness of the gook syndrome that one could not "feel with" Americans fighting the war without entering into it' (*Home from the War*, p. 212).

23 Parrish, *Autopsy*, p. xi.

24 John Parrish, *12, 20, & 5: A Doctor's Year in Vietnam* (New York: E. P. Dutton & Co. Inc., 1972), pp. 182–3.

25 Parrish, *12, 20 & 5*, p. 188.

26 Glasser, *365 Days*, p. 53.

27 Glasser, *365 Days*, p. 54. For a discussion of this caring in the First World War see Roper, *The Secret Battle*, ch. 4, 'Learning to care'.

28 Glasser, *365 Days*, p. 55.

29 Glasser, *365 Days*, p. x.

30 Peter Caldwell, *Bac-Si: A Doctor Remembers Vietnam* (Honolulu: Taote Publishing, 1991), p. 19.

31 Parrish, *12, 20 & 5*, p. 40.

32 Parrish, *12, 20 & 5*, p. 173.

33 Lunati, *Time Never Heals*, p. 70.

34 Parrish, *Autopsy*, p. 163.

35 Glasser, *365 Days*, p. 203.

36 Ben Sherman, *Medic! The Story of a Conscientious Objector in the Vietnam War* (New York: Balantine Books, 2002), pp. 4–5.

37 Parrish, *12, 20 & 5*, p. 239.

38 Parrish, *12, 20 & 5*, p. 251.

39 Hassan, *Failure to Atone*, p. 113.

40 Hassan, *Failure to Atone*, p. 117.

41 Hassan, *Failure to Atone*, p. 183.

42 Figley, *Mapping Trauma and Its Wake*, p. 52.

43 Lunati, *Time Never Heals*, p. 24.

44 Lunati, *Time Never Heals*, p. 35.

45 Parrish, *Autopsy*, p. 306.

46 Parrish, *Autopsy*, p. 285.

47 Parrish records a doctor taking an overdose during his tour of duty (*Autopsy*, p. 114). At the end of *A Doctor's Vietnam Journal*, Carl Bartecchi notes that back in the United States he was seeing PTSD in other physicians who had served in Vietnam: 'They, too, in many cases were undiagnosed and had not sought treatment' (Bartecchi, *A Doctor's Vietnam Journal*, p. 334).

48 Dr Byron E. Holley, *Vietnam 1968–1969: A Battalion Surgeon's Journal* (Lincoln, Nebr.: An Author's Guild BackPrint Edition, 2000; Ballantine Books, 1993).

49 Holley, *Vietnam 1968–1969*, p. 68. Holley's account is primarily made up of letters he wrote to his wife during his tour in Vietnam with some letters to his parents included and occasionally some later commentary.

50 Holley, *Vietnam 1968–1969*, p. 91.

51 Holley, *Vietnam 1968–1969*, p. 110–11. Holley returns to Rollins's death in his memoir, *Vietnam: A Battalion Surgeon Returns* (New York: Writers Club Press, 2001), p. 27.

52 Holley, *Vietnam 1968–1969*, p. 114.

53 Holley, *Vietnam 1968–1969*, p. 143.

54 Holley, *Vietnam: A Battalion Surgeon Returns*, p. 24.

55 Holley, *Vietnam 1968–1969*, p. 149.

56 Holley, *Vietnam 1968–1969*, p. 153.

57 Holley, *Vietnam 1968–1969*, p. 162.

58 Holley, *Vietnam 1968–1969*, p. 162.

59 Holley, *Vietnam 1968–1969*, p. 200. This is an account of his homecoming, not a letter to his wife Sondra.

60 Holley, *Vietnam: A Battalion Surgeon Returns*, p. vii.

61 Hackworth in Daniel E. Evans Jr, DVM and Charles W. Sasser, *Doc: Platoon Medic* (Lincoln, Nebr.: Writers Club Press, 2002), p. xviii.

62 Sherman, *Medic*, p. 150; our ellipses in square brackets.

63 Evans, *Doc*, p. 107.

64 Glasser, *365 Days*, p. 53. In his 2011 work, *Broken Bodies, Shattered Minds: A Medical Odyssey from Vietnam to Afghanistan* (Palisades, NY: History Publishing Company, 2011), Glasser reiterates this 'grace', especially found in the bravery of the medics, and connects the war in Vietnam to the wars in Iraq and Afghanistan: Vietnam was 'filled with confusing stories, outright lies, terrible decisions, bizarre unexplainable and unexpected results, distortions of the truth, foolishness, stupidity, courage, bravery, and in more cases than anyone would be willing to admit, a kind of dazzling grace. And nowhere was that grace more clearly seen than in the medics' (p. 38).

65 Evans, *Doc*, p. 253.

66 'When exploring questions of intimacy, for instance, the men talked a great deal about how much they suffered when they lost close buddies, how the knowledge that 'anybody might die' would cause them to try to limit and routinize their friendships. Yet the very nature of the combat situation made such restraint impossible. As one veteran explained:

When I was cold, *everyone* was cold. We were all hungry *together*. We were *all* scared shitless. When we were out of water, we were *all* out of water.'

(Lifton, *Home from the War*, p. 267)

67 Evans, *Doc*, p. 266.
68 Evans, *Doc*, p. 266.
69 Evans, *Doc*, p. 1.
70 Evans, *Doc*, p. 283.
71 Evans, *Doc*, p. 283.
72 Kinney, *Borrowed Time*, p. viii.
73 Sherman, *Medic*, p. 155. The connection with Macbeth and guilt returns in a *Guardian* newspaper report on the suicides of American veterans of the wars in Iraq and Afghanistan.

> Libby Busbee is pretty sure that her son William never sat through or read Shakespeare's *Macbeth*, even though he behaved as though he had. Soon after he got back from his final tour of Afghanistan, he began rubbing his hands over and over and constantly rinsing them under the tap.
> 'Mom, it won't wash off,' he said.
> 'What are you talking about?' she replied.
> 'The blood. It won't come off.'
> On 20 March last year, the soldier's striving for self-cleanliness came to a sudden end. That night he locked himself in his car and, with his mother and two sisters screaming just a few feet away and with Swat officers encircling the vehicle, he shot himself in the head. (Ed Pilkington, 'US Military Struggling to Stop Suicide Epidemic among War Veterans', *The Guardian*, 1 February 2013; www.theguardian.com/world/2013/feb/01/us-military-suicide-epidemic-veteran; accessed 9 October 2014).

74 Kinney, *Borrowed Time*, p. 117.
75 Kinney, *Borrowed Time*, p. 142.
76 Kinney, *Borrowed Time*, p. 142.
77 Shatan, 'Stress Disorders', p. 51. Recent research presented in the *Guardian* article on soldier suicides connects back to Shatan's hypothesis: 'Contrary to widely held assumptions, it is not the fear and the terror that service members endure in the battlefield that inflicts most psychological damage, Nash [US Navy psychiatrist] has concluded, but feelings of shame and guilt related to the moral injuries they suffer. Top of the list of such injuries, by a long shot, is when one of their own people is killed. "I have heard it over and over again from marines – the most common source of anguish for them was failing to protect their 'brothers'. The significance of that is unfathomable, it's comparable to the feelings I've heard from parents who have lost a child"' (Pilkington, 'US Military').
78 Sherman, *Medic*, p. 282.
79 Noting that there was no overall sense of 'the war's total lack of order or structure, the feeling that there was no genuine purpose, that nothing

could ever be secured or gained, that there could be no measureable progress', Lifton suggests that any 'action' became 'part of the general absurdity, the antimeaning' (*Home from the War*, p. 38). For a longer discussion of the effect of this antimeaning on the psyche of the returning soldier see pp. 38–40.

80 Parrish, *Autopsy*, 141.

81 Parrish, *Autopsy*, 141.

82 Lifton, *Home from the War*, p. 19. See also Lifton's comparison's to First World War experience on pp. 37 and 130–1.

83 Glasser, *365 Days*, pp. 278–9.

84 See especially 'Paraphernalia' in Borden's *The Forbidden Zone*.

85 Bartecchi, *A Doctor's Vietnam Journal*, p. 15.

86 Caldwell, *Bac-Si*, pp. 19–31 and 60.

87 Caldwell, *Bac-Si*, p. 66.

88 Caldwell, *Bac-Si*, p. 120.

89 Parrish, *12, 20 & 5*, p. 70. For a useful overview of the Vietnamese–American relationship and history immediately prior to the war from the perspective of an American physician, see George Tyler, MD, *Mist over the Dong Nai: A Doctor's War in Vietnam*, privately printed by George Tyler, 1980.

90 Jim Whitmore in Evans, *Doc*, p. 314.

91 Evans, *Doc*, p. 317.

92 Caldwell, *Bac-Si*, p. 134.

93 Hassan, *Failure to Atone*, p. 115.

94 Hassan, *Failure to Atone*, p. 155.

95 Hassan, *Failure to Atone*, p. 176.

96 Hassan, *Failure to Atone*, p. 182.

97 Hassan, *Failure to Atone*, p. 183.

98 Parrish, *Autopsy*, pp. 2–4.

99 Elbring in Steinman, *Women in Vietnam*, pp. 153–4.

100 Kinney, *Borrowed Time*, p. 142.

101 Kinney, *Borrowed Time*, p. 142.

102 Hassan, *Failure to Atone*, p. 180.

103 Glasser, *Broken Bodies, Shattered Minds*, pp. 220–1. Glasser's book devotes a longer discussion to the issue of medical personnel in war.

104 Lifton, *Home from the War*, p. 416.

105 Parrish, *12, 20 & 5*, p. 312.

106 Parrish, *Autopsy*, p. xii.

107 Parrish, *Autopsy*, p. 163.

108 Parrish, *Autopsy*, p. 167.

109 Parrish, *Autopsy*, p. 167.

110 Parrish, *Autopsy*, p. 167.

111 Parrish, *Autopsy*, p. 167.

112 Hassan, *Failure to Atone*, p. 113.

7

Fatal injury

In the autobiographical writings we have discussed so far the writers primarily represent themselves as isolated in their own pain, the traumatic nature of their experience rarely acknowledged even in their own profession. As we noted in our introduction, Iraq War veteran poet Brian Turner's poem 'AB negative (The Surgeon's Poem)' is unusual in bringing us into the physician's intimate physical and emotional relationship with war injury and death:

> And an exhausted surgeon in tears,
> His bloodied hands on her chest, his head
> Sunk down, the nurse guiding him as he cries,
> To a nearby seat and holding him as he cries
> Though no one hears it'. (lines 37–41)

If the emotional experience of medical personnel has been paid scant attention in the history of warfare, loss and the grief that attends it are even more rarely acknowledged as an aspect of that experience for those whose work places them in the particular kind of intimacy with death that Turner represents. Especially, death reflects their failure to prevent injury from being fatal, the whole purpose of their presence in the warzone. This chapter examines how memoirs of medical personnel from the Iraq War construct and reconstruct injury, particularly what these writers often refer to as fatal injury, as their writers respond to the injured and dead.[1] When soldiers are injured or die in combat their privileged mourners are their combatant comrades at the front and their families at home. The frontline hospital, the space crucial in their movement from injury in combat to home that we have noted as the 'center of an hourglass' in our introduction, whether on a medevac flight stretcher or in a flag-draped coffin, is often represented to the public as no more than a brief pause in the narrative. The medical personnel who receive and care for those bodies and form part of the honour guard for the dead are excluded from the mourning narrative. Yet it is through their stories, accounts by doctors, nurses and others, that we confront the constructions of death and injury that define this war, and the emotional burden borne by those who treat those injuries and grieve these deaths. While earlier chapters have explored the emotional trauma that attends the daily confrontation with wounding, sickness and deaths in war, this chapter looks more specifically at the response of medical personnel to death and how individuals represent themselves as participants in grief at the loss of the dead, even those they do not know. As the final chapter, although the discussion focuses on the war in Iraq, it also speaks to the larger issue of loss and grief that is a mostly unacknowledged consequence of medical work in a warzone. We have seen in Chapter 6 the impact of grief at the deaths of comrades for medics and battalion doctors, and the relationship between grief and guilt that attends the deaths of innocent victims, where the medical personnel are powerless to save them or effect change. In this chapter, however, we look more generally at the relationship between medical personnel and the deaths of those they care for and the post-war effects of this intimacy with death, keeping in mind Shatan's connection between grief and post-traumatic stress. Recently this issue has come to the fore in a *Guardian* article on American Iraq and Afghanistan War veteran suicides, where researchers have concluded that 'the most common source of anguish for [the Marines] was failing to protect their "brothers". The significance of that is unfathomable. It's comparable to the feelings I've heard from parents who have lost a child.'[2] Even if, for medical personnel, the connection is rarely as intimate, these accounts foreground loss and grief as a central element in the carer's experience and a lingering presence in its aftermath.

The first section of this chapter discusses the medical personnel relationship with soldier deaths in the context of the larger public discourses of sacrifice and heroism which the nation employs to give them meaning. The second part focuses on representations of non-American, particularly Iraqi civilian children's, injuries and deaths and their impact on one surgeon, Chris Coppola, whose focus, unusually, turns away from the soldier to the civilian child. The final section explores the way medical personnel represent their emotional response to caring for the wounded and dead, in the context of the need to mourn established at the beginning of the chapter, in relation to recent understanding of forms of trauma stress outlined in an interview with Dr Vaughn DeCoster, a medical social worker in Iraq, and through conclusions about medical personnel stress drawn by Richie-Melvan and Vines in their interviews with nurses who served in Iraq and Afghanistan.[3] As we have seen in earlier discussion, throughout we find that the focus, no matter whether it is on combatant or civilian death, centres round the psychic burden that results from engagement with injury and death.

In previous chapters we note how, in the emotion-driven politics of war, mourners tend to privilege their own. Perhaps even more than in earlier wars, these accounts from the Iraq War, even while they treat the so-called enemy and civilian casualties, foreground what Butler defines as 'grievable' lives ('that the life would be grieved if it were lost'),[4] in this case those of American combatants.[5] Yet it can be argued that in wartime the representation of the soldier's death as heroic sacrifice relies on an abstraction of death that obscures the unpalatable facts of bodily damage that causes the death, so that even 'grievable' lives are subject to a silencing that is a form of avoidance or disowning of injury. The process of repatriation during the Iraq War, where the flag-draped coffin and the elaborate military protocol and ritual surrounding the body's return home are presented as honouring the dead, at the same time works to erase the knowledge of the injured body and thus the physical horror of what death in war often means, as noted in Lifton's comments on the return of bodies from the Vietnam War.[6] The individual thus becomes 'grievable' only in terms of the prescription imposed by the state and the military. Central to medical memoirs from this particular warzone, which by their nature must own injury, is how they negotiate and bear witness to that injury in the larger context of the public wartime heroic narrative through which these dead and injured are remembered.

In spite of anti-war protests at the onset of the so-called 'Operation Iraqi Freedom', and some continuation of those protests in the early years of the war, this conflict carried very little of the angry and anti-government rhetoric that attended the Vietnam War. One important difference here has been that this war was fought by regular or reserve troops rather than conscripts or draftees, hence there was no disruption to the lives of those who did not have to confront the personal reality of the war. Although doctors may appear to be volunteers, in fact all the memoirists discussed here had some connection to the military, because they were reservists, had already served in some capacity, had a military scholarship for medical school or, like Dave Hnida, had joined the army specifically because they felt they should offer their medical services in Iraq. Perhaps because of this there is reluctance on the part of most of these memoirists to criticise it openly, unlike doctors in the Vietnam War; Chris Coppola is one of the few who lets us know directly that he does not support the war. This apparent reluctance may arise from editorial or self-censorship, given that these writings were published during the war. In addition, it is too soon to have a legacy of post-war writing at a reflective distance from the war. In spite of the way some writers link the medical experience to that of the Vietnam War, the political context in which this war was fought makes for a tone that is noticeably different from the writings from Vietnam, even those published during that war. At the same time, however, the accounts indicate a very high awareness of potential stress responses, from more recent definitions of acute stress response to the definitions of post-traumatic stress response that emerged after the Vietnam War. This means that in this context they are very much influenced by a post-Vietnam understanding of the psychological trauma that accompanies war. One noticeable difference from earlier wars, then, is the much more open discussion around post-war trauma, the stigma around mental breakdown and the support or lack of support for those returning from the warzone, including non-combatants, that has become part of public discourse. Most of the writers discussed here feel the need to explore what might be considered the traumatic, or at the very least the emotional, aspect of their service, if only to dismiss it. Yet in spite of this greater understanding of the psychological consequences of war service, and their willingness to address this as an issue, these writers seem more reticent about revealing their own emotional pain than medical personnel from the war in Vietnam. This leads to a visible tension between the awareness of traumatic response in these works and the unwillingness at the individual level to explore it in the depth we have seen in memoirs by Hassan and Parrish, for example, in Chapter 6, or by Vietnam nurses discussed in Chapter 5.

Heidi Kraft, a psychologist based at a combat support hospital in Iraq, in her memoir *Rule Number Two*, points to the comparisons between this war and earlier wars, and concludes by affirming that an important difference is in the current acknowledgement that 'war damages doctors too'. Kraft's title derives from an encounter in the film and TV series *M*A*S*H*.:

> I remember this one episode [of *M*A*S*H*] Hawkeye sees a friend of his from high school. He later operates on the friend and loses him on the table. He is distraught.
>
> ...

So after surgery, Henry comes to talk to Hawkeye. Henry tells him that when he went to school for commanding officers, he learned that there are two rules of war. Rule number one is that young men die. Rule number two is that doctors can't change rule number one.

...

That afternoon ... I wrote in my journal about the two rules. I found myself astonished that even fifty years after the Korean War, some things still seemed very much the same. We still heard the helicopters coming, waited for them, ducked our heads, and ran to bring our patients in on canvas stretchers. We still wrote on patients' chests with ink so their next doctors would know what we had done, and we still operated on gurneys made into OR tables.

There were differences too, of course. ... Rule number one might now state that war damages people. Rule number two, of course, would be unchanged.

I was certain of one truth, though, that Henry might not have learned in his course fifty years ago: War damages doctors, too. They are damaged by rule number two.[7]

If we consider that *M*A*S*H* is often seen as an oblique way of presenting the Vietnam War, especially given Kraft's use of the ubiquitous medevac helicopter as the image that links present with past, then we might wonder if this passage is unintentionally subversive: war, whatever the rhetoric, is about physical and psychic damage. However we read Kraft's intent here, what is especially important is her emphasis on the relationship between injury and death in war and the emotional burden this places on those who try to save lives. This emotional burden is examined more directly in Richie-Melvan and Vines's *Angel Walk: Nurses at War in Iraq and Afghanistan*, which explores nurses' experiences through multiple interviews and begins by linking these wars with the Vietnam War nursing experience. They expand Kraft's claim to include nurses and elaborate on the 'damage':

Those who care for troops who are experiencing pain and suffering are likely to experience some of the same emotional crises themselves ... their experiences in a combat zone left an indelible mark on their memory ... they were forever changed.

[T]here are many challenges in war and ... direct combat is but one of them. Those who must wage battles, often seemingly unending, to save the lives of those wounded or injured in wars are challenged repeatedly.[8]

The book opens with a direct connection between its purpose and the Vietnam War experience: 'I [Diane Vines] wanted to work on the book

with Dr Sharon because my generation of nurses had never truly reconciled the events of the Vietnam War and the terrible struggles of the
nurses and warrior vets after serving in Vietnam.'[9]

Unlike Kraft and Richie-Melvan and Vines, most of the writers discussed in this chapter do not make a direct connection between the war
in Iraq and the war in Vietnam but, whether spoken or unspoken, this
relationship between injury and death and the burden carried by medical
personnel is a common thread in the memoirs under discussion and is
arguably informed by post-Vietnam recognition that medical personnel
are damaged by 'rule number two'. In his memoir of the Iraq War, *Paradise
General*, surgeon Dave Hnida makes a direct connection between the
war's physical injuries and the psychological injuries of those who treat
them, asserting, 'We were wounded by what we did and what we saw'.[10]
Equally important to the discussion is Hnida's emphasis on the purpose
of his memoir which is to bring what he did and saw, the connection
between his work as a doctor and the injury and death of combatants,
into the public arena: 'I knew people back home saw and heard about the
deaths and wounds, but on a screen or in writing it was all sanitized and
sterile. Just numbers. ... They didn't see, feel or smell what a broken body
is like up close and personal.'[11]

All of the medical personnel discussed here to a greater or lesser
degree employ such sensory experience of the 'broken body' to place it
and their own experience as carers of that body at the centre of the narrative, bringing us back to Santanu Das's analysis of 'touch and intimacy' in
First World War nursing, discussed in previous chapters. Yet, at the same
time, we find that, like some of the First World War nurses' accounts, the
writers under discussion often also engage in the raised rhetoric of the
public domain where the body takes on heroic significance. As in the
First World War narratives, this rhetoric sits in uneasy juxtaposition with
the graphic uncovering of the damage war inflicts. Examining the tension
between heroic rhetoric and representation of injury and death, especially
as both discourses are central to the grief and mourning that the medical personnel claim as part of their experience, allows us to explore the
dilemma faced by those who bear witness to this most recent war. If the
act of retelling allows individuals to construct their experience in a way
that offers them meaning, especially as they mourn the deaths of those
they could not save, then we might interpret this as a deliberate attempt
to replace the violence committed on the human body with patriotic
platitudes. Yet in spite of the heroic discourse through which the deaths
are often constructed, these accounts foreground injury. And as with

earlier writings we find a range of responses, from Richard Jadick's fram-
ing of *On Call in Hell* with the heroic ideology of the First 8th Battalion
Marines, to the almost complete absence of a heroic narrative in Cheryl
Lynn Ruff's *Ruff's War* and Coppola's collection of e-mails home, *Made
a Difference for That One* and his memoir, *A Pediatric Surgeon in Iraq*.[12]

In exploring these accounts, we should keep in mind what Alastair
Thomson and Graham Dawson define as 'composure', which Dawson
tells us 'involves a striving, not only for a formally satisfying narrative or
a coherent narrative of events, but also for a version of the self that can
be lived with in relative psychic comfort – for, that is, subjective composure'.[13] As we have seen in some of the First World War nurses' accounts,
these memoirs from the Iraq War, in struggling with representation of
injury and death, would appear to be attempting to negotiate their way to
a form of composure – sought after but not quite achieved. For medical
personnel, reaching out for a reconciliation between what they did and
what they saw and its emotional legacy, this search for composure as it is
represented in the memoirs often reflects the medical debriefing that is
part of medical protocol after surgery. Yet, as a reaction to the emotional
consequences of treating the wounded, it persists long after the experience is over from a professional perspective, lingering at the end of these
accounts as a debriefing that can never be completed.

One account that highlights this relationship between medical debriefing and the search for composure in the context of death and grief is
Richard Jadick's memoir, *On Call in Hell*. As much an elegy to the dead
as a story of Jadick's time in Iraq, his account is dedicated to the 'brave
marines who died between June 2004 and Jan. 2005', who 'sacrificed all
that we may live in freedom and security'. He goes on to describe the
First Battalion 8th Marines as fighting to 'free Fallujah from the deadly
grasp of the Iraqi insurgents and foreign jihadis who held the city cap-
tive' and 'who performed their duty with courage and honor, and often,
tremendous personal sacrifice'.[14] Jadick's representation of the Marines
is unsurprising to any reader of his account; he wants to pay tribute to
their courage. This is part of the larger loyalty he feels to the Marine unit
he served with, a closeness that we have also seen in Holley's account of
his time as a battalion surgeon in the Vietnam War in Chapter 6. Unlike
the writing from the Vietnam War, however, Jadick's rhetoric reflects
the language in the United States public domain. This rhetoric is similarly reflected in the foreword to Kraft's *Rule Number Two* by Lieutenant
Colonel W. C. Gregson, retired, United States Marine Corps, in a tone
that fits uncomfortably with the actual memoir, which declares '[b]ehind

the newscasts and the headlines lie the real lives of the warrior class of America … *Rule Number Two* is the story of the strong men and women who are doing the nation's bidding so that others may pursue their lives undisturbed.'[15]

Heroic rhetoric collapses in the face of mass anonymous death, however. Navy nurse Cheryl Lynn Ruff cannot retrieve any meaning from her experience of mass casualties:

> The choppers continued arriving, bringing us more and more wounded. We saw untold gunshot wounds that had resulted in severe, devastating injuries to the head, face, neck, torso, abdomen, arms, and legs. Gaping, bloody holes were torn through every part of the body. Limbs dangled from bodies, held by a slight thread of flesh, or they had been ripped off completely. Faces smeared with a mixture of blood, sweat, and dirt were recognizable as human solely by the piercing eyes looking up in fear and pain. Others were suffering from sucking chest wounds, charred flesh, shattered bones, or partially blown-away skulls – their brain matter was missing, but the individual continued to breathe because the brain stem remained intact. Even small, relatively harmless-looking external bullet holes to the abdomen would reveal extensive internal damage to the bowel, bladder, stomach, liver, and spleen. It was a horrible, gruesome, and heart-wrenching sight.
>
> We received and treated all those who had become a casualty of this war: American fighting men, Iraqi soldiers, and the innocent Iraqi women and children who were at the wrong place at the wrong time. Their screams of excruciating pain filled the air, and the stench of destroyed flesh and death was revolting as it intensified in the sweltering Iraqi heat. I thought I had entered hell when I arrived at Camp Guadalcanal with its primitive conditions. Now I believed I had moved even deeper into hell, for I had truly entered the hell of war.
>
> As the wounded continued to arrive and the scenes of overwhelming and incomprehensible human devastation and destruction seemed as though they would never cease, I realized we were struggling and doing everything in our power to keep these people alive while others were struggling just as hard to kill them.
>
> …
>
> The sights we witnessed were haunting, and the smells of this hell invaded our senses and penetrated deep into our very souls.[16]

In a grotesque democracy of injury, bodies are fragmented into body parts and the intimate details of anatomy laid bare, with the final evocation of sight and smell returning us to Hnida's 'smell of a broken body'. Ruff exposes the impact of her immersion in this 'hell' as an experience that penetrates her physically, emotionally and spiritually. This detailed listing of body parts shows that the images have never left her. Unlike Jadick's representation of his marines, Ruff cannot impose an ideology of heroic sacrifice on what she witnesses. Without the focus on individuals there is no possibility of a narrative of courage or honour, or a ritual that would restore wholeness in the face of loss and grief. These injured and dead are nameless faceless victims of a larger violence that lacks the purpose needed to frame it with meaning.

For Ruff the sights and smells invade her. Such an intimacy with the body becomes the means by which the medical personnel discussed here express the underlying stress of their work. In these accounts the most pervasive signifier of injury is blood. As a metaphor blood is used to evoke the way the intimacy between medical personnel and patient permeates the doctors' or nurses' psyches as it permeates their clothing physically. Emotionally, as Hnida asserts, they, too, are wounded. Blood carries the emotional weight of witnessing death and injury and the accompanying stress of loss and failure. As a biological process against which they constantly fight, bleeding represents both the damage they try to repair and the futility that often attends their efforts, becoming the recurring image through which these men and women negotiate their role as they try to save the wounded, pumping blood back as it bleeds out, tying 'bleeders', restarting hearts in a desperate race against time. As in the image of the surgeon's bloody hands in Turner's poem 'AB Negative', blood especially represents the intimacy of the medical personnel with the fatally wounded body, at times becoming almost literally a part of the carer attending the body. Kraft devotes an entire chapter, 'Karen's Boots', to the blood on a nurse's boots which represents the emotional burden of nursing in a warzone; Jadick explains the biochemistry of the term 'bleeding out'; and Hnida places blood at the centre of a lengthy narrative of an individual he works to save.

Treating a massively injured combatant, Hnida uses the young soldier's blood to represents his purpose as a doctor in a warzone. Retrieving this one casualty from the many he treats during his tour of duty, Hnida uses the extended narrative of his medical care to represent the way he is defined by his intimate relationship with this soldier and by extension all of his patients, as well as to force home the point he makes at the beginning of the book and place his own intimacy with injury – the smell and feel of the broken body – in front of his audience.

> It was a bustling day in the ER [emergency room] when an unannounced
> chopper thundered in carrying a young soldier whose vehicle was blown

ten feet into the air by a well-hidden IED. His condition was one step past critical by the time he got to me. I had to ignore the raw stumps that minutes before were a complete arm and leg; tourniquets were on snugly and the oozing could wait. There was no time to waste before fixing the more important blood pouring from his neck, as well as trying to figure out why his abdomen was rapidly swelling like a balloon.

To look at his face, though, you would have thought life was fine. There was no sign of damage, just little smudges of dirt on his cheeks and peacefully closed eyes. With short-cropped blonde hair and a square jaw he reminded me of a typical twentysomething I would see in my practice for a winter's sore throat or a sprained ankle from a summer evening softball game. From the neck down, this kid was in bad shape. The force of the blast had ruptured his liver and spleen and I was squirming as I gazed at the small holes burned into his neck by hot chunks of shrapnel. ... I shut out images of home and the faces I'd left behind. Forcing myself into medical autopilot, I went to work trying to keep the soldier alive.

It took twenty-eight minutes of medical improv to get him stable enough for surgery. We made up treatments as we went along; pumping in countless units of blood and vials of medications, cautiously peeking under, then changing saturated bandages, and adjusting tubes and dials to force oxygen into his reluctant lungs. I was soaked with his blood by the time we were done, but it would be hours and hours until I could shower and change my uniform. The warm stickiness didn't bother me, though, and even served an important purpose: reminding me there was a young man who belonged to that blood, and now he belonged to me.

...

The surgery was tough, but the next task was even tougher; Rick [fellow surgeon] volunteered to go outside into the dark heat and talk to the soldiers in the kid's unit. ... He was hurting and so was I, but we couldn't show that hurt to anyone besides each other. Often here, a projected 'never say die' attitude really meant 'we're futilely trying to cheat death'. We needed to hold each other up as we staggered down the thin line separating life and death.[17]

The chief nurse hands Hnida a wallet that has fallen out of the young soldier's pocket:

I shouldn't have taken a look.

Right inside the fold of the sweat-stained wallet was a photo of the soldier and his family. He had a bright bubbly wife with arms around two kids dressed up in their Easter best ... All smiling. All happy. All together.

Now things were too personal. ... I couldn't stop picturing my kids on respirators with missing limbs and holes in their necks. Then came snapshot images of teenagers lying on a sidewalk after being shot while fleeing a school.[18] I shook my head back and forth, violently trying to get the images the hell out of my brain. … I usually did a good job of blocking out personal details when a life was on the line, it was the only way to ensure the psych bell didn't toll for me. That's why I made it a rule *not* to look at the names of those soldiers teetering on the line between life and death. They were 'the leg,' the pelvis,' or in this case 'the neck'. … I avoided looking at this soldier's name. I DID NOT want to know it. But unfortunately, I did. He was 'Honey' and 'Daddy'. And I was one step from losing my sanity. The photo had blown a giant hole in my protective armor. …

…

Back at my barracks I showered for ten minutes longer than the mandated two, watching blood swirl down the drain until the water flowed clear. I felt I'd never truly wash his blood off my skin, just like I could never get the pungent odor of charred flesh to leave my nostrils; they were my scars of his battle.[19]

Hnida's narrative bears a striking resemblance to Van Devanter's story of 'Gene', from the medical particulars to the photograph that replaces the anonymous damaged body with the human being. Like Van Devanter, Hnida uses this account to explore the psychic stress that is visited on the surgeon, the necessity of maintaining professional distance, and the potential for breakdown once that distance is breached. Blood here represents his responsibility as a surgeon in a warzone. He embraces that reminder, 'the warm stickiness … reminding me there was a young man who belonged to that blood, and now he belonged to me'. Later, showering, the blood defines his ownership of the young man, something 'I'd never truly wash off my skin … my scars of his battle'. While initially Hnida works to save an anonymous combatant, maintaining his 'medical autopilot', like Van Devanter the appearance of the photograph reminds him of the soldier's humanity represented by a wife and small children. Unlike Van Devanter, however, Hnida's encounter does not result in a reaction against the war. Yet although he appears to find some 'composure' in knowing that his surgery saved the young man long enough to bring him home to die, it can be argued that the narrative structure that directs him to offer closure at the end of the chapter is undermined by the central image of injury that is at the heart of the story. The blood that can never truly be washed off represents the burden of remembering that Hnida must carry as a consequence of owning the intimacy rather than maintaining emotional distance.

Richard Jadick's narrative of Marine heroism is also permeated by blood, and he uses blood to confront not only the intimacy between the doctor and his patients, but also what failure means in the context of that intimacy. Losing his temper with his medics when they leave blood on the floor of the forward aid station, he writes,

> [I]t was the blood on the floor that made me crack. We had lost too many good men and the blood was like a rebuke, like an accusation of failure. … It's not just the pain of failure; it's the pain of knowing that you're sending a patient home to his family in a box, and that they are going to have terrible Thanksgivings and terrible Christmases for years to come as a result of your failure.[20]

It is, perhaps, the paradoxical situation in which these medical personnel work that elicits pain and anger. The burden they carry is their inability to overcome 'rule number two' while at the same time seeing it as their responsibility to do so. Failure provokes a questioning of procedure that continues in these accounts long after the tour of duty is officially over. As noted earlier, it is as if the burden they carry home is a continuation of the medical protocol or debriefing that follows a death. The bleeding that they cannot control, but which pervades the senses so that it is *their* wound, thus becomes a metaphor for the memories that persist. Failing to keep the terribly injured Lance Corporal Brown alive, Jadick describes his death first in terms of medical failure: his complete loss of blood: 'Brown was literally drained … eventually there was nothing left to try', and then in terms of his human loss: 'It was a crushing loss. I put my arms around Markeley, both of us crying. "I'm sorry". I said, I didn't do it, couldn't do it. I'm sorry.'[21] But then he immediately returns to compulsively revisiting the medical procedures that explain to us the dilemmas of choice for the surgeon: 'Did he not have blood because he had pericardial tamponade? I didn't lap his heart, but it didn't hit me.'[22] His questioning continues into the present tense so that the death persists into the moment of writing: 'I don't know, I just don't know. Demarkus Brown, Lonny Wells – when they come in alive and then they die, you question everything you did, time and time again.'[23] As combatants carry the psychological impact of combat home with them, so medical personnel bear the burden of their decisions and apparent failures. Jadick's extension of this narrative suggests he cannot leave it behind; he is compelled to explain in detail the biochemistry of bleeding out:

> Doctors call it exsanguination or hypovolemia, Marines call it bleeding out, but what it comes down to is that there's a lot more in bleeding to death than just sort of draining away. Blood is a pretty complex fluid, and when you lose too much of it you start to get into three specific kinds of trouble.

Trauma specialists call it the 'lethal triad' – hypothermia, coagulopathy, and acidosis. The cycle starts when blood levels in the body drop to a point where the tissues aren't getting enough of the oxygen blood carries, so the metabolism starts to shut down and body-heat generation goes with it. ... Once the body enters this triad, it tends to spiral out of control rapidly; the heart spasms and gives out, the vessels relax, and the fluids release – 'declamping syndrome', some people call it – and the patient dies.[24]

This scientific naming is both an attempt to control the process by explaining it and to show its uncontrollability. The focus on individual deaths and on the precise outlining of the biochemical cause of death is a particular characteristic of writings from this war where, generally, because of the lower number of casualties, there is more time than in previous wars for medical personnel to contemplate individual death. It also points to the connection between contemporary expectations of medical procedures and physician control: the preoccupation with this moment of no return, when the doctor confronts his failure, is also the moment when he must acknowledge a loss of medical control. This loss of control is also foregrounded by Hnida who moves beyond the current scientific naming to place 'bleeding out' in a historical context, telling us that in the American Civil War the moment the body releases its fluids in death was termed 'the rude unhinging of the machinery of life'.[25] Unlike the American Civil War, however, in this war there is a strong sense that the trauma surgeon is under pressure to repair all damage. Even given the massive injury that causes death in a warzone, as with Jadick's musings above, the pressure on surgeons is increased when they experience their inability to repair the damage as their own failure rather than as a consequence of rules numbers one and two.

For medical personnel, not only does the death of a patient carry an enormous sense of failure in the immediate term, but their unwillingness to accept 'rule number two' in the face of medical technology that can save lives that would have been lost in earlier wars means they carry an additional emotional burden in the aftermath. Their sole purpose, as they see it, is to intervene between injury and death. As Jadick writes: 'the only reason you exist is to be the guy who steps in and interrupts that wounded man's demise'.[26] Positioning themselves as mediators between home and front, then, they bear witness to injury and mourn the dead. When Hnida writes that 'we were wounded by what we did and what we saw', like medical personnel in the one hundred years before him, he immediately places his claim for himself in the context of others: 'but no more than those we cared for'.[27]

Even as he claims this intimacy with the wounded and their blood, and uses it to bring his audience as far as possible into that same intimacy, Hnida employs that blood to avoid confronting the politics of the war. Although the war's damage is central to his memoir, in a chapter he calls 'Dante's Infirmary' he acknowledges, '[a]s for the war itself, we didn't have arguments or discussions. There was no desire, or for that matter, energy. We were too busy trying not to slip and fall in the bloody puddles on the floor.'[28] The doctors' preoccupation with trying to keep their metaphoric balance prevents them from confronting what the blood stands for and its political source. The focus on blood in these two accounts thus directs attention away from the source of the injury even as the focus on injury colludes in a refusal to question. Yet avoiding the question may be necessary for psychological survival. This points to the dilemma faced by medical personnel in warzones throughout history and brings us back to the exchange between nurses in Lesley Smith's First World War memoir, *Four Years out of Life*, where the women recognise that 'keeping busy' in order not to think about the origins of their work is a form of cowardice.[29] The easier path is to immerse oneself in the work. It is not just the raised rhetoric of sacrifice then that can obscure injury, but the focus on injury can itself become a form of avoidance, since it prevents surgeons like Hnida from confronting the source of the blood beyond the broken body. Unlike Van Devanter, for example, for whom the broken body demands a confrontation with the politics that have caused its injury even after the return home, for Hnida and Jadick at least, it would seem that this body, a constant reminder of their failure as doctors, stands in the way of any interrogation of the politics behind the bloodletting.

Although the intimacy between the physician and the wounded stands in the way of a critical distance that would allow them to confront the politics of the war, the opening of the damaged body to public view is an owning of injury that in itself arguably makes a subversive political statement, albeit perhaps at times an unconscious one. Moreover, while constructing a heroic context for that body relies on a rhetoric which is at odds with the representation of injury, in these narratives it would seem to arise out of the immediate need for a coping mechanism similar to some First World War nurses, and like them comes out of a very human desire to return dignity to the individual. It is not entirely cowardice then that causes these writers to avoid interrogating the cause or validity of the war, but the position Jadick represents above that makes it difficult for medical personnel to confront the larger context. Exposing injuries that are otherwise unseen, both actually and metaphorically, is the larger story central to these accounts. Since medical personnel are witness to the most intimate of injuries to the interior of the body and thus the only individuals who can communicate this injury, their position gives them the burden of bearing witness to the injured body which is subjected not only to the indignity of terrible wounding, but also to the medical treatments that open the body to public view during treatment or autopsy. In the same way that the story of the body is retold as it is washed and dressed in military uniform, so the doctor's story is a redressing. Describing the death of a young soldier, Hnida's telling deliberately moves us from the initial impression which reveals no injury, to the revelation visible only to the medical staff who bear witness:

> The pressure waves from those blasts don't always leave a mark on the outside but can shatter bones and rupture organs on the inside. As the staff rolled him on his side to examine his back, only the upper half of his body moved; his legs and feet pointed at the ceiling. The force of the blast had shattered his pelvis, and his spine disconnected from the legs.
>
> It was always a fatal injury.
>
> We lost him.[30]

Hnida relates a series of events as part of a longer account of the medical debriefing, revealing the injury that would otherwise be unseen. Moreover, even though the injury is fatal, he still claims the death as a collective responsibility and loss, 'We lost him'.

In the case of the death described above, Hnida follows the injury narrative with a description that restores wholeness: 'The soldier was gently cleaned and all signs of medical trauma were repaired. He was redressed in his uniform. The staff lined up and stood at attention as the soldier was wheeled out of the emergency room.'[31] This specific account mirrors the larger process by which trauma to the body is at once revealed and concealed. As dignity is returned to the individual in this process of transformation from soldier to mutilated body back to soldier, injury is arguably erased. While military ritual honours the dead, at the same time it translates the cause of death into a heroic narrative in the same way as the nation's flag covers the coffin that holds the body. Yet the motivation behind this 'redressing' is a grieving ritual:

> There would be an empty cot in [the] barracks that night. Loved ones back home would have an empty room. And countless lives would forever have a big hole that could never be filled.

The next day we got together as a group in the musty tent and beat ourselves up over everything we had done and maybe could have done better. But in the end, though, we realized we had done everything right in a case that was destined for wrong. ...

Nevertheless, the death of the young soldier hurt with a pain none of us could put into words. We are not gods. Sometimes we make mistakes. And even when we don't, we suffer because we are not able to undo the damage one human can inflict on another. Each of us would see this young man's face the rest of our lives. But his family would be the ones that missed his face the most.[32]

Hnida offers his own leave-taking and grief over the death of the soldier, drawing the reader not only into the injury, the broken body that he wants to place in full view of his audience, but also into grief at the loss of this one individual and the impossibility of expressing it adequately to those outside. Yet although Hnida brings us into his own dilemma, 'we suffer because we are not able to undo the damage one human can inflict on another', his position as the 'sufferer' would seem to obscure the context in which the suffering occurs. He ends this chapter, 'Death of an American Soldier', by describing a therapeutic game of catch and suggesting that 'maybe all world leaders step onto the lawn of the UN and toss a ball around until they solve out their self-manufactured troubles'.[33] This is the nearest he comes to direct criticism of the war that has killed the soldier, and yet it avoids examining the obvious issue: the UN did not support the United States invasion of Iraq.

The military rituals attending a soldier's death in war are designed to honour the dead unquestioningly. As noted earlier, the language that narrates heroic death offers meaning and consolation to those who mourn the loss. Chris Hedges asserts that the cause 'can't be questioned without dishonoring those who gave up their lives. ... There is a constant act of remembering and honoring the fallen during war. These ceremonies sanctify the cause.'[34] Yet arguably, in these medical memoirs, the covering of the body with the uniform is an ineffective veneer for those who have witnessed the injury; one could posit that the readers' participation in this witness takes them beyond the sterility of media reporting to a confrontation with the broken body which Hnida states is the impetus behind his memoir. Although he details the guard of honour for the soldier, Hnida ends his account by returning to the collective sense of failure that attends the impossibility of repairing injury: 'we suffer because we are not able to undo the damage.'[35] What we find then is a tension between the desire to return dignity to the injured body and allow the military ritual to honour the death, and the deep sense of loss and power-lessness that attends it. It would seem from Jadick's and Hnida's accounts that in spite of the power of the public language to persuade the people at home of the validity of the death and thus of the war, no construction of heroism can mitigate the burden these deaths force medical personnel to carry.

Jadick goes even further than Hnida in consciously taking on the bur-den of remembrance as well as the personal guilt involved in that remem-bering: 'I made sure to look every Marine in the face; there's something about seeing their faces. It's too easy to start thinking about our deceased as numbers – and forget that each one was a vital human being.'[36] Remembering the dead thus becomes both personally and politically fraught. If to remember involves military ritual and patriotic rhetoric, then accounts by Hnida and Jadick arguably conspire with the public representation that Hedges asserts perpetuates war by 'sanctifying the cause'. At the same time, these voices own injury and hold it up to public view and in doing so they become witnesses for whom remembering is a mourning ritual far more complex than that conveyed through military rhetoric and protocol. Jadick's final chapters articulate the lack of closure that all medical personnel carry with them. The habit of medical debrief-ing persists to become a form of mourning. But in taking responsibility for the deaths, Jadick seems to absolve the real source, the war itself. His questioning of his personal responsibility in the following passage illus-trates the extent to which the burdens of war are carried not by those who mandate it, but by those individuals who have been the most immediate witnesses to trauma.

> I'll know I'll never stop thinking about our marines … and I can't overlook
> the fact that we lost men in Iraq, men who came to us alive looking for help,
> who we couldn't save. Lonny Wells, Nicholas Ziolkowski, Demarkus Brown.
> I can't help thinking, over and over again, is there something I could have
> done, something I could have done differently? What would have happened
> if I'd made just one change in the whole long chain of events leading to their
> deaths, would it have changed the outcome? I don't know, and I don't think
> I'll ever know.[37]

For writers like Jadick, the heroic narrative is crucial to mourning and remembering American Marines' deaths, especially as it offers meaning in the face of his own failure to prevent the death. Yet the American sol-dier must be created a hero in the context of his fight against 'the bad guys'. Iraqi deaths, especially those of so-called 'insurgents' are usually seen in this context: although the doctor must be and is willing to treat their injuries, he cannot mourn their deaths, since they are the cause of his mourning.

Not all the writers considered here construct the war from this position, however. As we have seen in Ruff's account, injured and dead bodies lose the us/them binary that is necessary to the construction of war. For Ruff the specific image of an Iraqi child points to the common humanity that transcends these binaries. Seeing an injured boy screaming for his mother she writes: '[e]ven though he spoke a different language from our own, the cry for "Mom" was universal ... the vision of that helpless, innocent mangled child still haunts me'.[38] Others, however, like Navy surgeon Zsolt Stockinger in *Fragments from Iraq*, honestly confront their inability to feel the same emotion over the deaths and injuries of an 'insurgent' as they would feel for an American soldier. After major surgery to try and save the life of an Iraqi, Stockinger notes that the emotions that attend the death are not those that his team experience after the death of a 'US Army soldier': 'who he was should make no difference, but of course it does. This is war after all. And as we know, war is insane: we attempt to kill people by shooting them, but if we do a bad job of it, we do everything we can to save them. I guess that's what makes us the good guys'.[39] Stockinger's claim that American doctors are the 'good guys' because they try to save those they have failed to kill may be distasteful, but it does acknowledge the absurdity of war where doctors like him are confronted with its outcome. Yet lest his or Jadick's representation of Iraqi death be seen as representative of American medical personnel we must turn to surgeon Chris Coppola's memoir, *A Pediatric Surgeon in Iraq*, and the edited collection of his e-mails home, *Made a Difference for That One*. Unlike Stockinger, Coppola confronts the discomfort he feels at the apparent contradiction between his roles as doctor and officer as he considers the death of an Iraqi 'insurgent' he tries to save:

> I look for signs in his swollen face for malice, but all I see is a dying man who needs our treatment.
>
> ...
>
> His death leaves me cold.
> As a team we feel like a failure whenever we lose a patient who arrives at our hospital alive ... How am I supposed to comprehend his death when my duty as a doctor to heal contradicts my duty as an officer to defend?[40]

The point where the doctor and the officer are not in contention is in the treatment of injured Iraqi children. Coppola's accounts, unlike most of the others discussed here, mourn the injured and dead children of Iraq. The injured child, not the American soldier, is at the centre of his narratives. At times, the child literally takes over the soldier narrative, as when Coppola chooses to finish skin grafts on a burned Iraqi child over an order to respond immediately to a MASCAL (mass casualty). Where surgeons like Jadick and Hnida privilege the injuries and deaths of American soldiers, Coppola's accounts foreground Iraqi children and through them he establishes a narrative of connection between American and Iraqi that attempts to transcend the forms of separation and otherness we find in most of the American accounts. Coppola's writings thus take us into another arena of war: the injured and dead child and that child's humanity, and by extension the common humanity between Americans and Iraqis that is his focus. Coppola opens his description of Iraq by representing it not as barren and inhospitable, inhabited by an enemy, as so many other memoirs do, but as a place where he finds commonalities with home in the image of the children:

> The sun is rising over the Tigris river, and far-off palm trees line its bank. Outside the wire [of the US base] the local farmers work the land. ... Men and women work together. Everywhere the ground explodes with growth in green rows. Life seems to go on as if war were something far away and of little concern to the people of Balad. Children go on being children. They wear brightly colored clothes; one rides a donkey. Two others chant in raised voices and laugh at the end of each verse.[41]

In contrast with other memoirs where the first shock of receiving a casualty is of a wounded American soldier, Coppola

> look[s] down at the patient lying on the stretcher. It is a child who looks to be about two years old. I had expected to see a soldier ... and the sight of a child is jarring ... I ask the medic if he knows how this baby was shot, but he only answers, 'Crossfire at a checkpoint'.[42]

Coppola's memoir includes an image of the X-ray showing the bullet lodged in the child's skull. As a 'photograph' from the medical perspective it takes the place of other possible photographic images of the child. Its stark black and white statement of injury allows us literally to see through Coppola's medical lens as it reveals the interiority of the damage to the child's body. We are privileged to enter the injury from the surgeon's perspective; undistracted by outer appearance, we are left with the outline of a small skull with a bullet silhouetted at the point of entry. For Coppola this is war, both professional and personal at the same time. And he brings professional and personal together in a detailed description of the operation he and another surgeon perform on the boy. Reading his own children's e-mails soon after he responds: 'When I think of the boy with the fresh incision in his head, it is easy to be thankful for my healthy family.'[43] For Coppola the child bridges any sense of the Iraqi people as other. Later, treating a boy injured in the first election, he reflects that 'something about the Cupid's bow arches of his upperlip and the round chubbiness of his pink cheeks makes him look like my four- year-old son, Griffin.'[44]

The child who becomes the main focus of Coppola's memoir and the subject of several of his e-mails home is a two-year-old girl, Leila, who has suffered severe burns as the result of an incendiary device thrown into her home: 'She whimpers weakly, barely conscious as her hands struggle to keep their grip on a quilted pink security blanket well worn with use. I feel an incredible tenderness toward her.'[45] Coppola's equally human response to the child's mother and father breaks down any possible 'otherness':

> The mother looks back and forth between her two children. Her face wet with tears ... I find her father with a small group of soldiers, some US troops, some Iraqi. ... Except for the national insignia and the thick black moustaches, the Iraqi soldiers look much the same as the Americans – sweaty, dusty men in layers of muted camouflage and armor.[46]

Leila's long-drawn-out treatment and eventual death become an extended elegy for the children who are casualties of war. Her presence dominates Coppola's account, cutting across the rhetoric of courage borne out of violence through which military death is constructed. He notes as he is preoccupied with planning her skin grafts that he is 'only half paying attention to the discussions of the previous night's work on the military casualties received'. During the delicate and time-consuming graft procedure 'I hear a familiar and devastating noise: an incoming MASCAL is announced over the hospital loudspeakers'.[47] Ordered to evacuate the operating room, since civilian treatment takes a lower priority to military, Coppola refuses and races to finish the grafts. Standing outside the bounds of military-medical protocol he asserts that 'battlefield support may be military priority, but I feel no doubt in my heart that my highest duty in this moment is to finish this girl's operation'.[48] When Leila eventually dies in spite of treatment, Coppola inserts into his memoir the original, unedited e-mail about her death, as if unable to revisit it and rewrite it into the memoir anew as he does with other events. The poignancy of her death is heightened by his representation of her personality: 'I knew her long enough to learn that her favourite stuffed animal was a pink bear, she loved chips and snacks, and her giggles brought joy to her mother and father.'[49] Coppola cannot end the e-mail with any sense of affirmation. This death cannot be reimagined through a rhetoric of heroism. 'Tomorrow, I will go back to work and try to help the others who come my way. But tonight I am broken.'[50]

All of these writers confront their responses to death and injury on a personal level, often taking us into the immediate moments where they admit defeat as doctors and wrestle with the burden of failure. As already noted, unlike medical personnel writing about their Vietnam War experience, they are less likely to use representation of injury as a political tool. Coppola is the only writer here who directly voices opposition to the war. Yet at the same time their writing is very conscious of the connection between their work and the potential for it to cause some form of post-trauma stress. In spite of this heightened awareness, we see less admission of breakdown in these accounts from Iraq than in memoirs from the Vietnam War.

Individual attitudes range from Kraft's 'war damages doctors too' to the scepticism of Stockinger who comments, after attending a mandatory lecture on combat stress, 'the publicity about combat stress is half the problem: you tell people that they are going to get it, they will.'[51] Later he acknowledges its reality and notes that 'the standard management for combat stress cases (shell shock, battle fatigue, whatever you want to call it) is "three hots and a cot"; the soldier is pulled out of the front line for a day or two to rest and sleep with an expectation he will return to the front.'[52] Stockinger focuses only on *combat* stress, and his referral to it as 'shell shock' suggests an unwillingness to speak in terms that recognise the more recent understanding of war stress, or perhaps even of a war experience that cannot be constructed in terms of a 'front line'. He does not consider the psychological consequences of his own work.

A much more nuanced understanding of wartime stressors and response is evident in an interview with medical social worker, Dr Vaughn DeCoster. DeCoster was an officer in charge of a small combat stress team in Iraq, an indication that the military take post-trauma stress and other forms of mental health more seriously than in previous wars.[53] What is important in DeCoster's interview is his assertion that 'As far as, like post-traumatic stress, the reality is most people over there you're not post anything. It's kind of my favourite line, I keep, we'd always tell soldiers that a lot of it was a normal reaction to combat.'[54] He also notes that soldiers under immediate combat stress were having nightmares or flashbacks relating to previous deployments.[55] Asked what he thinks some of the main causes of PTSD are, De Coster emphasises that it is a 'normal' reaction:

> I think there's events that anyone will experience post-traumatic stress disorder if the event is horrific enough. ... I think there's a normal post-traumatic stress that we go through as our brains sort of adjust and we make sense and sort of incorporate that experience into our being and into our existence. You know, 'cause it's a stark reminder that our realities are breached.[56]

DeCoster acknowledges continuing stigma around these mental health issues in the military, but also notes that this is less of an issue than formerly, in large part because of a change in cultural attitudes: 'mental health and emotions and psychology is much more in our culture, it's more normal, than it was ten years ago or twenty years ago.'[57] While De Coster and his interviewer mostly focus on combat as a stressor, when asked about his own coping strategies he responds that

> exercise would probably be the number one. Running and working out with weights ... having time to reflect, is what I did a lot in Iraq when I had time ... I used to journal a lot ... I used to say one of the things we would encourage soldiers to do is to journal, to write it out, 'cause it's a way for your mind to process what's going on rather than just letting it bounce around in your head.[58]

Yet in spite of the presence of psychiatric social workers such as DeCoster, the chasm between those who experience war and injury and those who work behind the lines remains. Medevac medic Sergeant Schacht, interviewed while serving in Afghanistan, speaks to this gap in understanding. Noting that he and his medevac comrades rely heavily on each other's emotional support to deal with the events they witness he says, 'there are sometimes when we have really bad missions and we can talk to each other and we're fine.' On the army combat stress teams he comments,

> the fact that they're not out there, they're not getting shot at, they're not dealing with the death, they're not dealing with the wounded. They're not dealing with soldiers crying and wanting to go home, they want to see their Mom, they're sorry for everything they've done wrong, they don't hear that and when you try to explain to them about your nightmares, and about your, you get these feelings and all they can do is nod their head, yes we

understand, no you don't understand – it's very frustrating to deal with and that's why we're relying heavily on each other ... we would die for each other. Unless you're there it's hard to explain about that.[59]

Schacht is under no illusions as to the psychological repercussions of his work:

I love this job; this is the best job I probably have ever had. The problem is I will pay for it later on in life. I pay for it now. I have the dreams, I have the, it's hard. The brain does not forget the stuff you see ... With the Medevac you see the ugly of war every single day ... It's like, man, will this never stop.[60]

Schacht is very direct about his own traumatic response – 'the brain does not forget the stuff you see' – an answer coming a century later to Stimson's questions in the First World War: 'These frightful sights would work havoc with one's brain ... what will we think when we get through with it all? How are we going to stand the mental strain?'[61] The accounts discussed in this chapter suggest that these writers do not really begin to process their experience until they return home. If 'war damages doctors too', these writers represent and negotiate their own damage in their memoirs as part of the process of 'writing it out' in the aftermath of their tour. While these memoirs are much more than therapy, the process of writing, as we have seen in relation to earlier accounts, can be therapeutic. Although the gap between the experience and the date of writing the memoir might be too short for individuals to reflect on the long-term effects of their war experience, the accounts themselves, especially the acknowledgement of loss, grief and despair at their inability to save the injured, allow emotion a place in the narrative. At times they also acknowledge intense reaction, as in Coppola's admission after the death of Leila, 'tonight I am broken'. At other points possible traumatic response may be hinted at obliquely, as when Hnida describes the blood that permeates his uniform. The image stands for the trauma that itself remains unspoken. As we discuss earlier, emotion may also be obscured by the rhetoric around death itself. Thus Coppola is 'broken' by the death of a civilian child, but has no language or ritual to impose meaning on the death and allow him consolation. Yet when he describes his role in the Patriot Detail [Honour Guard] of a soldier's death he pays tribute to the dead in spite of acknowledging his refusal to believe in the rightness of the war. In his e-mail home Coppola describes how, at the 'loading [of the] flag-draped containers I tried to give these heroes a salute worthy of their service and sacrifice. It is so hard, even as I write this four days later, to contain the emotions that rush forth.'[62] But when he returns to the event in his memoir he interrogates the reasons behind the deaths: 'I have to ask if we've gained anything that equals the value of one of their lives.'[63] Lacking a belief in the cause means for Coppola that his work is a form of damage control that carries no larger meaning: 'It just seems like I'm working as fast as I can to mop up a mess that will never be cleaned up ... we don't belong here.'[64] Nowhere however, do we find the openness around acknowledging the emotional turmoil that is so important to the Vietnam medical memoirs.

Treating the injured may be the only source of meaning open to Coppola. Yet even for a surgeon like Richard Jadick, who establishes meaning through the rhetoric of courage and heroism in which he narrates the story of his Marines, it is not enough to sustain him or offer composure as he confronts those deaths after the war. He establishes that his main goal is to prevent these deaths. It is this role that brings him into close contact with them, exacerbating the pain of loss when he fails to save them. Of all the writers discussed here, and in spite of the rhetoric of heroism through which he elegises the deaths, Jadick expresses most fully the burden of grief and sense of failure he carries home, admitting at the end of his account, '[t]hey don't tell you about the emotions and garbage you have to carry around with you afterward'.[65] Jadick's motivation for creating an FAS [forward aid station] and thus putting himself in harm's way during the battle of Fallujah goes back to his reason for becoming a doctor: witnessing the death of his baby brother from sudden infant death syndrome and the grief of his mother. His purpose unites the emotional with the practical. Having learned about controlling bleeding from one death, he is able to save the life of another:

> But there was another lesson, and I was determined we would learn that one, too. Volpe made it by the very slimmest of margins. He was moments, literally seconds away from leaving an agonizing emptiness in his mother's heart. I had come to this war for one reason – to keep as many mothers from feeling that pain as I could – and it was now clear what we had to do. ... *We needed to get closer.*[66] [original italics]

Positioning himself with his medics in the fighting paradoxically allows Jadick to save lives while at the same time increasing the emotional burden of grief and loss as he witnesses first-hand the deaths of those he could not save. However, this burden is the result of the relatively low number of casualties these medical personnel are treating, in comparison with the other wars discussed here. Jadick can name his wounded and dead and explain in detail the surgical work he did to treat their wounds. In an extended narrative where he retraces the procedures of treating Lance Corporal Demarkus Brown, Jadick allows the reader to understand the doctor's burden. The constant use of the conditional tense moves us back and forth between the event itself and the present point of recollection which must confront the failure:

> I couldn't save him, that was my job too and I failed. I don't know if we ever had a chance. ... Should I have cracked his chest ... Maybe ... Maybe I should've just gone for a central line ... I didn't have a central line kit, but I could've figured some way to get in there. ... I don't know. I just don't know. Demarkus Brown, Lonny Wells – when they come in alive and then they die, you question everything you did, time and time again. ...
>
> You don't always have time for that right away, but the losses still affect you.[67]

Jadick refuses to avoid confronting death. He takes on the role of personalising and mourning each death as part of his job as physician, rather than trying to find resilience in avoidance. While Hnida writes that 'blocking out personal details' was the only way 'to ensure the psych bell didn't toll for me',[68] Jadick makes sure to 'look every Marine in the face'. This embracing of loss and the desire to memorialise the dead mean carrying the emotional weight of the war. In his penultimate chapter, 'What comes home', Jadick lets us into what that does mean:

> The worst thing that can happen for a doctor is to lose a patient on the table and that is certainly the case in combat; your job, the only reason you exist, is to be the guy who steps in and interrupts that wounded man's demise ... I can't help thinking, over and over again, is there something I could have done, something I should have done differently?
>
> ...
>
> I had some rough nights after I came back.[69]

Hnida too acknowledges 'traveling back in sweat-soaked dreams on our darkest nights';[70] Cheryl Lynn Ruff writes that 'at times I cannot help but relive the painful experiences I witnessed'.[71] Jadick concludes: 'I suppose that all of us had PTSD – post-traumatic stress disorder – to some extent or another by the time we were done.'[72] He connects that trauma to seeing friends injured and killed and to treating them to the point where 'the emotional strain is just too much'.[73] Of the necessary psychic numbing and inability to regain emotional feelings he writes, 'But men suffer ... when the combat is over and even mourning can become nearly impossible. No matter how tough you are, those demons are going to find a way to come out and haunt you.'[74] Resilience may ultimately be undermined by intrusive, uncontrollable demons. Emotional pain and the isolation it causes haunt the endings of these memoirs even though they are not explored further.

Richie-Melvan and Vines focus on the psychological response of medical personnel, especially nurses, post-war. The title of their book, *Angel Walk*, describes the ritual leave-taking medical personnel engage in as a dead soldier leaves the hospital. The book itself then demonstrates the close connection between death and loss and post-trauma stress that Jadick contends with. Arriving in Germany with a medevac patient, the normality of the environment precipitates a breakdown for Captain Marie: 'I broke down. I never cried so much in my life. After I left the patient I fell apart … everything here was normal … That's when I said to myself, "Nobody knows what's going on over there. Nobody knows all the pain that we have, all the sadness, all the loneliness, all the misery." '[75] And later: 'I was glad about coming home. But when you come home it's like the whole world doesn't see what's going on over there.'[76]

In spite of what would appear to be a greater recognition on the part of veterans and the larger society both in and outside the military that suffering some form of trauma stress is normal, certainly compared to veterans from earlier wars, and Vaughn DeCoster affirms a greater understanding of mental health issues, Richie-Melvan and Vines emphasise the ongoing presence of stigma around acknowledging psychic wounds and seeking help. One returning nurse admitted not initially seeking care because of 'a fear of being stigmatized by her peers and of being seen as "less than" by some superior officers'.[77] A male nurse, Captain Simon, initially avoided treatment but suffered severe 'nightmares, flashbacks, emotional crying, and paranoia'.[78]

> CPT Simon was the second ANC officer I met who had been diagnosed with and received treatment for post-traumatic stress disorder (PTSD). Both nurses [he and CPT Marie] said they initially felt shame that they 'couldn't handle it alone'. Both also admitted that they delayed seeking help because of fears that if anyone in their chain of command learned of their 'emotional problems', that it would jeopardize their professional career. The female nurse was able to receive private, confidential care with her primary care physician without anyone in her chain of command being noticed.[79]

But the male nurse, Simon, 'feels he has been "shunned" by a few senior officers who didn't seem to be concerned about his health and welfare'.[80] This shunning would suggest a gendering of responses to the condition that feeds back into stereotypes about masculine and feminine reaction to stress. Men, in military positions especially, are expected to cope, to be able to exert control over their emotions and exhibit a greater degree of resilience than women.

Richie-Melvan and Vines emphasise the need to learn from previous wars, especially noting the concept of 'impacted grief' as a crucial element in wartime trauma. And since finding that the lack of any ritual engagement for medical personnel after the deaths of patients contributed to post-war trauma, they affirm that 'we can't overstress the importance of a chance to see and take care of the dead body as a healing process for the nurses and warriors'.[81] This would apply equally to physicians. The main problem they define as distressing is that 'in Vietnam, as is the case in Iraq and Afghanistan, there was often no time to mourn in safety or mourning was and is often delayed or never facilitated'.[82] Such lack of facilitation would suggest a further complication in the understanding between those who function as facilitators and those who actually experience the trauma that the medic Schacht describes.

Like DeCoster, Richie-Melvan and Vines stress that a major coping skill to aid resiliency is 'journaling': 'the nurses [they interviewed] felt that journaling was about thoughts and feelings that the nurses were experiencing and that the intensive focused training should be about dealing with trauma and being realistic to prepare them before deployment'.[83] Especially, they note that the nurses interviewed believed that through journaling and talking about their experiences they could help nurses who were coming behind them.[84] If we extend this to include all medical personnel, we can suggest that the writing of diaries or journals in the immediate term, or memoirs later, is the means by which individuals both work to develop their own resilience and pass on their experience to others, not just within this one war, but through the generations of medical personnel whose writing we discuss throughout the book. Schacht's comments about the common understanding of experience and its trauma that marks his relationship with his comrades is important in considering the connection between experience across wars. Those who have experienced war as medical personnel can communicate across time through their writing and achieve a connection forged through similar experience.

Narratives of patient death, whether of soldiers or civilians, are, as we have seen throughout our discussion, central to the trauma borne by medical personnel for whom these deaths define a grief that is the most unspoken aspect of this work. When individuals come to write their journals and memoirs these become sites of war mourning that occur privately during their tour of duty or, more publicly, loss that could not be articulated at the time is expressed in a memoir in the war's aftermath. Revisiting and rewriting in detail of specific deaths and naming the dead become a mourning ritual. As mourning is continual, so all the writers here state or suggest that writing a memoir is a process of remembering that reflects the continued presence of their experience.

Notes

1 The accounts here are by Americans as unfortunately were were unable to find any accounts by British medical personnel.
2 Ed Pilkington, 'US Military'. Struggling to Stop Suicide Epidemic Among War Veterans', *The Guardian*, 1 February 2013, www.guardian.co.uk/world/2013/feb/01/us-military-suicide-epidemic-veteran.
3 Dr Vaughn DeCoster worked as a medical social worker and officer in charge of a small combat stress team at a forward operating base (FOB) in Baghdad. Interview transcript, Vaughn DeCoster Collection (AFC/2001/001/60194), Veterans History Project, American Folklife Center, Library of Congress, Washington, DC; Sharon Richie-Melvan and Diana Vines, *Angel Walk: Nurses at War in Iraq and Afghanistan* (Portland, Oreg.: Arnica Publishing, 2010).
4 Judith Butler, 'Precarious Life, Grievable Life' in *Frames of War: When is Life Grievable* (London and New York: Verso, 2009), p. 15.
5 See Butler, 'Precarious Life', pp. 1–32.
6 See Chapter 6.
7 Heidi Kraft, *Rule Number Two: Lessons I Learned in a Combat Hospital* (New York and London: Little, Brown and Company, 2007), pp. 133–4.
8 Richie-Melvan and Vines, *Angel Walk*, p. xiii.
9 Richie-Melvan and Vines, *Angel Walk*, p. xxi. It is noteworthy given Kraft's and others connecting of the two wars that these accounts are being published even as memoirs such as Hassan's *Failure to Atone* (2006) and Parrish's *Autopsy of War* (2012) are still exploring the psychological burden carried by doctors who worked in the Vietnam War.
10 Dave Hnida, *Paradise General: Riding the Surge at a Combat Hospital in Iraq* (New York: Simon & Schuster, 2010), p. 165.
11 Hnida, *Paradise General*, p. 165.
12 Richard Jadick, *On Call in Hell* (New York: Caliber, 2007); Cheryl Lynn Ruff, *Ruff's War: A Navy Nurse on the Frontline in Iraq* (Annapolis, Md.: Naval Institute Press, 2005); Chris Coppola, *A Pediatric Surgeon in Iraq* (Chicago: NTI Upstream, 2009) and *Made a Difference for That*

One A Surgeon's Letters Home from Iraq (compiled by Meredith Coppola) (New York: iUniverse, Inc., 2005).

13 Graham Dawson, *Soldier Heroes: British Adventure, Empire and the Imagining of Masculinities* (London and New York: Routledge, 1994), p. 22; Alastair Thomson, *Anzac Memories: Living with the Legend* (Melbourne and Oxford: Oxford University Press, 1995).

14 Jadick, *On Call*, p. 5.

15 Gregson in Kraft, *Rule Number Two*, pp.ix–x. For further examples of heroic rhetoric see George Sheldon's *Their Last Words: A Tribute to Soldiers Who Lost Their Lives in Iraq* (New York: Berkley Caliber Books, 2005). In interrogating such representations of the soldier, Lifton argues that 'warriors and their myths are readily absorbed by specific societies, to be re-created in their own hierarchical, power-centred image. We then encounter the phenomenon of the warrior class, or what I shall call the socialized warrior. Now the allegedly heroic act, the killing of the enemy with whatever accompanying ritual, is performed to consolidate and reaffirm the existing social order' (*Home from the War*, p. 27).

16 Ruff, *Ruff's War*, pp. 129–30, 133.

17 Hnida, *Paradise General*, pp. 91–5.

18 Hnida was one of the doctors at the scene after the Columbine School shootings and personally knew many of the victims.

19 Hnida, *Paradise General*, pp. 94–5. While Hnida ultimately does not save this patient, the young man lives long enough to be flown home for his family to say goodbye to him. Hnida ends the chapter: 'Several days later, they turned off his life support and the family donated his organs to others in need. And we suited back up into our mental armor, waiting to see who we would work on next' (p. 115).

20 Jadick, *On Call*, p. 198.

21 Jadick, *On Call*, p. 212.

22 Jadick, *On Call*, p. 212.

23 Jadick, *On Call*, p. 213.

24 Jadick, *On Call*, p. 223.

25 Hnida, *Paradise General*, p. 89.

26 Jadick, *On Call*, p. 244.

27 Hnida, *Paradise General*, p. 165.

28 Hnida, *Paradise General*, p. 165.

29 Smith, *Four Years Out of Life*, p. 67.

30 Hnida, *Paradise General*, p. 181.

31 Hnida, *Paradise General*, p. 182.

32 Hnida, *Paradise General*, pp. 182–3.

33 Hnida, *Paradise General*, p. 185.

34 Chris Hedges, *War is a Force that Gives Us Meaning* (New York: Anchor Books, 2003), p. 145.

35 Hnida, *Paradise General*, p. 182.
36 Jadick, *On Call*, p. 229.
37 Jadick, *On Call*, p. 244.
38 Ruff, *Ruff's War*, p. 133.
39 Zsolt T. Stockinger, MD, *Fragments from Iraq: Diary of a Navy Trauma Surgeon* (Jefferson, NC, and London: McFarland & Company, 2012), pp. 54–5.
40 Coppola, *A Pediatric Surgeon*, pp. 48–9.
41 Coppola, *A Pediatric Surgeon*, p. 15.
42 Coppola, *A Pediatric Surgeon*, p. 18.
43 Coppola, *A Pediatric Surgeon*, p. 28.
44 Coppola, *A Pediatric Surgeon*, p. 39.
45 Coppola, *A Pediatric Surgeon*, p. 65.
46 Coppola, *A Pediatric Surgeon*, p. 65.
47 Coppola, *A Pediatric Surgeon*, p. 69.
48 Coppola, *A Pediatric Surgeon*, p. 70.
49 Coppola, *A Pediatric Surgeon*, p. 91; *Made a Difference*, p. 71.
50 Coppola, *A Pediatric Surgeon*, p. 100; *Made a Difference*, p. 72.
51 Stockinger, *Fragments*, p. 114.
52 Stockinger, *Fragments*, p. 223.
53 DeCoster interview transcript, p. 5.
54 DeCoster interview transcript, p. 5.
55 DeCoster interview transcript, p. 6.
56 In *Battlefield Angels: Saving Lives Under Enemy Fire from Valley Forge to Afghanistan* (Oxford: Osprey Publishing, 2011), a study of medics in war, Scott McGaugh defines immediate trauma response as 'COSR (Combat Operational Stress Response) which is generally considered to be an expected emotional reaction to combat stress, while PTSD is a more protracted psychological condition' (p. 230).
57 DeCoster interview transcript, p. 10.
58 DeCoster interview transcript, p. 19. Two nurses interviewed by Scannell-Desch and Doherty report using similar strategies to deal with stress in Iraq: 'I spent my personal time reading, exercising, doing needlepoint, and writing almost every day in my journal'; 'I was running 6 days a week. It really helped me cope and got me in great shape. At 5 o'clock in the morning I was out there with our commander, a family practice doctor, running in gravel and sand. We started a running club' (Elizabeth Scannell-Desch and Mary Ellen Doherty, *Nurses in War: Voices from Iraq and Afghanistan* (New York: Springer Publishing, 2012), pp. 98, 99).
59 The Ugly of War' (video) online at www.guardian.co.uk./world/video/2008/sep/08/sixmonthsinafghanistan.afghanistan?intcomp=239 (accessed 9 October 2014).
60 'The Ugly of War'.

61 Stimson, *Finding Themselves*, p. 84.
62 Coppola, *Made a Difference*, p. 33.
63 Coppola, *A Pediatric Surgeon*, p. 146.
64 Coppola, *A Pediatric Surgeon*, p. 130.
65 Jadick, *On Call*, p. 255.
66 Jadick, *On Call*, p. 160.
67 Jadick, *On Call*, pp. 212–13.
68 Hnida, *Paradise General*, p. 94.
69 Jadick, *On Call*, p. 244.
70 Hnida, *Paradise General*, p. 276.
71 Ruff, *Ruff's War*, p. 205.
72 Jadick, *On Call*, p. 254.
73 Jadick, *On Call*, p. 255.
74 Jadick, *On Call*, p. 255.
75 Richie-Melvan and Vines, *Angel Walk*, p. 53.
76 Richie-Melvan and Vines, *Angel Walk*, p. 54.
77 Richie-Melvan and Vines, *Angel Walk*, p. 57.
78 Richie-Melvan and Vines, *Angel Walk*, p. 58.
79 Richie-Melvan and Vines, *Angel Walk*, p. 58.
80 Richie-Melvan and Vines, *Angel Walk*, pp. 58–9.
81 Richie-Melvan and Vines, *Angel Walk*, pp. 74–5.
82 Richie-Melvan and Vines, *Angel Walk*, p. 75.
83 Richie-Melvan and Vines, *Angel Walk*, p. 89.
84 Richie-Melvan and Vines, *Angel Walk*, p. 89.

Conclusion: 'Shared experiences and meanings'

In our Introduction we note how Lynda Van Devanter positions her memoir between the past, those women who nursed and suffered injury in previous wars, and a future that will acknowledge the invisible psychological wounds which she and others suffer. In doing so her purpose is to highlight the relationship between telling her story and her own emotional recovery and survival. Moreover, in placing her memoir in the context of other accounts – those who came before and those who will come after – she illustrates how experiences of one war overlap and merge with those from another, so that they can be said to be in dialogue. This dialogue allows what Stanton *et al.* call 'shared experiences and meanings'[1] across time and culture. When we set the medical personnel accounts discussed throughout this book side by side, in the same way that Stanton *et al.* bring together nursing experiences from the Vietnam War with the wars in Iraq and Afghanistan, we can move beyond the traditional historical treatment of each war experience as separate. In *Angel Walk*, similarly, collecting experiences of nurses from the Vietnam War and the wars in Iraq and Afghanistan, Richie-Melvan and Vines, as we note in Chapter 7, extend their Vietnam experiences so that they merge with and offer practical help for nurses currently dealing with the war experience. It would seem that this relational concern for others comes out of the nurses' training we considered in Chapter 5 and generates their desire to forge links between generations of war nurses. Notably, our research has not found any similar collective created by doctors. The different culture of nurses (primarily female) and doctors (primarily male) would partially seem to explain this difference.[2] The surgeon, especially in wartime, as we have seen so often throughout the accounts discussed here, belongs in a culture that stresses toughness and self-reliance and the ability to remain in control at all times. While female nurses also carry this burden to some extent, their training and culture include nurturing and connection as well as self-reliance, values underlined by the relationships represented in the Vietnam Women's Memorial in Washington, DC.

While medical histories have traditionally focused on the factual and concrete, our analyses of the accounts discussed here emphasise the interdependence of experience and emotion, and it is in exploring this interdependence that we find reflected specific commonalities. Although we separate the wars under discussion into their own chapters, in bringing them together collectively, similarities, more than differences, become increasingly visible. Looking at the experiences of trauma and the attendant methods of coping through which the medical personnel discussed here survive such trauma, allows these accounts to speak to each other across time and culture. Although, as we note in the introduction, psychiatric historians emphasise difference in definitions of trauma, stressing the cultural role in its construction – for example, the shell shock of the First World War cannot be the post-traumatic stress syndrome of the Vietnam era – it is equally important to note how much these accounts point to common traumatic experience that allows us to investigate similarities of response over the decades. Remarque's assertion that 'a hospital alone shows what war is' applies as much to the combat hospital in Iraq in the twenty-first century as it does to the hospital on the Western Front of the First World War. It reveals what medic Sergeant Schacht calls 'the ugly of war'. Drawing out these similarities, as we show throughout, means reading beyond the representations of exterior mental toughness needed to perform within these most extreme conditions to reveal the emotion that the writers may be reluctant to acknowledge. Retrieving the often deeply embedded invisible wounds of the medical personnel, obscured behind the injury narrative of those they care for, and bringing together their experiences, our object is to legitimise the emotions of the experience not only for the specific writers discussed here, but more generally for all medical personnel serving in warzones, past or future. Although individuals are often silent about their own pain or refer to it only obliquely, taking these accounts out of the isolation in which they were often written, we can read not only the trauma that accompanies the experience, but its paradoxical nature, in which intense satisfaction in the work of healing can coexist with fear and horror and despair.

More specifically, we find that the intimacy between the carer and the sufferer is the common element in all of the narratives discussed here and the source of the emotional pain that we find represented throughout, whether directly or indirectly. This is the 'world of hurt' in which all of these individuals work and which remains with them long after the work itself is over. As Stanley Pavillard put it, demobilisation did not come with 'new unmarked memories to match' their new civilian clothes; 'the scars inflicted on us during those terrible days are there for life.'[3] While professional detachment is a means of surviving this world, the common element we find throughout is that this is often unsustainable. Once soldiers are no longer soldiers but 'men in soldiers' uniforms', once the enemy is no longer 'other' but a suffering human being, and when that suffering individual can no longer be defined merely as an injury, then the psychic defences of the carer are breached. Out of this intimacy with the wounded, sick and dead comes the desire to bear witness to such suffering, which in turn results in the narratives under discussion. Whether or not they can be constructed as necessary for the greater good, the suffering itself and the emotional pain it causes those who bear witness to it must be transformed into a narrative that allows the writer to contain it, either in the immediate term or much later. At the same time, as we see in a range of writings such as Mary Borden's admission that she is 'incapable of a nearer approach to the truth' in her war stories in *The Forbidden Zone* or Ronald Glasser's bald statement that there is no narrative in the Vietnam War, this is an experience that even in its telling is often conscious of the inadequacy of language to articulate the experience. Yet it is, of course, through the attempts to overcome these limitations that we find the story. The impetus to write remains, and in the telling, no matter how incomplete and fragmented, or ordered and controlled, we find not only the foregrounded story of the sufferer, but behind it the story of its teller.

If this writing bears witness to pain and suffering, essential to that is the grief and loss borne by medical personnel as they struggle to insert their medical skill between the patient and death, whether it is in the desperate attempts to prevent 'bleeding out' on the operating table, or through careful nursing over days or weeks. The resultant physical and mental exhaustion is perhaps the most commonly articulated experience across all of these accounts. And even where there are fewer casualties, as in the Iraq War, the emotional investment in the injured and dead seems to become greater. If the writing comes out of a desire to impose order and control over an often uncontrollable environment and to bear witness to pain and suffering, then it also becomes, whether consciously or not, a site of mourning, not just for the dead and injured, but for the past 'innocent' self that can never be recovered.

The traumatic experience of medical personnel in warzones thus comes directly out of the suffering and injury of others. All of these accounts, whether consciously or not, bear witness to this suffering, often represented through the concept of 'seeing' and 'sight' as we note throughout; beginning with Stimson's concern about the after-effects of 'these frightful sights' in the First World War and extending to Hnida's desire for the American public to 'see' the 'broken body', these narratives reveal the medical personnel to be both participant in and observer of the damage wrought by war. While such individuals take on themselves the task of revealing such suffering through their writing, their work itself demands detachment. This tension between witnessing suffering and the need for a detachment that would allow them to mitigate that suffering and articulate it is central to the writings discussed throughout this book, the crucial point where these very diverse accounts intersect, and often the source of the emotional stress they reveal.

As we note in Chapter 3, Stuart Mawson shows how this tension is part of the larger dynamic surrounding resilience and breakdown in his description of his medical aid station during the Battle of Arnhem: 'Let it not be wondered at, if the fabric sometimes cracks, rather that in the main it holds tolerably together.' While we have emphasised the concept of traumatic 'seeing' as a repeated motif in these accounts, seeing of course goes far beyond witnessing the terrible nature of warzone injury. Medical work in a warzone involves a high degree of mental and emotional stress that is less concretely identifiable. The wounds belong to individual human beings and it is the difficulty of remaining detached from this connection that is repeatedly represented as the cause of emotional breakdown. The context of war exacerbates this: the required triage in mass casualty situations means that medical personnel often feel that they are 'playing God', making choices as to who would live and who would die. In the longer term, they were also responsible for sending patients they had healed back to a warzone where they were likely to be killed or injured. For those too badly injured to return to the fighting, there is the concern over their integration on their return home, an issue repeated throughout nurses' accounts across the wars under discussion.

In addition to these emotions, in most instances warzone medical practice stressors have always involved the physical exhaustion of working seemingly impossible hours, compounded by lack of sleep. Doctors and nurses often deal with inadequate medical supplies, and an added stress, 'moral distress', is knowing that an individual might have been saved if there had been more time and resources available. In addition, the living environment is often primitive and dangerous. Because medical personnel training emphasises casualty needs over those of the carer, as we have seen throughout, it is difficult for carers to acknowledge their own distress and needs more generally. In many instances, the successful implementation of professional detachment that aids in resilience in the warzone breaks down once the danger and stress of the environment are over, leaving individuals unprepared for the post-war trauma they carry home. Combined with a training that emphasises self-abnegation and emotional control, this trauma may be silenced. Our aim, therefore, goes beyond the disembedding of trauma from these texts, to making the trauma visible more generally and thus legitimising it in this particular group.

As we have seen in the quotation from Mawson cited above, resilience is necessarily defined in the context of traumatic breakdown. If breakdown occurs when coping skills are overwhelmed by traumatic events, then resilience is the ability to withstand an experience that threatens the ability to struggle through. Resilience is not the opposite of breakdown, however. In the accounts discussed here, breakdown and resilience exist on a continuum. At times individuals break down; at times they show resilience. As exposure to a severely traumatic environment increases, so does the likelihood of breakdown. However, as with combatant breakdown, we also see that it may be mitigated or avoided through appropriate rest periods, and the recognition that carers need respite from their work. The problem arises when the larger wartime culture fails to recognise the potential for medical personnel breakdown, since traumatic experience is so often defined in terms of combat and thus, as we note in the Introduction, medical personnel trauma is obscured by it. In the absence of official support, we see that individuals develop their own coping mechanisms (often seemingly instinctive), ranging from extreme forms of detachment that could be defined as dissociation, to conventional forms of recreational escape. Writing letters can allow individuals both to articulate their painful experiences and to mitigate emotional isolation. Correspondence, exchanges with those outside the warzone, as well as parcels from home, therefore, become extremely important, indicating as they do that those 'over there' have not been forgotten. In the case of Japanese POWs, we can see how the complete lack of letters and Red Cross parcels exacerbated the already brutal conditions and their sense of being completely cut off from and abandoned by the outside world. But letters can also emphasise the gap in understanding between those at home and those at the front, further increasing a sense of alienation. Even when letters, and more recently e-mails, do offer support, connection with home can increase emotional vulnerability, as we find, for example, in Coppola's communications between his own children and the Iraqi children he cares for.

If external support can be fickle, individuals often need to rely almost completely on their own inner resources. The writing of the diaries that have become so important to our discussion here are, in themselves, means of coping, as we note throughout, offering a way of working through the experiences and creating a private space in which one can escape from external pressures. Moreover, it is through them that we see recorded other forms of coping: listings of books read, POWs finding solace in contemplating the natural scenery around them, and First World War nurses and doctors taking long walks in the Belgian and French countryside to remove their minds from the suffering on their hospital wards. More recently, what had been common practices in the past have become integrated into the advice given by combat stress teams working in Iraq and Afghanistan, so that individuals in warzones are advised to write journals or blogs or to exercise regularly. At the war front, depending on the context, romances and flirtations too become useful distractions, though they can also contribute to emotional pain. Thus romances end when an individual is killed, returns home in the case of the one-year tour of duty in Vietnam, or is transferred abruptly to another theatre of war. Throughout our discussion we find that the most important source of coping is often the support of peers; an acknowledgement of shared pain becomes crucial for emotional survival, as we see in the very different experiences of Brenda McBryde, nursing in the Second World War, and Sergeant Schacht, a medic in Afghanistan. Such unspoken but tacit understanding is an essential element in the comradeship forged out of wartime hardship.

Whether or not these strategies aid long-term resilience is difficult to ascertain. What we do see, however, is that the creation of the narrative, in spite of the shortcomings we note earlier, and while it demands that the individual dwell on the painful experience, may be a particularly powerful method in achieving control over the trauma. When the writing itself fulfils a larger purpose for the writer, such as Van Devanter's desire to make public her own experience so she can offer help to others, then not only what is said but how and why it is told can be especially important. Thus using her experience to highlight her own uninitiated naivety and to warn against another war, we find First World War American nurse Shirley Millard ending her memoir: 'Now the world is once again beating the drums of war. To my son Coco, his friends and their mothers I offer this simple record of the dark caravan that winds endlessly through the memory of my youth.'[4] In a very different cultural and historical position, the individual may conclude with a quiet celebration of survival, as we find at the end of POW Aidan MacCarthy's 1979 memoir: 'But the greatest gift I have had is the appreciation of life around me. To be able to love my wife and children, to breathe the air, to see a tree in the golden stillness of a Cork evening, to take a glass of Irish whiskey ... and to see the dawn come up again on a new day.'[5]

Such writing, as we have seen throughout this discussion, is a way of ordering and controlling, to a greater or lesser degree, the chaos that is the war experience, both for the self and for others. As Alastair Thomson concludes, '[w]e compose our memories to make sense of our past and present lives'. He goes on to examine what he defines as the need for 'composure' that is determined by the public context as well as private need: 'we compose or construct memories using the public languages and meanings of our culture. In another sense we compose memoirs that help us feel relatively comfortable with our lives and identities.'[6] Graham Dawson defines this more specifically as 'subjective composure', wherein the 'story' the individual tells him or herself derives from the desire both to 'compose' a narrative and to achieve 'composure' in doing so: 'the telling creates a perspective for the self within which it endeavours to make sense of the day, so that its troubling, disturbing aspects may be "managed", worked through, contained, repressed.'[7] He sets this private narrative in the context of its social importance: 'The story that is actually told is always the one preferred amongst other possible versions, and involves a striving, not only for a formally satisfying narrative or a coherent narrative of events, but also for a version of the self that can be lived with in relative psychic comfort – for, that is, subjective composure.'[8]

It can be argued then, that to attain composure is part of the process of resilience, a coming to terms with the traumatic experience and using it, as MacCarthy and Millard do, to enlarge the experience for a greater purpose, especially in memoirs written long after the war. Yet although the writers discussed here tend to move towards a 'subjective composure' in their accounts, there is a constant tension between that composure and the experiences that are told. In letters and diaries the act of 'writing out' the experience is, arguably, an impulse towards 'composure', but these cannot offer the considered control we might expect to find in post-war memoirs. In the immediate term, diaries and letters show how individual stories are shaped and controlled in a way that contains the traumatic events related within the parameters of that specific letter or diary entry. Conversely, they often convey more effectively than memoirs the chaotic day-to-day environment that belies control. It has thus been important that we examine a range of forms and genres here, as well as published and unpublished accounts. The satisfying conclusion of MacCarthy's memoir must be considered alongside the diary that ends abruptly or the collection of letters that concludes during the war, and cannot offer 'composure' either to the writer or the reader. Thus Stimson's collection of letters ends in the spring of 1918, so we do not know what kind of future 'havoc' those 'frightful sights' may have worked 'on [her] brain', and whether or not they were assuaged by her very full and accomplished post-war work as a superintendent of the Army Nurse Corps, as Dean of the Army School of Nursing, and as president of the American Nurses' Association in addition to her contribution on nursing to the multi-volume history of the US Army medical department.[9]

Whether in the two world wars or in more recent wars in Vietnam, Afghanistan and Iraq, the intended outcomes of 'battling for the noblest principles of liberty and justice' were not always easily reconcilable with the loss of life or the physical as well as the psychological casualties. The sense of purpose, the 'heroic joy' and feeling 'as a normal being should', as 'Mademoiselle Miss' put it in 1916, but which can be applied to those of later generations, was predicated on experiences replete with horror, with 'blood and anguish'. This was continually negotiated by the medical personnel we have considered here and by countless others who left no written record. When medical personnel write their memoirs, the idea of composure often seems to elude them even as they struggle towards it, as we see in accounts by doctors from the Vietnam War, and in some of the accounts by doctors from Iraq who find it difficult to move beyond the deadly legacy of the war. Many of the writers discussed here reiterate the impossibility of really preparing individuals for working in the 'world of hurt' that is the warzone. Bringing together these diverse voices cannot do that job either, but it may at least tell others that they belong to a community that shares their experience.

Notes

1 Marietta P. Stanton, Sharon S. Dittmar, Mary Ann Jezewski and Suzanne S. Dickerson., 'Shared Experiences and Meanings of Military Nurse Veterans', *Journal of Nursing Scholarship* 28: 4 (Winter 1996): 343–6; p. 347.

2 Although many of the nurses in the wars in Iraq and Afghanistan are male, the initiative here comes from female Vietnam veteran nurses.
3 Pavillard, *Bamboo Doctor*, p. 206.
4 Millard, *I Saw Them Die*, p. 115.
5 MacCarthy, *A Doctor's War*, p. 159.
6 Thomson, *Anzac Memories*, p. 8.
7 Dawson, *Soldier Heroes*, p. 22.
8 Dawson, *Soldier Heroes*, p. 23.
9 Stimson, 'The Army Nurse Corps', p. 309.

Bibliography

Archives

Army Medical Services Museum Archives

Gibbens, Trevor, 'Captivity: Trevor Gibbens' Experiences as Prisoner of War in Germany, 1940–1945'

Hanson, Allan, 'The Story of POW 12415. 1940–1945' (revised 1995) (RAMC/PE/1/607/HANS M70)

Reid, J. B., 'A Guest of the Fuehrer (POW)', typescript (RAMC/PE/1.611/REID M 70)

Watson, W. 'An Account of My Work in South Africa, as an Hospital Orderly attached to the Royal Army Medical Corp during the Boer Campaign from December 1899 to December 1900. Including a version of my experiences from Preston to Pretoria' (ACDMS: 2001: 42)

Welsh, R. B. C., 'POW Diary of Captain R. B. C. Welsh: A RAMC Doctor on the Burma/Siam Railway 26 January 1942–24 October 1945'

Westlake, David, RAMC, 'An Account of Life as a POW', typescript

Imperial War Museum, London, Department of Documents

Brown, M, Personal Papers (88/7/1)

Essington-Nelson, Alice, Personal Papers (86/48/1)

Morris, Mary, 'A Nurse's War Time Diary', Personal Papers (80/38/1)

Nicolson, Joan Eileen, Oral interview (12075)

Seed, P. G. The Second World War papers of Captain P. G. Seed (91/35/1)

Tattersall, Norman, 'Gallipoli Diary', Personal Papers (98/24/1)

Westren, J., Personal Papers (91/4/1)

Library and Archives Canada

Hoerner, Sophie, Nursing Sister (R2495-0-7-E)

Bibliography

Liddle Collection, Brotherton Library, University of Leeds

Ferguson, Katherine, 'War Experiences' (WO, 134)
Hitchens, Nurse, Tape transcript 548, First World War Women's Recollections
McKerrow, C., Unpublished diary, Liddle/WW1/GS/1020

Veterans History Project, American Folklife Center, Library of Congress, Washington, DC

Carter, Grover, 'Diary', Carter Grover Collection (AFC/2001/001/44233)
Cunningham, Ann Catherine, Ann Catherine Cunningham Collection (AFC/2001/001/48446)
DeCoster, Vaughn, Vaughn DeCoster Collection (AFC/2001/001/60195)
Hopkins, Elizabeth. Elizabeth Hopkins Collection (AFC/2001/001/9639)
McGregor, Mildred, Mildred McGregor Collection (AFC/2001/001/55277)

Wellcome Trust Library and Archives, London

Knocker, Mary, unpublished memoir, 'Through Shadows and Sunshine 1914–18', papers of Mary Ethel Cory Knocker (later Love) (1883–1970) (CMAC/GC/258)

Published works

Abrams, S., 'Go Down to Suffering and Raise it Up', *Public Health Nursing* 28: 1 (2010): 103–4
Adams, Ken, *Healing in Hell: The Memories of a Far Eastern POW Medic* (Barnsley, Pen & Sword Books, Ltd., 2011)
Albertson, Audrey, Audrey Albertson collection (AFC/2001/001/26868), Veterans History Project, American Folklife Center, Library of Congress, Washington, DC
Aldrich, Mildred, *A Hilltop on the Marne* (Boston and New York: Houghton Mifflin Company, 1915)
Allport, Alan, *Demobbed: Coming Home after the Second World War* (New Haven, Conn., and London: Yale University Press, 2009)
Ambrosius, L. E., 'Woodrow Wilson and George W. Bush: Historical Comparisons of Ends and Means in Their Foreign Policies', *Diplomatic History* 30: 3(2006): 509–43
Andrews, Lucilla, *No Time for Romance* (London: Corgi Books, 1978; Harrap & Sons, 1977)
Antze, Paul and Michael Lambed (eds), *Tense Past: Cultural Essays in Trauma and Memory* (New York and London: Routledge, 1996)
Atherton, Gertrude, *Life in the War Zone* (New York: New York Times, 1916)
Babington, Anthony, *Shell-Shock: A History of Changing Attitudes to War Neurosis* (London: Leo Cooper, 1997)

Bibliography

Bagnold, Enid, *A Diary Without Dates* (London: Virago 1978; Heinemann, 1918)

Barker, Pat, *Regeneration* (London: Viking, 1991)

Barker, Pat, *The Eye in the Door* (London: Viking, 1993)

Barker, Pat, *The Ghost Road* (London: Viking, 1995)

Barron Norris, Marjorie, *Sister Heroines: The Roseate Glow of Wartime Nursing, 1914–1918* (Alberta: Bunker to Bunker Publishing, 2002)

Bartecchi, Carl E., *A Doctor's Vietnam Journal* (Bennington, Vt.: Merriam Press, 2006)

Bayne, Breckeinridge, J., *Bugs and Bullets* (New York: Richard R. Smith, 1944)

Beck, James M., *The War and Humanity: A Further Discussion of the Ethics of the World War and the Attitude and Duty of the United States* (New York and London: G. P. Putnam's Sons/The Knickerbocker Press, 1917)

Benson, Krystina, 'Archival Analysis of the Committee on Public Information: The Relationship between Propaganda, Journalism and Popular Culture', *International Journal of Technology, Knowledge and Society*, 6: 4 (2010): 151–64

Black, Elizabeth Walker, *Hospital Heroes* (New York: Charles Scribner's Sons, 1919)

Blythe, Ronald, *Private Words: Letters and Diaries from the Second World War* (London: Penguin/Viking, 1991)

Borden, Mary, *The Forbidden Zone* (London: Heinemann, 1929)

Brittain, Vera, *One Voice: Pacifist Writings from the Second World War* (London and New York: Continuum, 2005)

Brittain, Vera, *Testament of Youth* (London: Virago, 1982; Macmillan, 1933)

Brown, Kevin, *Fighting Fit: Health, Medicine and War in the Twentieth Century* (Stroud: History Press, 2008)

Burdett, Carolyn, *Olive Schreiner and the Progress of Feminism: Evolution, Gender and Empire* (Basingstoke: Palgrave Macmillan, 2001)

Burnell, Karen J., Peter G. Coleman and Nigel Hunt, 'Coping with Traumatic Memories: Second World War Veterans' Experience of Social Support in Relation to the Narrative Coherence of Memories', *Ageing and Society* 30: 1 (2010): 57–78

Burnham, John C., *What Is Medical History?* (Cambridge: Polity, 2005)

Buswell, Leslie, *Ambulance No. 10: Personal Letters from the Front* (London and Boston: Constable & Co., 1917)

Butler, Judith, *Frames of War: When Is Life Grievable* (London and New York: Verso, 2009)

Caldwell, Peter, *Bac-Si: A Doctor Remembers Vietnam* (Honolulu: Taote Publishing, 1991)

Camion Letters: From American College Men Volunteers of the American Field Service in France, 1917 (New York: Henry Holt & Co, 1918)

Cancian, Sonia, *Families, Lovers and Their Letters: Italian Postwar Migration to Canada* (Winnipeg: University of Manitoba Press, 2010)

Bibliography

Carden-Coyne, Ana, *Reconstructing the Body: Classicism, Modernism, and the First World War* (Oxford: Oxford University Press, 2009)

Carpentier, Nico, *Culture, Trauma, and Conflict: Cultural Studies Perspectives on War* (Newcastle: Cambridge Scholars Publishing 2007)

Caruth, Cathy, *Unclaimed Experience: Trauma, Narrative, and History* (Baltimore and London: Johns Hopkins University Press, 1996)

Cochrane, A. L., Capt. RAMC. 'Notes on the Psychology of Prisoners of War', *British Medical Journal* (23 February 1946): 282–4

Cooter, Roger, Mark Harrison and Steve Sturdy (eds), *War, Medicine and Modernity* (Stroud: Sutton Publishing, 1998)

Coppola, Dr Chris, *Made a Difference for That One: A Surgeon's Letters Home from Iraq* (compiled by Meredith Coppola) (New York: iUniverse, Inc., 2005)

Coppola, Dr Chris, *A Pediatric Surgeon in Iraq* (Chicago: NTI Upstream, 2009)

Crofton, Eileen, *The Women of Royaumont: A Scottish Women's Hospital on the Western Front* (East Linton: Tuckwell Press, 1997)

Cushing, Harvey, *From a Surgeon's Journal: 1915–1918* (Boston: Little, Brown and Co, 1941)

Das, Santanu, *Touch and Intimacy in the First World War* (Cambridge: Cambridge University Press, 2005)

Dawson, Graham, *Soldier Heroes: British Adventure, Empire and the Imagining of Masculinities* (London and New York: Routledge, 1994)

Dearden, Harold, *Medicine and Duty: A War Diary* (London: William Heinemann Ltd., 1928)

Deland, Margaret, *Small Things* (New York: D. Appleton & Co., 1919)

Dent, Olive, *A VAD in France* (London: Grant Richards, 1917)

Derby, Richard, *'Wade in, Sanitary!' The Story of a Division Surgeon in France* (New York and London: G. P. Putnam's Sons/The Knickerbocker Press, 1919)

Eakin, Paul John, 'Relational Selves, Relational Lives: The Story of the Story', in G. Thomas Couser and Joseph Fichtelberg (eds.) *True Relations: Essays on Autobiography and the Postmodern* (Westport, Conn.: Greenwood Press, 1998)

Erikson, Kai, *Everything in Its Path* (New York: Simon and Schuster, 1976)

Evans, Daniel E. Jr, DVM and Charles W. Sasser, *Doc: Platoon Medic* (Lincoln, Nebr.: Writers Club Press, 2002)

Fell, Alison S., and Christine E. Hallett (eds), *First World War Nursing: New Perspectives* (New York and London: Routledge, 2013)

Ferguson, Ion, *Doctor at War* (London: Christopher Joseph, 1955)

Fessler, Diane Burke, *No Time for Fear: Voices of American Military Nurses in World War II* (East Lansing: Michigan State University Press, 1996)

Figley, Charles R. (ed.), *Mapping Trauma and Its Wake: Autobiographic Essays by Pioneer Trauma Scholars* (New York and London: Routledge, 2006)

Finzi, Kate, *Eighteen Months in the War Zone* (London: Cassell & Co., 1916)

Fitzgerald, A. L. F. [The Edith Cavell nurse from Massachusetts], *A Record of One Year's Personal Service with the British Expeditionary Force in France, Boulogne: The Somme, 1916-1917*, with an account of the imprisonment, trial and death of Edith Cavell (Boston: W. A. Butterfield, 1917)

Fivush, Robyn and Catherine A. Haden (eds), *Autobiographical Memory and the Construction of a Narrative Self: Developmental and Cultural Perspectives* (Mahwah, NJ, and London: Lawrence Erlbaum Associates, 2003)

Florez, C. de, *'No. 6': A Few Pages from the Diary of an Ambulance Driver* (New York: E. P. Dutton & Co., 1918)

Foley, Barbara Jo, Ptlene Minick and Carolyn Kee, 'Nursing Advocacy during a Military Operation', *Western Journal of Nursing Research* 22: 4 (2000): 492–507

Foote, Katherine [An American VAD], *Letters from Two Hospitals* (Boston: Atlantic Monthly Press, 1919)

Friedenberg, Zachary, *Hospital at War: The 95th Evacuation Hospital in World War II* (College Station: Texas A&M Press, 2004)

Friends of France: The Field Service of the American Ambulance described by its Members (Boston and New York: Houghton Mifflin Co, 1916)

Fry, Sara T., Rose Harvey, Ann Hurley and Barbara Foley, 'Development of a Model of Moral Distress in Military Nursing', *Nursing Ethics* 9: 4 (2002): 373–87

Furey, Joan, Interview with Donald Anderson, 'Visions of War, Dreams of Peace: A Conversation with Joan A. Furey', *War, Literature, and the Arts* (Fall/Winter 1999): 118–33

Gask, George, *A Surgeon in France: The Memoirs of Professor George E. Gask CMG, DSO, FRCS 1914-1918* (Liskeard: Liskeard Books, 2002)

Gill, D. C., *How We Are Changed by War: A Study of Letters and Diaries from Colonial Conflicts to Operation Iraqi Freedom* (New York and London: Routledge, 2010)

Glasser, Ronald J., *365 Days* (New York: George Braziller, 1971)

Glasser, Ronald J. MD, *Broken Bodies, Shattered Minds: A Medical Odyssey from Vietnam to Afghanistan* (Palisades, NY: History Publishing Company, 2011)

Grenfell, Joyce, *The Time of My Life: Entertaining the Troops: Her Wartime Journals*, ed. James Roose-Evans (London: Hodder and Stoughton, 1989)

Gruhzit-Hoyt, Olga, *A Time Remembered: American Women in the Vietnam War* (Novato, Calif.: Presidio, 1999)

Hall, Joanne M. and Patricia E. Stevens, 'A Nursing View of the United States–Iraq War: Psychosocial Health Consequences' *Nursing Outlook* 40:3 (May / June 1992): 113–20

Hallett, Christine, *Containing Trauma: Nursing Work in the First World War* (Manchester: Manchester University Press, 2009)

Hallett, Christine, 'Portrayals of Suffering: Perceptions of Trauma in the Writings of First World War Nurses and Volunteers', *Canadian Bulletin of Medical History* 27:1 (2010): 65–84

Bibliography

Hampton, Lynn, *The Fighting Strength: Memoirs of a Combat Nurse in Vietnam* (New York: Warner Books, 1990)

Hanna, Martha, *Your Death Would Be Mine: Paul and Marie Pireaud in the Great War* (Cambridge Mass.: Harvard University Press, 2006)

Harrison, Mark, *Medicine and Victory: British Military Medicine in the Second World War* (Oxford: Oxford University Press, 2004)

Hartley, Jenny (ed.), *Hearts Undefeated: Women's Writing of the Second World War* (London: Virago: 1994)

Hassan, Allan, *Failure to Atone: The True Story of a Jungle Surgeon in Vietnam* (Sacramento, Calif.: Failure to Atone Press, 2006)

Hearder, Rosalind, *Keep the Men Alive: Australian POW Doctors in Japanese Captivity* (Sydney: Allen & Unwin, 2009)

Hedges, Chris, *War Is a Force that Gives Us Meaning* (New York: Anchor Books, 2003)

Hemingway, Ernest, *A Farewell to Arms* (New York, Scribner's, 1929)

Herman, Judith, *Trauma and Recovery* (New York: Basic Books, 1992)

Higonnet, Margaret, 'Authenticity and Art in Trauma Narratives of World War One', *Modernism/Modernity* 9: 1 (2002): 91–107

Higonnet, Margaret (ed.), *Nurses at the Front: Writing the Wounds of the Great War* (Boston: Northeastern University Press, 2001)

Hinton, James, *Nine Wartime Lives: Mass-Observation and the Making of the Modern Self* (Oxford: Oxford University Press, 2010)

Hnida, Dave, *Paradise General: Riding the Surge at a Combat Hospital in Iraq* (New York: Simon & Schuster, 2010)

Hobhouse, Emily, *The Brunt of War and Where It Fell* (London: Methuen & Co., 1902)

Holder, V. L., 'From Hand-Maiden to Right Hand: World War I – The Mud and the Blood', *AORN Journal* 80: 4 (2004): 652–65

Holley, Byron E., *Vietnam 1968–1969: A Battalion Surgeon's Journal* (Lincoln, Nebr.: An Author's Guild BackPrint Edition, 2000; Ballantine Books, 1993)

Holley, Byron, E., *Vietnam: A Battalion Surgeon Returns* (New York: Writers Club Press, 2001)

Hunt, Nigel, *Memory, War and Trauma* (Cambridge: Cambridge University Press, 2010)

Hunt, Nigel and Sue McHale, 'Memory and Meaning: Individual and Social Aspects of Memory Narratives', *Journal of Loss and Trauma* 13:1 (2008): 42–58

Imbrie, Robert Whitney, *Behind the Wheel of a War Ambulance* (New York: Robert McBride & Co., 1918)

Inder, W. S. *On Active Service with the SJAB, South African War 1899–1902: A Diary of Life and Events in a War Hospital* (Kendal: Atkinson, 1903)

Jadick, Richard, *On Call in Hell* (New York: Caliber, 2007)

Jones, Edgar, 'Doctors and Trauma in the First World War: The Response of British Military Psychiatrists', in Peter Gay and Kendrick Oliver (eds), *The Memory of Catastrophe* (Manchester: Manchester University Press, 2004)

Jones, Edgar, and Simon Wessely, *Shell-Shock to PTSD: Military Psychiatry from 1900 to the Gulf War*, Maudsley Monographs 47 (Hove and New York: Psychology Press, 2005)

Jones, Edgar and Simon Wessely, 'War Syndromes: The Impact of Culture on Medically Unexplained Symptoms,' *Medical History* 49: 1 (2005): 55–78

Keynes, Geoffrey, *The Gates of Memory* (Oxford: The Clarendon Press, 1981)

Kinney, Charles M., *Borrowed Time: A Medic's View of the Vietnam War* (Victoria, BC: Trafford Publishing, 2003; 2005)

Kirmeyer, Laurence, 'Landscapes of Memory: Trauma, Narrative and Dissociation' in Paul Antze and Michael Lambek (eds), *Tense Past: Cultural Essays in Trauma and Memory* (New York and London: Routledge, 1996)

Kraft, Heidi Squier, *Rule Number Two: Lessons I Learned in a Combat Hospital* (New York, Boston and London: Little, Brown and Company, 2007)

Krebs, Paula M., *Gender, Race and the Writing of Empire: Public Discourse and the Boer War* (Cambridge: Cambridge University Press, 1999)

LaCapra, Dominic, *Writing History, Writing Trauma* (Baltimore and London: Johns Hopkins University Press, 2001)

La Motte, Ellen N., *The Backwash of War: The Human Wreckage of the Battlefield as Witnessed by an American Hospital Nurse* (New York: The Knickerbocker Press, 1916)

Leese, Peter, *Shell Shock: Traumatic Neurosis and the British Soldiers of the First World War* (Basingstoke: Palgrave Macmillan, 2002)

Lifton, Robert Jay, *Home from the War: Vietnam Veterans: Neither Victims nor Executioners* (New York: Simon and Schuster, 1973)

Lowry, Donal (ed.), *The South African War Reappraised* (Manchester: Manchester University Press, 2000)

Luard, K. E. [published anonymously], *Diary of a Nursing Sister on the Western Front 1914–1915* (Edinburgh and London: Blackwood & Sons, 1915)

Luard, K. E., *Unknown Warriors* (London: Chatto and Windus, 1930)

Luckhurst, Roger, *The Trauma Question* (London and New York: Routledge, 2008)

Lukey, Brian J. and Victoria Tepe (eds), *Biobehavioural Resilience to Stress* (Boca Raton, Fl., London and New York: CRC Press/Taylor & Francis, 2008)

Lunati, Frank (as told to Gene Ligotti), *Time Never Heals: The Memoirs of Capt. Frank Lunati, Battalion Surgeon 2/5 1st Cavalry Division (Air Mobile) 1965–1966* (Bloomington, Ind.: Xlibris, 2003)

MacCarthy, Aidan, *A Doctor's War* (Cork: The Collins Press, 2005; Robson Books, 1979)

'Mademoiselle Miss': Letters from an American Girl Serving with the Rank of Lieutenant in a French Army Hospital at the Front (Boston: W. A. Butterfield, 1916)

Mawson, Stuart, *Arnhem Doctor* (London: Orbis Publishing, 1981)

Mawson, Stuart, *Doctor after Arnhem: Witness to the Fall of the Third Reich* (Stroud: Spellmount, 2006)

Mayhew, Emily, *Wounded: From Battlefield to Blighty 1914–1918* (London: Bodley Head, 2013)

McBryde, Brenda, Interview in *The Age* (Wednesday 18 March 1981)

McBryde, Brenda, *A Nurse's War* (New York: Universe Books, 1979)

McBryde, Brenda, *Quiet Heroines: Nurses of the Second World War* (London: Chatto and Windus, 1985; Waldon: Cakebreads Publication, 1989)

McEwen, Yvonne, *It's a Long Way to Tipperary: British and Irish Nurses in the Great War* (Dunfermline: Cualann Press, 2006)

McGaugh, Scott, *Battlefield Angels: Saving Lives under Enemy Fire from Valley Forge to Afghanistan* (Oxford and New York: Osprey Publishing, 2011)

McGregor, Mildred, *World War Two: Front Line Nurse* (Ann Arbor: University of Michigan Press, 2007)

McManners, Hugh, *The Scars of War* (London: HarperCollins, 1993)

McNally, Richard J., *Remembering Trauma* (Cambridge, Mass. and London: Belknap Press/Harvard University Press, 2003)

Menard, Shirley and Lois Johns, 'The Military Nurse Experience in Vietnam: Stress and Impact', *Journal of Clinical Psychology* 45: 4–6 (1989): 736–44

Meyer, Jessica, *Men of War: Masculinity and the First World War in Britain* (Basingstoke: Palgrave Macmillan, 2009)

Millard, Shirley, *I Saw Them Die: Diary and Recollections of Shirley Millard,* ed. Adele Comandini (New York: Harcourt, Brace and Company, 1936)

Milne, Esther, *Letters, Postcards, Email: Technologies of Presence* (New York and London: Routledge, 2010)

Morris, Mary, *A Very Private Diary: A Nurse in Wartime*, ed. Carol Acton (London: Weidenfeld and Nicolson, 2014)

Morrissette, Patrick J., *The Pain of Helping: Psychological Injury of Helping Professionals* (New York: Brunner-Routledge, 2004)

Mortimer, Maud, *A Green Tent in Flanders* (Garden City, NY: Doubleday, Page and Co., 1917)

Nichols, John and Tony Rennell, *Medic: Saving Lives – from Dunkirk to Afghanistan* (London: Penguin Books, 2009)

Noble, I., *Nurse Around the World: Alice Fitzgerald* (New York: Messner, 1964)

Norman, Elizabeth, *Women at War: The Story of Fifty Military Nurses who Served in Vietnam* (Philadelphia: University of Pennsylvania Press, 1990)

Nussbaum, Felicity. 'Toward Conceptualizing Diary', in James Olney (ed.), *Studies in Autobiography* (New York and Oxford: Oxford University Press, 1988)

Orcutt, Philip Dana, *The White Road of Mystery: The Note-Book of an American Ambulancier* (New York: John Lane; London: John Lane, The Bodley Head, 1918)

Owen, Wilfred, *Selected Letters,* ed. John Bell (Oxford: Oxford University Press, 1985)

Parrish, John, *12, 20 & 5: A Doctor's Year in Vietnam* (New York: E. P. Dutton & Co. Inc., 1972)

Parrish, John, *Autopsy of War: A Personal History* (New York: Thomas Dunne Books/St Martin's Press, 2012)

Parsons, R. Peabody, 'Have We Kept the Faith?', *Atlantic Monthly* (August 1923): 666–72

Paul, Elizabeth A., 'Wounded Healers: A Summary of the Vietnam Nurse Veteran Project', *Military Medicine* 150: 11 (November 1985): 571–6

Paulson, Daryl S. and Stanley Krippner, *Haunted by Combat: Understanding PTSD in War Veterans Including Women, Reservists, and Those Coming Back from Iraq* (London and Westport, Conn.: Praeger Security International, 2007)

Pavillard, Stanley S., *Bamboo Doctor* (London: Macmillan & Co., Ltd., 1960)

Phibbs, Brendan, *The Other Side of Time* (Boston: Little, Brown, 1987)

Philps, Richard, *Prisoner Doctor: An Account of the Experiences of a Royal Air Force Medical Officer during the Japanese Occupation of Indonesia, 1942–1945* (Hove: The Book Guild, 1996)

Pilkington, Ed, 'US Military Struggling to Stop Suicide Epidemic among War Veterans', *The Guardian*, 1 February 2013, www.guardian.co.uk/world/2013/feb/01/us-military-suicide-epidemic-veteran

Poirier, Suzanne, *Doctors in the Making: Memoirs and Medical Education* (Iowa City: University of Iowa Press, 2009)

Powell, Mary Reynolds, *A World of Hurt: Between Innocence and Ignorance in Vietnam* (Cleveland, OH: Greenleaf, 2000)

Price, D. H. and J. Knox, 'Women Vietnam Veterans and Post Traumatic Stress Disorder: Implications for Practice', *Affilia*, 11:1 (Spring 1996): 61–75

Quinn, P. J. and S. Trout (eds), *The Literature of the Great War Reconsidered: Beyond Modern Memory* (Basingstoke: Palgrave Macmillan, 2001)

Randolph, E, *An Unexpected Odyssey: The Chronicle of a Field Ambulance Private, 1940–1945*, IWM 3504 (Perth, WA: E. Randolph, 1981)

Reid, Fiona, *Broken Men: Shell-Shock, Treatment and Recovery in Britain 1914–1930* (London: Continuum, 2010)

Remarque, Erich Maria, *All Quiet on the Western Front* (St Albans: Triad/Mayflower Books, 1977; Putnam & Co., 1929)

Rice, Philip Sidney, *An Ambulance Driver in France* (Wilkes-Barre, PA: Philip Sidney Rice, 1918)

Richie-Melvan, Sharon and Diane Vines, *Angel Walk: Nurses at War in Iraq and Afghanistan* (Portland, Oreg.: Arnica Publishing, Inc., 2010)

Rinehart, Mary Roberts, *Kings, Queens and Pawns* (New York: George H. Doran & Co., 1915)

Rippl. Gabriel, Phillip Schwieghauser and Therese Steffen (eds), *Haunted Narratives: Life Writing in an Age of Trauma* (Toronto: University of Toronto Press, 2013)

Bibliography

Robinett, Jane, 'The Narrative Shape of Traumatic Experience', *Literature and Medicine* 26: 2 (Fall, 2007): 290–311

Roper, Michael, *The Secret Battle: Emotional Survival in the Great War* (Manchester: Manchester University Press, 2009)

Rothblum, Esther and Ellen Cole (eds), *A Woman's Recovery from the Trauma of War: Twelve Responses from Feminist Therapists and Activists* (New York and London: Haworth Press, 1986)

Ruff, Cheryl Lynn, *Ruff's War: A Navy Nurse on the Frontline in Iraq* (Annapolis, Md.: Naval Institute Press, 2005)

Rushton, Patricia, *Gulf War Nurses: Personal Accounts of 14 Americans 1990–1991 and 2003–2010* (Jefferson, NC, and London: McFarland & Company, Inc., 2011)

Rutherford, N. J. C., *Soldiering with a Stethoscope* (London: Stanley Paul & Co., 1937)

Sassoon, Siegfried, *The War Poems,* Rupert Hart-Davis ed. (London: Faber & Faber, 1983)

Scannell-Desch, Elizabeth, 'Lessons Learned and Advice from Vietnam War Nurses: A Qualitative Study', *Journal of Advanced Nursing* 49:6 (2005): 600–7

Scannell-Desch, Elizabeth and Mary Ellen Doherty, *Nurses in War: Voices from Iraq and Afghanistan* (New York: Springer Publishing, 2012)

Scarry, Elaine, *The Body in Pain: The Making and Unmaking of the World* (Oxford: Oxford University Press, 1985)

Schrire, I., *Stalag Doctor* (London: Allan Wingate, 1956)

Scurfield, Raymond and Katherine Platoni (eds), *War Trauma and Its Wake: Expanding the Circle of Healing* (New York and Hove: Routledge, 2013)

Sewell, Patricia (ed.), *Healers in World War II: Oral Histories of Medical Corps Personnel* (Jefferson, NC, and London: McFarland & Company Inc., 2001)

Seymour, James William Davenport, *Memorial Volume: American Field Service in France* (Boston: AFS, 1921)

Shatan, Chaim F., 'Stress Disorders among Vietnam Veterans: The Emotional Content of Combat Continues', in Charles Figley (ed.), *Trauma and Its Wake*, vol. II (New York: Brunner/Mazel, 1978)

Sheldon, Sayre P. (ed.), *Her War Story: Twentieth Century Women Write about War* (Carbondale and Edwardsville: Southern Illinois University Press, 1999)

Shephard, Ben, *A War of Nerves: Soldiers and Psychiatrists in the Twentieth Century* (Cambridge, Mass.: Harvard University Press, 2001)

Sherman, Ben, *Medic! The Story of a Conscientious Objector in the Vietnam War* (New York: Balantine Books, 2002)

Sister X, *The Tragedy and Comedy of War Hospitals* (New York: E. P. Dutton, 1906)

Smith, Lesley, *Four Years Out of Life* (Glasgow: Phillip Allen, 1932)

Smith, Winnie, *Daughter Gone to War: The True Story of a Young Nurse in Vietnam* (New York: Warner Books, 1992)

Stanton, Marietta P., Sharon S. Dittmar, Mary Ann Jezewski and Suzanne S. Dickerson, 'Shared Experiences and Meanings of Military Nurse Veterans', *Journal of Nursing Scholarship* 28: 4 (Winter 1996): 343–6

Starnes, Penny, *Nurses at War: Women on the Frontline 1939–45* (Stroud: Sutton Publishing, 2000)

Stein, Dan J., Soraya Seedat, Amy Iversen and Simon Wessely, 'Post-Traumatic Stress Disorder: Medicine and Politics', *The Lancet* 369: 9556 (13–19 January 2007): 139–44

Steinman, Ron, *Women in Vietnam: The Oral History* (New York: TV Books, 2000)

Stevenson, William Yorke, *At the Front in a Flivver* (Boston and New York: Houghton Mifflin Co, 1917)

Stevenson, William Yorke, *From 'Poilu' to 'Yank'* (Boston and New York: Houghton Mifflin Co., 1918)

Stimson, Julia, 'The Army Nurse Corps', in *The Medical Department of the United States Army in the World War*, vol. XIII, part two (Washington, DC: US Government Printing Office, 1927)

Stimson, Julia, *Finding Themselves: The Letters of an American Army Chief Nurse in a British Hospital in France* (New York: Macmillan, 1918)

Stockinger, Zsolt T., MD, *Fragments from Iraq: Diary of a Navy Trauma Surgeon* (Jefferson, NC, and London: McFarland & Company, 2012)

Stonebridge, Lyndsey, 'Theories of Trauma', in Marina MacKay (ed.), *The Cambridge Companion to the Literature of the Second World War* (Cambridge: Cambridge University Press, 2009)

Stur, Heather, *Beyond Combat: Women and Gender in the Vietnam War Era* (Cambridge: Cambridge University Press, 2011)

Summerfield, Penny, *Reconstructing Women's Wartime Lives* (Manchester: Manchester University Press, 1998)

Tal, Kali, *Worlds of Hurt: Reading the Literatures of Trauma* (Cambridge: Cambridge University Press, 1996)

Tanielian, Terri and Lisa H. Jaycox (eds), *Invisible Wounds of War: Psychological and Cognitive Injuries, Their Consequences, and Services to Assist Recovery* (Santa Monica, Calif.: RAND Corporation, Center for Military Health Policy Research, 2008)

Taylor, Eric, *Front-line Nurse: British Nurses in World War II* (London: Robert Hale, 1997)

Thomson, Alastair, *Anzac Memories: Living with the Legend* (Melbourne and Oxford: Oxford University Press, 1995)

Toman, Cynthia, *An Officer and a Lady: Canadian Military Nursing and the Second World War* (Toronto and Vancouver: UBC Press, 2007)

Treves, Sir Frederick, *The Tale of a Field Hospital* (London: Cassell and Co., 1912)

Turner, Brian, 'AB Negative (The Surgeon's Poem)', in *Here Bullet* (Hexham: Bloodaxe Books, 2005; 2007)

Bibliography

Tyrer, Nicola, *Sisters in Arms: British Army Nurses Tell Their Story* (London: Phoenix, 2009)

'The Ugly of War' (video), online at www.guardian.co.uk./world/video/2008/sep/08/sixmonthsinafghanistan.afghanistan?intcomp=239

Van Bergen, Leo, *Before My Helpless Sight: Suffering, Dying and Military Medicine on the Western Front, 1914–1918*, trans. Liz Walters (Farnham: Ashgate, 2009)

Van Devanter, Lynda, with Christopher Morgan, *Home before Morning: The Story of an Army Nurse in Vietnam* (New York: Warner Books, 1983)

van Vorst, Marie, *War Letters of an American Woman* (New York: John Lane Co. and London: John Lane, The Bodley Head, 1916)

Vuic, Kara Dixon, *Officer, Nurse, Woman: The Army Nurse Corps in the Vietnam War* (Baltimore: Johns Hopkins University Press, 2010)

Walker, Keith, *A Piece of My Heart: The Story of Twenty-Six American Women Who Served in Vietnam* (New York: Ballantine Books, 1985)

Walsh, Patricia, *River City: A Nurse's Year in Vietnam, Memoir* (Boulder, Colo.: TOA Press, 2009)

Wandrey, June, *Bedpan Commando* (Holland, OH: Elmore Publishing Company, 1989)

Watts, Lt. Col. J. C., *Surgeon at War* (London: Allen and Unwin Ltd., 1955)

Wharton, Edith, *Fighting France: From Dunkerque to Beaufort* (New York: Charles Scribner's Sons, 1915)

Whitehead, Ian R., *Doctors in the Great War* (Barnsley: Leo Cooper, 1999)

Wildwind, Sharon Grant, *Dreams that Blister Sleep: A Nurse in Vietnam* (Edmonton, Alberta: River Books, 1999)

Wilson, Woodrow, *President Wilson's Great Speeches and Other History Making Documents* (Chicago: Stanton & Van Vliet Co., 1919)

Winship, Michael, 'At a Military Hospital, Warriors Are Not the Only Wounded' http://billmoyers.com/2012/05/15/at-a-military-hospital-warriors-are-not-the-only-wounded/

Wolfe, Jessica, P. J. Brown, J. Furey and K. B. Levin, 'Development of Wartime Stressor Scale for Women', *Psychological Assessment* 5: 3 (1993): 330–5

Wolfe, Jessica, Kelly R. Chrestman, Paige Crosby Ouimette, Danny Kaloupek, Rebecca M. Harley and Maria Bucsela, 'Trauma-Related Psychophysiological Reactivity in Women Exposed to War-Zone Stress', *Journal of Clinical Psychology* 56: 10 (2000): 1371–9

Young, Allan, *The Harmony of Illusions: Inventing Post-Traumatic Stress Disorder* (Princeton, NJ: Princeton University Press, 1995)

Zeiger, Susan, *In Uncle Sam's Service: Women Workers with the American Expeditionary Force, 1917–1919* (Ithaca, NY: Cornell University Press, 1999)

Zeiss, Robert A. and Dickman, Harold R., 'PTSD 40 Years Later: Incidence and Person-Situation Correlation in Former POWs', *Journal of Clinical Psychology* 45: 1 (January 1989): 80–7

Index

Note: 'n.' after a page number indicates the number of a note on that page.